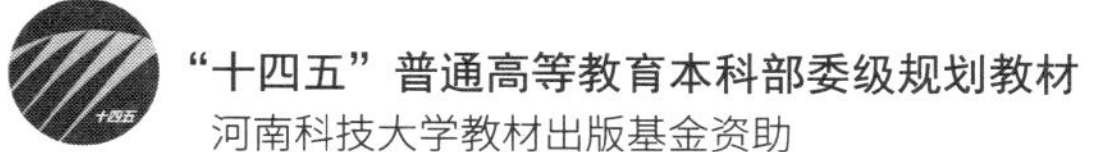

"十四五"普通高等教育本科部委级规划教材
河南科技大学教材出版基金资助

中国文化典籍英译选读

English Translation of Chinese Classics Selected Readings

张优　主　编
吕煜 陈昊 许晓玲　副主编

中国纺织出版社有限公司

内 容 提 要

本书通过展示中国文化典籍翻译的独特魅力，旨在使学习者领悟中华文化的精髓、掌握中华典籍外译的原理、提高中国优秀传统文化的对外传播能力。

本书共分五篇，涵盖中国先秦至近代各时期历史、文化、哲学、军事、科技领域最具代表性的典籍英译作品。“哲学思想篇”重点介绍儒家、道家经典英译；“历史军事篇”重点介绍编年史和方略典籍英译；“文学艺术篇”涵盖先秦汉魏诗、唐宋诗词、元曲、小说等英译作品；“育人处世篇”重点介绍蒙学、家训、处世经典英译；“自然科学篇”重点介绍中医、数学、农业、地理游记典籍英译。

本书适用于高校英语专业、翻译专业本科生和研究生，也可供非英语专业学生和其他英语爱好者学习参考。

图书在版编目（CIP）数据

中国文化典籍英译选读 / 张优主编；吕煜，陈昊，许晓玲副主编 -- 北京：中国纺织出版社有限公司，2022.12

“十四五”普通高等教育本科部委级规划教材

ISBN 978-7-5180-9946-7

Ⅰ. ①中… Ⅱ. ①张… ②吕… ③陈… ④许… Ⅲ. ①古籍－英语－翻译－中国－高等学校－教材 Ⅳ. ① H315.9

中国版本图书馆 CIP 数据核字（2022）第 194581 号

责任编辑：华长印　王安琪　　　责任校对：王蕙莹

责任印制：王艳丽

中国纺织出版社有限公司出版发行

地址：北京市朝阳区百子湾东里 A407 号楼　邮政编码：100124

销售电话：010—67004422　传真：010—87155801

http://www.c-textilep.com

中国纺织出版社天猫旗舰店

官方微博 http://weibo.com/2119887771

唐山玺诚印务有限公司印刷　各地新华书店经销

2022 年 12 月第 1 版　第 1 次印刷

开本：787 × 1092　1/16　印张：20.75

字数：358 千字　定价：69.80 元

序言

PREFACE

“典籍”一词最早出于《孟子》。《孟子·告子下》曰：“诸侯之地方百里；不百里，不足以守宗庙之典籍。”赵岐注曰：“谓先祖常籍法度之文也。”可见，那时“典籍”的概念还泛指文献，未必单指书册典籍。早在孔子生活的春秋时期，已产生了传说中的《三坟》《五典》《八索》《九丘》等典籍，但这些典籍乃长期蓄积而成，内容重复，文辞烦浮，并非出自一人之手，且未成体系。直到孔子以教育家的身份登上历史舞台，欲广泛行教，宣传古道，“举其弘纲撮其机要”，才不得不整理那些已有的典籍以成新籍——《易》《书》《诗》《礼》《乐》《春秋》，从此揭开了中国典籍发展的序幕。

伴随战国时期的“百家争鸣”，产生了大批的私人著作，使我国的典籍创作进入了一个崭新的时期，出现了我国历史上典籍生产的高潮。早期有儒家、道家、墨家，战国中叶以后儒家又有孟子、荀子；道家又有尹文子、慎子、庄子；新生的法家商鞅、吴起、申不害、韩非子；名家公孙龙、惠施；阴阳家邹衍等，都留下了大量思想巨著。与此同时，科技方面也出现了医书《内经》、药物书《本草》，文学方面则出现了不朽的名著《离骚》。此外在天文、历法、农业、畜牧、历史、地理等方面也出现了专著。此后虽有秦始皇焚书坑儒、三武灭佛、元人毁道、清廷禁书，以及兵燹回禄之灾，典籍屡遭厄运，但自两汉以来，中经盛唐、两宋，旁及辽、金、西夏，直至元、明、清，特别是在纸张被广泛应用、印刷术通行以后，中国典籍旧有新传，代有新作，多如丘山，浩如烟海，将中华民族的容智思维物化了出来，凝结成了灿烂的华夏文化。

典籍是一种特殊的社会产品，它既具备物质形态，同时又具备意识形态。凡是典籍，无论是关于人文科学、社会科学，还是科学技术都是人们某种意识的反映。而人们的意识任何时候都要受社会政治、经济、文化、军事的影响；受时代的局限；受阶级、阶层、个人社会地位、生活经历的制约；受社会风尚、地域习俗的浸染。

我国古代文化典籍的分类有多种，按照经、史、子、集四部分类法是目前学界最能接受和认可的古籍分类方法。其中，经部包括儒家经典及对其解释注疏之书、阅读经书使用的字词工具书；史部包括历史、地理、目录之书；集部包括文学之书，除此之外的典籍都归入子部。作为为大学生编著的我国古代文化典籍通识读本，本书并未采用划分朝代列举的方法，主要意在突出清晰的文化主题线索。本书适当参照传统的四部分类法，时间大致自春秋时期迄清末，选取六十余种较能代表我国传统文化的典籍及其代表性英译之作，分为哲学思想、历史军事、文学艺术、育人处世和自然科学五类主题。其中，哲学思想篇包括儒家典籍和道家典籍；历史军事篇包括编年史书和兵法典籍；文学艺术篇包括先秦诗歌、汉魏晋诗、唐诗、宋词、元曲和古典小说；育人处世篇包括蒙学典籍和家训典籍；自然科学篇包括中医典籍、数学典籍、农业典籍和地理游记。

全书内容涉及面广，结构完整，在译者和译本的选择上，不仅选取了国内外著名译者的经典译文，同时兼顾了时代特征和译者主体的不同风格，力求在有限的篇幅范围内，较为全面地展现中国典籍英译的精粹，帮助学习者了解和掌握中国传统文化典籍知识及其翻译策略，培养具有家国情怀、文化自信、全球视野的中国文化国际传播人才。本书所选的译者既有开中国典籍英译滥觞的海外汉学名家，也有多年来致力于我国传统文化对外传播的中国学者。通过对比展示不同译者对中国文化典籍的解读，使读者体会不同主题典籍的独特语言特点和翻译过程中开放的阐释视角。由于中国典籍言简意赅，含义丰富，不同身份的译者对典籍的解读也难免受到意识形态、宗教信仰、文化背景等方面的影响，因此，在赏析典籍英译的过程中，就需要结合原文、历史背景和译者主体来批判性分析译文的特点。

在结构上，本书每一章节均包括教学目标、文化背景、文化关键词、典籍简介、典籍原文、白话译文、英文翻译、赏析重点及拓展训练，附录中的拓展训练参考译文以及参考文献，便于学习者做进一步研读。

相比国内同类教材，本书编排有三大特色：首先，将国学典籍的翻译学习与中国文化对外传播和交流相结合。通过汉英对照的“文化背景”和“典籍简介”，提高学生运用英语向世界传播中国优秀传统文化的能力；其次，倡导研讨式典籍翻译学习模式。本书在所选英文译作之后没有提供传统意义上的学术性译本分析，而是通过基于问题导向的赏析重点，引导学习者从文化解读和语言转换角度对比思考中西方译者的翻译策略和方法，适于启发式教学，锻炼学生自主学习能力，激发创造性思维；最后，提高文化外宣的翻译实践能力。本书在每一章配备“文化外宣汉英翻译”拓展训练，通过丰富的中国典籍文化知识翻译训练，提升学习者的双语转换能力和跨文化沟通能力。

本书的出版得到了河南科技大学 2021 年教材出版基金和中央支持地方高校改革发展资金（河南黄河文化国际交流研究院）的资助。典籍英译博大精深，鉴于编者水平有限，在编写过程中难免存在疏漏、不足之处，敬请各位读者批评指正。

编者

2021 年 12 月于洛阳

目录

CONTENTS

第一篇 哲学思想篇

Philosophy and Thoughts

第一章　儒家经典英译

Translation of Confucian Classics

一、学习目标

（1）用英文介绍儒家核心思想基本内容。

（2）掌握儒家文化核心概念汉英翻译。

（3）鉴赏儒家代表性典籍汉英翻译方法。

二、文化背景

儒家思想是中国古代最具影响力的学术和思想流派。儒家文化作为华夏固有价值系统的一大代表，并不是通常意义上的学术或流派，一般来说，儒学并不优越于其他学派，尤其是在先秦时期，儒学只是数百个学术流派之一。汉代以来，儒家思想被大力发扬，成为用于教育和社会管理的主要学术思想和卓越的意识形态。直到今天，中国仍深受儒家思想的影响。

Confucianism is China's most influential academic and ideological school in ancient time. As the representative of Chinese inherent value system, Confucianism is absolutely superior to the customary meaning and role of academic schools. Generally, especially before Qin dynasty, Confucianism was just one of hundreds of academic schools and did not have a superiority or privilege over other schools. Since Han dynasty, Confucianism has been largely promoted to be the dominant academic thought and prominent ideology used for educating and administrating the society. Even up to today, China is still under the extensive influence of Confucianism.

儒家始终坚持"亲亲""尊尊"的立法原则，维护"礼治"，提倡"德治"，重视"人治"。儒家的经典著作最终由孔子修订，但不同朝代的人们对这些经典的看法和理解不同。在汉代，儒家经典过于社会化，造成一些滥读滥解释，直接导致后代对它的误读、混淆和看法分歧。到宋代，以朱熹（1130—1200）为代表的儒家学者吸收了道教和佛教思想重新解释这些经典著作，使儒家思想的发展进入一个新阶段，这在学界被称为新儒学。

Confucian fundamentally insisted on the legislative principle of "getting close to man who deserves to be closed up" and "respecting the men who is respectable to uphold his basic idea", maintaining "rule by rites", advocating "rule by morality", and valuing "rule by man". Confucian's classics were finally revised by Confucius, but in different dynasties people had different views and understanding these classics. In Han dynasty, Confucian classics were over-socialized or misunderstood, which directly caused misreading, confusion and difference in the view of following generations. In Song dynasty, a large group of Confucian represented by Zhu Xi (1130–1200) re-explained these classics via taking in some thoughts from Taoism and Buddhism, which made Confucianism develop into a new stage. It is called Neo-Confucianism in academic circle.

现在，全世界都面临着许多问题，如全球变暖、能源危机、环境污染、文明冲突，以及加剧人类生存危机的紧迫性问题。儒家思想基于其复杂的意识形态系统重新发挥着缓解这些危机甚至提供解决办法的作用。儒家思想为全人类维护和平与和谐，为自然和地球上的其他物种共存指明了方向。

Today, the whole world is facing many problems like global warming, energy crisis, environmental pollution, clash of civilization and the urgency that may worsen the crisis of human survival. Basing itself on its sophisticated ideological systems, Confucianism replays its key role of alleviating these crises and even supplying the solutions. Confucianism has pointed out the direction for human staying in peace and harmony as well as coexisting with nature and other species on the earth.

三、文化关键词

仁　Ren (benevolence, humanity, mercy, kindness)

义　Yi (justness, righteousness, obligation, friendliness)

礼　Li (rituals, ceremony, manners, courteousness)

智　Zhi (wisdom, resourcefulness, intelligence, well-educatedness)

信　Xin (royalty, reliability, responsibility, faithfulness)

诸子百家　The Hundred Schools of Thought

《大学》 *The Great Learning*

《中庸》 *The Doctrine of the Mean*

《论语》 *The Analects*
《孟子》 *Mencius*
《诗经》 *The Book of Poetry*
《尚书》 *The Book of Documents*
《礼记》 *The Book of Rites*
《易经》 *The Book of Changes*
《春秋》 *The Spring and Autumn Annals*

第一节 《大学》
The Great Learning

一、典籍简介

《大学》是一篇论述儒家修身治国平天下思想的散文，原是《小戴礼记》第四十二篇，相传为曾子所作，实为秦汉时儒家作品，是一部中国古代讨论教育理论的重要著作。主要概括总结了先秦儒家道德修养理论，以及关于道德修养的基本原则和方法，对儒家政治哲学也有系统的论述，对做人、处事、治国等有深刻的启迪性。经北宋程颢、程颐竭力尊崇，南宋朱熹又作《大学章句》，最终和《中庸》《论语》《孟子》并称“四书”。宋、元以后，《大学》成为学校官定的教科书和科举考试的必读书，对中国古代教育产生了极大的影响。

The Great Learning is a prose that discusses Confucianism's self-cultivation of the country's thoughts. It was originally the 42nd article of *Xiao Dai Liji*. It was said that it was made by Zeng Zi. It is actually a Confucian work in the Qin and Han dynasties. It is an ancient Chinese discussion on education theory. It mainly summarizes the pre-Qin Confucian moral cultivation theory, as well as the basic principles and methods of moral cultivation. It also systematically discusses Confucian political philosophy and has profound enlightenment on being a person, doing things, and managing the country. After the Northern Song dynasty, Cheng Hao and Cheng Yi tried to respect it. In the Southern Song dynasty, Zhu Xi made another *The Great Learning*, and eventually and *The Doctrine of the Mean*, *The Analects* and *Mencius* were also called "Four Books." After the

Song and Yuan dynasties, *The Great Learning* became a must-read for the school's official textbooks and imperial examinations, which had a great impact on ancient Chinese education.

二、作者简介

曾子（前 505—前 435），春秋末年思想家，孔子晚年弟子之一，儒家学派的重要代表人物。倡导以“孝恕忠信”为核心的儒家思想，“修齐治平”的政治观，“内省慎独”的修养观，“以孝为本”的孝道观至今仍具有极其宝贵的社会意义和实用价值。曾子参与编制了《论语》，撰写《大学》《孝经》等作品。

Zeng Zi (505 BC–435 BC), a thinker of the late Spring and Autumn Period, was one of Confucius's disciples in his later years, also an important representative of the Confucian school. He advocated the Confucianism with "filial piety and faithfulness" as the core, the political concept of "cultivating Qi Zhi Ping", the concept of "introspection and self-discipline", and the "filial piety-based" idea still has extremely valuable social significance and practical value. Zeng Zi participated in the compilation of the *Analects of Confucius*, writing *The Great Learning*, *The Classic of Filial Piety* and other works.

三、典籍英译赏析

【原典 1】

大学之道在明明德，在亲民，在止于至善。

【今译】

大学的宗旨在于弘扬光明正大的品德，在于使人弃旧图新，在于使人达到最完善的境界。

【理雅各英译】

What the Great Learning teaches is: to illustrate illustrious virtue; to renovate the people; and to rest in the highest excellence.

【辜鸿铭英译】

The object of a Higher Education is to bring out [明] the intelligent [明] moral power [德] of our nature; to make a new and better society (lit. people); and to enable us to abide in the highest excellence.

【赏析重点】

（1）对比分析排比结构“在明明德，在亲民，在止于至善”的翻译方法。

（2）对比分析文化关键词“大学之道”“明德”“亲民”“至善”的翻译方法。

【原典2】

知止而后有定；定而后能静；静而后能安；安而后能虑；虑而后能得。

【今译】

知道应达到的境界才能够志向坚定；志向坚定才能够镇静不躁；镇静不躁才能够心安理得；心安理得才能够思虑周详；思虑周详才能够有所收获。

【理雅各英译】

The point where to rest being known, the object of pursuit is then determined; and, that being determined, a calm unperturbedness may be attained to. To that calmness there will succeed a tranquil repose. In that repose there may be careful deliberation, and that deliberation will be followed by the attainment of the desired end.

【辜鸿铭英译】

When a man has a standard of excellence before him, and only then, will he have a fixed and definite purpose; with a fixed and definite purpose, and only then, will he be able to have peace and tranquillity of mind; with tranquillity of mind, and only then, will he be able to have peace and tranquillity of soul; with peace and serenity of soul, and only then, can he devote himself to deep, serious thinking and reflection; and it is only by deep, serious thinking and reflection that a man can attain true culture.

【赏析重点】

（1）对比分析逻辑结构“……而……”的翻译思路。

（2）对比分析文化关键词“定”“静”“安”“虑”“得”的翻译用词。

【原典3】

物有本末；事有终始。知所先后，则近道矣。

【今译】

每样东西都有根本、有枝末，每件事情都有开始有终结。明白了这本末始终的道理，就接近事物发展的规律了。

【理雅各英译】

Things have their root and their branches. Affairs have their end and their beginning. To know what is first and what is last will lead near to what is taught in the Great Learning.

【辜鸿铭英译】

In human affairs, there are springs of actions and consequences. When a man knows that he must first attend to the one before he can deal with the other, he is then not far from the truth.

【赏析重点】

（1）分析“知所先后，则近道矣”的逻辑关系和翻译方法。

（2）对比分析文化关键词“本末”“终始”“先后”的翻译用词。

【原典 4】

古之欲明明德于天下者，先治其国；欲治其国者，先齐其家；欲齐其家者；先修其身；欲修其身者，先正其心；欲正其心者，先诚其意；欲诚其意者，先致其知，致知在格物。

【今译】

古代那些要想在天下弘扬光明正大品德的人，先要治理好自己的国家；要想治理好自己的国家，先要管理好自己的家庭和家族；要想管理好自己的家庭和家族，先要修养自身的品性；要想修养自身的品性，先要端正自己的心思；要想端正自己的心思，先要使自己的意念真诚；要想使自己的意念真诚，先要使自己获得知识；获得知识的途径在于认识、研究万事万物。

【理雅各英译】

The ancients who wished to illustrate illustrious virtue throughout the kingdom, first ordered well their own States. Wishing to order well their States, they first regulated their families. Wishing to regulate their families, they first cultivated their persons. Wishing to cultivate their persons, they first rectified their hearts. Wishing to rectify their hearts, they first sought to be sincere in their thoughts. Wishing to be sincere in their thoughts, they first extended to the utmost their knowledge. Such extension of knowledge lay in the investigation of things.

【辜鸿铭英译】

Men in old times when they wanted to further the cause of enlightenment and civilization in the world began first by securing good government in their country. When they wanted to secure good government in their country, they began first by putting their house in order. When they wanted to put their house in order, they began first by ordering their conversation aright. When they wanted to put their conversation aright, they began first by putting their minds in a proper and well-ordered condition. When they wanted to put their minds in a proper and well-ordered condition, they began first by getting true ideas. When they wanted to have true ideas, they began first by acquiring knowledge and understanding. The acquirement of knowledge and understanding comes from a systematic study of things.

【赏析重点】

（1）对比分析文化关键词“治国”“齐家”“修身”“正心”“诚意”“致知”“格物”的翻译用词特点。

（2）分析“欲……，先……”的语法结构特点和翻译方法。

【原典5】

物格而后知至，知至而后意诚，意诚而后心正，心正而后身修，身修而后家齐，家齐而后国治，国治而后天下平。

【今译】

通过对万事万物的认识、研究后才能获得知识；获得知识后意念才能真诚；意念真诚后心思才能端正；心思端正后才能修养品性；品性修养后才能管理好家庭和家族；管理好家庭和家族后才能治理好国家；治理好国家后天下才能太平。

【理雅各英译】

Things being investigated, knowledge became complete. Their knowledge being complete, their thoughts were sincere. Their thoughts being sincere, their hearts were then rectified. Their hearts being rectified, their persons were cultivated. Their persons being cultivated, their families were regulated. Their families being regulated, their States were rightly governed. Their States being rightly governed, the whole kingdom was made tranquil and happy.

【辜鸿铭英译】

After a systematic study of things, and only then, knowledge and understanding will come. When knowledge and understanding have come, and only then, will men have true ideas. When men have true ideas, and only then, will their minds be in a proper and well-ordered condition. When men's minds are in a proper and well-ordered condition, and only then, will their conversation be ordered aright. When men's conversations are ordered aright, and only then, will their houses be kept in order. When men's houses are kept in order, and only then, will there be good government in the country. When there is good government in all countries, and only then, will there be peace and order in the world.

【赏析重点】

（1）对比分析儒学关键词“物格”“知至”“意诚”“心正”“身修”“家齐”“国治”“天下平”的翻译用词。

（2）分析“……而后……”的句法结构和翻译方法。

第二节 《中庸》

The Doctrine of the Mean

一、典籍简介

《中庸》是儒家经典的“四书”之一。原是《小戴礼记》第三十一篇，作者现学术界普遍认为是子思及其弟子多人所作。也有学者认为可能是由儒家学者在战国写成。宋朝学者对《中庸》非常推崇，而将其从《礼记》中抽出独立成书，朱熹则将其与《论语》《孟子》《大学》合编为“四书”。《中庸》在字面上的解释即是“中道及常理”之意。而执中又当求“中和”，在一个人还没有表现出喜怒哀乐的平静情绪为“中”，表现出情绪之后经过调整而符合常理为“和”。其主旨在于修养人性。

The Doctrine of the Mean is one of the “Four books” of the Confucian classics. Originally known as the thirty-first article of *Xiao Dai Liji*, the classic is generally considered by the academic community to be made by Zi Si and his disciples. Some scholars believe that it may have been written by Confucian scholars in the Warring States. Scholars of the Song dynasty highly praised *the Doctrine of the Mean*, and extracted it from *the Book of Rites*, and Zhu Xi co-edited it with *The Analects*, *Mencius* and *The Great Learning* which were called “Four books”. The literal interpretation of *The Doctrine of the Mean* is the meaning of “middle way and common sense.” In the pursuit of the fairness, a man should also seeks “neutralization”. When a person has not shown the emotions, he is “middle”. After expressing emotions, he is adjusted to conform to common sense as “harmony.” Its main purpose is to cultivate humanity.

二、作者简介

子思，春秋战国之际儒家学派的主要代表人物之一，历史上称为“述圣”，他开创的学派被称为“子思之儒”，与孟子并称为思孟学派。其主要作品有《汉书·艺文志》著录《子思》二十三篇。

Zi Si, one of the main representatives of the Confucian school in the Spring and Autumn Period and the Warring States Period, was called Shu Sheng (narrator of the sacred) in history. The school he founded was called “Confucianism of Zi Si”, and the thoughts of Zi Si and Mencius was called the Si-Meng School. His main works include *Yiwen Zhi from Hanshu*, which recorded twenty-three articles of *Zi Si*.

三、典籍英译赏析

【原典 1】

天命之谓性，率性之谓道，修道之谓教。道也者，不可须臾离也，可离非道也。

【今译】

天所赋予人的东西就是性，遵循天性就是道，遵循道来修养自身就是教。道是片刻不能离开的，可离开的就不是道。

【辜鸿铭英译】

The ordinance of God is what we call the law of our being (性). To fulfill the law of our being is what we call the moral law (道). The moral law when reduced to a system is what we call religion (教). The moral law is a law from whose operation we cannot for instant in our existence escape. A law from which we may escape is not the moral law.

【安乐哲英译】

What (*tian* 天) commands (*ming* 命) is called natural tendencies (*xing* 性); drawing out these tendencies is called the proper way (*dao* 道); improving upon this way is called education (*jiao* 教). As for this proper way, we cannot quit it even for an instant. Were it even possible to quit it, it would not be the proper way.

【赏析重点】

（1）对比分析文化关键词“天命”“性”“率性”的翻译用词特点。

（2）分析“……之谓……”的句式特点和翻译方法。

【原典2】

是故君子戒慎乎其所不睹，恐惧乎其所不闻。莫见乎隐，莫显乎微。故君子慎其独也。

【今译】

因此，君子在无人看见的地方也要小心谨慎，在无人听得到的地方也要恐惧敬畏。隐蔽时也会被人发现，细微处也会昭著，因此君子在独处时要慎重。

【辜鸿铭英译】

Wherefore it is that the moral man (君子) watches diligently over what his eyes cannot see and is in fear and awe of what his ears cannot hear. There is nothing more evident than what cannot be seen by the eyes and nothing more palpable than what cannot be perceived by the senses. Wherefore the moral man watches diligently over his secret thoughts.

【安乐哲英译】

It is for this reason that exemplary persons (*junzi* 君子) are so concerned a bout what is not seen, and so anxious about what is not heard. There is nothing more present than what is imminent, and nothing more manifest than what is inchoate. Thus, exemplary persons are ever concerned about their uniqueness.

【赏析重点】

(1) 对比分析文化关键词“戒慎”“恐惧”“慎独”的翻译用词。

(2) 分析“是故……”的句式特点和翻译方法。

【原典3】

喜怒哀乐之未发，谓之中；发而皆中节，谓之和。中也者，天下之大本也；和也者，天下之达道也。致中和，天地位焉，万物育焉。

【今译】

喜怒哀乐的情绪没有表露出来，这叫作中。表露出来但合于法度，这叫作和。中是天下最为根本的，和是天下共同遵循的法度。达到了中和，天地便各归其位，万物便生长发育了。

【辜鸿铭英译】

When the passions, such as joy, anger, grief and pleasure, have not a wakened, that is our true self (中) or moral being. When these passions awaken and each and all attain due measure and degree, that is the moral order (和). Our true self or moral being is the great reality（大本 lit. great root) of existence, and moral order is the universal law（达道）in the world. When true moral being and moral order are realised, the universe then becomes a cosmos and all things attain their full growth and development.

【安乐哲英译】

The moment at which joy and anger, grief and pleasure, have yet to arise is called a nascent equilibrium (*zhong* 中); once the emotions have arisen, that they are all brought into proper focus (*zhong* 中) is called harmony (*he* 和). This notion of equilibrium and focus (*zhong* 中) is the great root of the world; harmony then is the advancing of the proper way (*dadao* 达道) in the world. When equilibrium and focus are sustained and harmony is fully realized, the heavens and earth maintain their proper places and all things flourish in the world.

【赏析重点】

（1）对比分析文化关键词"中""和""达道"的翻译用词。

（2）分析"天地位焉，万物育焉"的句法特点和翻译方法。

【原典 4】

仲尼曰："君子中庸，小人反中庸。君子之中庸也，君子而时中。小人之中庸也，小人而无忌惮也。"

【今译】

仲尼说："君子中庸，小人违背中庸。君子之所以中庸，是因为君子随时做到适中，无过无不及；小人之所以违背中庸，是因为小人肆无忌惮，专走极端。"

【辜鸿铭英译】

Confucius remarked, "The life of the moral man is an exemplification of the universal moral order. The life of the vulgar person, on the other hand, is a contradiction of the universal moral order. The moral man's life is an exemplification of the universal order, because he is a moral person who constantly lives his true self or moral being. The vulgar person's life is a contradiction of the universal order, because he is a vulgar person who in his heart has no regard for, or fear of, the moral law."

【安乐哲英译】

Confucius said, "Exemplary persons (*Junzi* 君子) focus (*zhong* 中) the familiar affairs of the day; petty persons distort them. Exemplary persons are able to focus the affairs of the day because, being exemplary, they themselves constantly abide in equilibrium (*zhong* 中). Petty persons are a source of distortion in the affairs of the day because, being petty persons, they lack the requisite caution and concern."

【赏析重点】

（1）对比分析文化关键词"君子""小人""中庸""时中"的翻译用词。

（2）分析"君子之中庸也，君子而时中"的逻辑关系和翻译方法。

【原典5】

子曰："道之不行也，我知之矣：知者过之，愚者不及也。道之不明也，我知之矣：贤者过之，不肖者不及也。人莫不饮食也，鲜能知味也。"

【今译】

孔子说："中庸之道不能实行的原因，我知道了：聪明的人自以为是，认识过了头；愚蠢的人智力不及，不能理解它。中庸之道不能弘扬的原因，我知道了：贤能的人做得太过分；不贤的人根本做不到。就像人们每天都要吃喝，但却很少有人能够真正品尝滋味。"

【辜鸿铭英译】

Confucius remarked, "I know now why there is no real moral life. The wise mistake moral law to be something higher than what it really is; and the foolish do not know enough what moral law really is. I know now why the moral law is not under stood. The noble natures want to live too high, high above their moral ordinary self; and ignoble natures do not live high enough, i.e., not up to their moral ordinary true self."

"There is no one who does not eat and drink. But few there are who really know the taste of what they eat and drink."

【安乐哲英译】

The Master said, "I know why this proper way (*dao* 道) is not traveled. The wise stray beyond it while the simple - minded cannot reach it. I know why this proper way is not evident. Those of superior characters stray beyond it while those who are unworthy cannot reach it. Everyone character eats and drinks, but those with real discrimination are rare indeed.

【赏析重点】

（1）对比分析文化关键词"知者""愚者""贤者""不肖者"的翻译用词。

（2）分析"过之""不及"的语义特点和翻译方法。

第三节 《论语》

The Analects

一、典籍简介

《论语》是孔子及其弟子的语录结集，涵盖了中国哲学家孔子及其弟子的言论与思想，由孔子弟子及再传弟子编写而成，至战国前期成书，是儒家学派的经典著作之一。全书以语录体为主，集中体现了孔子的政治主张、伦理思想、道德观念及教育原则等，是中国古代典籍“四书”之一。两千年来，《论语》受到广泛研读，持续影响着中国乃至整个东亚的思想和价值观。

The Analects (literally: Edited Conversations)also known as *The Analects of Confucius*, is a collection of sayings and ideas attributed to the Chinese philosopher Confucius and his contemporaries, traditionally believed to have been compiled and written by Confucius's followers. It is believed to achieve its final form in the early Warring States period (475 BC–221 BC). *The Analects* is a work of quotation expounding Confucius' views on political propositions, ethical thoughts, morality concepts and educational principles. It was recognized as one of the "Four Books". *The Analects* has been one of the most widely read and studied books in China for the last 2,000 years, and continues to have a substantial influence on Chinese and East Asian thought and values today.

班固的《汉书·艺文志》说：“《论语》者，孔子应答弟子、时人及弟子相与言而接闻于夫子之语也。当时弟子各有所记，夫子既卒，门人相与辑而论纂，故谓之《论语》。”由此可知：“论语”的“论”是“论纂”的意思，“论语”的“语”是语言的意思。“论语”就是把“接闻于夫子之语”“论纂”起来的意思。《论语》是记载孔子及其若干学生言语行事的一部书。自汉代以来，便有不少人注解它。《论语》和《孝经》是汉朝初学者必读之书，一定要先读这两部书，才进而学习“五经”。“五经”就是今天的《诗经》《尚书》《周易》《礼记》和《春秋》。因此，《论语》是汉人启蒙书的一种。

In Descriptive Accounts of Books, *The History of the Han Dynasty* by Ban Gu, there is a record as follows: "*The Analects* is a book of the answers Confucius gave to his disciples and contemporaries as well as the dialogues between the disciples and their Master. The disciples had their own records. When Confucius passed away, his disciples got to gather and edite these words, so the book is called the Confucian Analects." Lun, means to collect up, to gather; yu, speech, words; lun yu, to collect up, to edit the words relative to Confucius. The *Analects* is a book about dialogues and actions of Confucius and some of his students. And the book was called Lun Yu then. It is the original title. Since the Han dynasty, many people have been making their commentaries to it. The beginners must first read *the Analects* and *the Classic of Filial Piety* in the Han dynasty before they started to read the "Five Classics", namely, *The Book of Poetry*, *The Book of Documents*, *The Book of Changes*, *The Book of Rites*, *The Spring And Autumn Annals*. Evidently *the Analects* served as one of the Children's primers in the Han dynasty.

二、作者简介

孔子（前 551—前 479），名丘，字仲尼，尼：神圣的山。公元前 551 年出生于鲁国的一个贫困家庭。他的父亲是鲁国的一个地方长官，在孔子出生三年后逝世。孔子经历了贫困和屈辱的少年后长大成人，曾做过管理仓库和照看牧场等琐碎工作（吾少也贱，故多能鄙事）。不过孔子接受过良好的教育。他 19 岁时结婚，并生了一个儿子和两个女儿。50 岁时，孔子被任命为鲁国的大司寇，后来被迫离职流放。他离开鲁国，周游列国，想寻找一个重用他的统治者，却遭冷遇。公元前 484 年，他回到鲁国边整理古代经典著作，边从事教学度过余生。孔子有弟子 3000 名，其中 72 个弟子为著名的儒学家。

Confucius (551 BC–479 BC), given name: Qiu; academic name: Zhongni (Ni:a sacred hill), was born in a poor family in the state of Lu in the year 551 BC. His father, commander of a district in Lu, died three years after Confucius was born. He had endured a poverty-stricken and humiliating youth upon reaching manhood, and been forced to undertake such petty jobs as warehouse management and caring for livestock (I was of humble station when young. That is why I am skilled in many menial things). But Confucius received a fine education. He was married at the age of 19 and had one son and two daughters. At the age of 50, he was appointed Minister of Crime of the Lu State, then forced to leave office and go into exile. He left Lu and traveled in the states looking for a ruler who might employ him but meeting instead with indifference. In 484 BC, he returned to Lu and spent the rest of his life teaching, putting in order ancient classics. Then he became a professional teacher with 3,000 students, and among them 72 disciples were famous Confucians.

孔子是中国古代著名教育家、文学家、政治家、思想家，他倡导仁、义、礼、智、信，是儒家学派创始人，并于晚年修订“五经”。孔子的主张与中国许多传统信仰相通，他在祭祖、长幼关系、夫妻关系、家国关系等众多方面都提出了看法，并提出了著名的人际交往黄金法则“己所不欲，勿施于人”。孔子是历史上对“人道”影响极为深远的人之一。他的哲学与教义，如今仍深刻地影响着人们的生活。

Confucius was a Chinese teacher, editor, politician, and philosopher of the Spring and Autumn period of Chinese history. The philosophy of Confucius, also known as Confucianism, emphasized personal and governmental morality, correctness of social relationships, justice and sincerity. Confucius is traditionally credited with having authored or edited many of the Chinese classic texts including all of the Five Classics. Confucius's principles have commonality with Chinese tradition and belief. He championed strong family loyalty, ancestor veneration, and respect of elders by their children and of husbands by their wives, recommending family as a basis for ideal government. He espoused the well-known principle "Do not do to others what you do not want done to yourself", the Golden Rule. Throughout history, Confucius is widely considered as one of the most important and influential individuals in affecting the lives of humanity. His teachings and philosophy greatly impacted people around the world and still linger in today's society.

三、典籍英译赏析

【原典 1】

子曰：“学而时习之，不亦说乎？有朋自远方来，不亦乐乎？人不知，而不愠，不亦君子乎？”

【今译】

孔子说：“学了又时常温习和练习，不是很愉快吗？有志同道合的人从远方来，不是很令人高兴的吗？人家不了解我，我也不怨恨、恼怒，不也是一个有德的君子吗？”

【辜鸿铭英译】

Confucius remarked, "It is indeed a pleasure to acquire knowledge and, as you go on acquiring, to put into practice what you have acquired. A greater pleasure still it is when friends of congenial minds come from afar to seek you because of your attainments. But he is truly a wise and good man who feels no discomposure even when he is not noticed of men."

【安乐哲英译】

The Master said, "Having studied, to then repeatedly apply what you have learned—is this not a source of pleasure? To have friends come from distant quarters—is this not a source of enjoyment? To go unacknowledged by others without harboring frustration—is this not the mark of an exemplary person (*junzi* 君子)?"

【赏析重点】

（1）对比分析文化关键词"学""习""说""愠"的翻译用词。

（2）分析"不亦说乎？不亦乐乎？不亦君子乎？"的句式特点和翻译方法。

【原典2】

有子曰："其为人也孝弟，而好犯上者，鲜矣；不好犯上，而好作乱者，未之有也。君子务本，本立而道生。孝弟也者，其为仁之本与！"

【今译】

有子说："孝顺父母，顺从兄长，而喜好触犯上层统治者，这样的人是很少见的。不喜好触犯上层统治者，而喜好造反的人是没有的。君子专心致力于根本的事务，根本建立了，治国做人的原则也就有了。孝顺父母、顺从兄长，这就是仁的根本啊！"

【辜鸿铭英译】

A disciple of Confucius remarked, "A man who is a good son and a good citizen will seldom be found to be a man disposed to quarrel with those in authority over him; and men who are not disposed to quarrel with those in authority will never be found to disturb the peace and order of the State. A wise man devotes his attention to what is essential in the foundation of life. When the foundation is laid, wisdom will come. Now, to be a good son and a good citizen—do not these form the foundation of a moral life?"

【安乐哲英译】

Master You said, "It is a rare thing for someone who has a sense of filial and fraternal responsibility (*xiaodi* 孝弟) to have a taste for defying authority. And it is unheard of for those who have no taste for defying authority to be keen on initiating rebellion. Exemplary persons (*junzi* 君子) concentrate their efforts on the root, for the root having taken hold, the way (*dao* 道) will grow therefrom. As for filial and fraternal responsibility, it is, I suspect, the root of authoritative conduct (*ren* 仁)."

【赏析重点】

（1）对比分析文化关键词"孝弟""犯上""作乱""本立""道生"的翻译用词。

（2）分析“鲜矣”“未之有也”的句式特点和翻译方法。

【原典 3】

子曰：“巧言令色，鲜矣仁！”

【今译】

孔子说：“花言巧语，装出和颜悦色的样子，这种人的仁心就很少了。”

【辜鸿铭英译】

Confucius remarked, “With plausible speech and fine manners will seldom be found moral character.”

【安乐哲英译】

The Master said, “It is a rare thing for glib speech and an insinuating appearance to accompany authoritative conduct (*ren* 仁).”

【赏析重点】

（1）对比分析文化关键词“巧言”“令色”“仁”的翻译用词。

（2）分析“鲜矣仁”的句式特点和翻译方法。

【原典 4】

曾子曰：“吾日三省吾身：为人谋而不忠乎？与朋友交而不信乎？传不习乎？”

【今译】

曾子说：“我每天多次反省自己，为别人办事是不是尽心竭力了呢？同朋友交往是不是做到诚实可信了呢？老师传授给我的学业是不是复习了呢？”

【辜鸿铭英译】

A disciple of Confucius remarked, “I daily examine into my personal conduct on three points; First, whether in carrying out the duties entrusted to me by others, I have not failed in conscientiousness; Secondly, whether in intercourse with friends, I have not failed in sincerity and trustworthiness; Thirdly, whether I have not failed to practice what I profess in my teaching.”

【安乐哲英译】

Master Zeng said, “Daily I examine my person on three courts. In my undertakings on behalf of other people, have I failed to do my utmost (*zhong* 忠)? In my interactions with colleagues and friends, have I failed to make good on my word (*xin* 信)? In what has been passed on to me, have I failed to carry it into practice?”

【赏析重点】

（1）对比分析文化关键词“省身”的翻译用词。

（2）分析“为人谋而不忠乎”的逻辑关系和翻译方法。

【原典 5】

子曰：“道千乘之国，敬事而信，节用而爱人，使民以时。”

【今译】

孔子说：“治理一个拥有一千辆兵车的国家，就要严谨认真地办理国家大事而又恪守信用，诚实无欺，节约财政开支而又爱护官吏臣僚，役使百姓要不误农时。”

【辜鸿铭英译】

Confucius remarked, “When directing the affairs of a great nation, a man must be serious in attention to business and faithful and punctual in his engagements. He must study economy in the public expenditure, and love the welfare of the people. He must employ the people at the proper time of the year.”

【安乐哲英译】

The Master said, “The way (*dao* 道) to lead a thousand-chariot state effectively is to carry out your official duties respectfully and make good on your word (*xin* 信); be frugal in your expenditures and love your peers; and put the common people to work only at the proper time of year.”

【赏析重点】

（1）对比分析文化关键词“乘”“敬事”“节用”的翻译用词。

（2）分析“敬事而信，节用而爱人”的逻辑特点和翻译方法。

第四节　《孟子》

Mencius

一、典籍简介

《孟子》，“四书”之一，是儒家学派思想家、哲学家孟子抒发自己政治、教育、哲学、伦理等思想观点的语录集。此书记录了孟子于战国时期周游列国，与各国统治者及孟子的学生们的谈话。此书由孟子及其弟子编作，成书于公元前四世纪晚期。此书为语录体，它所倡导的"人性本善"，贯穿于整本书的谈话之中，而对于具体问题的论述，则在孟子给统治者提出的建议当中有所体现。《孟子》是儒家学派经典著作，与《论语》相比，它的论述体现出了一定的进步性。

Mencius, one of the "Four Books", is a collection of anecdotes and conversations of the Confucian thinker and philosopher Mencius on topics in moral and political philosophy, often between Mencius and the rulers of the various Warring States. *Mencius* records his travels and audiences with the various rulers of the Warring States period, his students, and his other contemporaries. A number of linguistic and textual clues suggest that the text was not only written by Mencius himself but also by his disciples, probably during the late 4th century BC. *Mencius* comprises alternating short sayings and extensive dialogues on specific philosophical arguments. Its fundamental positions, such as Mencius' famous argument in chapter 6 that human nature is inherently good, are usually presented as conversations between Mencius and contemporaneous thinkers, while arguments on specific issues usually appear in records of his advice and counsel to various rulers. *Mencius* was one of the most important texts of early Confucianism, and represents a notable advance over *the Analects of Confucius* in terms of sophistication of argument.

《孟子》一书对中国文化的影响是巨大而深远的。但在成书之后，却一直被列为子部。按经史子集来分类，与经的地位悬殊。直到南宋，经"二程"（程颢、程颐兄弟）提倡，特别是朱熹所撰的《四书集注》，称《孟子》为"出处大概，高不可及"，并称"六经"为"千斛之舟"，而孟子是"运舟之人"。这时《孟子》一书才与"五经"并列。明清以降，朱注《孟子》更是作为开科取士的必读书。在儒学的发展史上孟子是孔子最重要的继承人，有"亚圣"之称。两千多年来，儒家学说对中国文化的影响可谓浃髓沦肌，渊远而流长。它不但支配了意识形态的各个领域，还影响到社会生活的各个方面。《孟子》一书自然就成了儒家学说的有机组成部分。它既作为重要的学术著作，同时又被视为文学作品（列入文学史和文学选读）。由于其文章巧于辩论，语言流畅，富有文采和感染力，对于后世的散文也有较大的影响。

The influence of *Mencius* to the Chinese culture is self-evident. But after the book was completed, although in Western and Eastern Han dynasties it had occupied the same position with Confucius' *The Confucian Analects*, yet it had long been catalogued in "philosophical works" the third class according to the traditional divisions of a Chinese library, i.e. classical works, historical works, philosophical works and belles-lettres. Therefore it was far inferior to the position of classical works. Not until Southern Song dynasty, through the recommendation of the two Confucian idealist philosophers, Cheng Yi and Cheng Hao, especially the great scholar Zhu Xi who wrote *A Variorum of the Four Books* in which he appraised *Mencius* "so great that nobody can catch up with him" and compared him to the helmsman of a gigantic ship, did Mencius become equal to the Five Classics. Through Ming and Qing dynasty Mencius became a required book for the imperial examination system. In the history of the development of the Confucian School, Mencius is the most important inheritor of Confucius and is called "the Second Sage". In past 2,000 years and more, the theory of the Confucian School has had a very deep-going influence of long standing and well established. It not only governs each field of the ideology, but also affects every aspect of the social life. Naturally, *Mencius* has become an organic component of the theory of the Confucian School. It has been considered as academic works and also literary works as well (included in the history of Chinese literature and its selected works) as a result of the fact that this book is rich in skilful arguments, written with ease and grace, full of literary talent and appeal, it has had greater influences on the proses of the later.

《孟子》在语言（包括书面语和口语）方面对后世的影响也是不可忽视的。时至今日，汉语中的许多成语典故，都源于《孟子》，例如，"五十步笑百步""缘木求鱼""揠苗助长""王顾左右而言他""出尔反尔""为渊驱鱼，为丛驱雀上有好者，下必甚焉"等，至今还经常出现于文章和口语中，其中有许多成为千古名句。

Mencius also bears an influence on the Chinese language (both written and oral) of the later years which can not be ignored. Up to now, there are many idioms and phrases in the Chinese language whose origins are in this book, for instance, "fifty paces and a hundred paces (all the same) ", "trying to find fish by climbing a tree (a fruitless approach) ", "pulling the seedlings upward to help the plants grow (spoiling things by excessive enthusiasm) ", "the King looked to the right and left and changed the subject (to evade an embarrassed scene) ", "moving to tall trees (moving to a better place) ", "going back on ones word (contradicting oneself) ", "driving the fish into deep waters (driving friends over to the side of the enemy) " and "When people of high rank like something, people below them will surely like", and so on and so forth. Many of these appear in articles and oral Chinese even nowadays, and some become very popular and famous.

二、作者简介

孟子（约前 372—前 289），中国伟大的思想家、教育家，被尊称为“亚圣”，仅次于孔子。孟子名轲，战国时期邹国（今山东邹城市）人。作为儒家学派的代表人物，孟子曾经游历多国宣传他的政治主张。一般认为，孟子“受业子思（孔子的孙子）之门人”。据记载，孟子游历各国的时长前后有二十多年，他主张“仁政”“民本”的思想，并以此为基，为君主提出建议。

Mencius or Mengzi (372 BC–289 BC) was a Chinese philosopher who has often been described as the “Second Sage”, that is after only Confucius himself. Mencius, also known by his birth name Meng Ke, was born in the State of Zou, now locating in the territory of Shandong Province. He was an itinerant Chinese philosopher and sage, and one of the principal interpreters of Confucianism. Supposedly, he was a pupil of Confucius's grandson, Zisi. Like Confucius, according to legend, he travelled throughout China for twenty years to offer advice to rulers for reform.

三、典籍英译赏析

【原典 1】

孟子见梁惠王。王曰：“叟！不远千里而来，亦将有以利吾国乎？”

【今译】

孟子拜见梁惠王。梁惠王说：“老先生，你不远千里来到这里，一定是有什么对我的国家有利的建议要告诉我吧？”

【理雅各英译】

Mencius went to see king Hûi of Liang. The king said, “Venerable sir, since you have not counted it far to come here, a distance of a thousand li, may I presume that you are provided with counsels to profit my kingdom?”

【赵甄陶英译】

Mencius went to see King Hui of Liang, who said, “Venerable sir, since you have made light of the distance of a thousand li, you may have some way to profit my state, mayn't you?”

【赏析重点】

（1）对比分析文化关键词“叟”“利”的翻译用词。

（2）分析“亦将有以利吾国乎”的逻辑结构特点和翻译方法。

【原典2】

孟子对曰："王！何必曰利？亦有仁义而已矣。"

【今译】

孟子回答说："大王！何必说利呢？只要说仁义就行了。"

【理雅各英译】

Mencius replied, "Why must your Majesty use that word 'profit'? What I am provided with, are counsels to benevolence and righteousness, and these are my only topics."

【赵甄陶英译】

Mencius answered, "Why should Your Majesty have mentioned the word 'profit'? What counts is benevolence and righteousness."

【赏析重点】

（1）对比分析文化关键词"仁义"的翻译用词。

（2）分析"亦有仁义而已矣"的句式特点和翻译方法。

【原典3】

王曰：'何以利吾国？'大夫曰：'何以利吾家？'士庶人曰：'何以利吾身？'上下交征利而国危矣。

【今译】

大王说，怎样才对我的国家有利？大夫说，怎样才对我的封地有利？一般人士和老百姓说，怎样对我自己有利？结果是从上到下互相争夺利益，国家就危亡了！

【理雅各英译】

If your Majesty say, 'What is to be done to profit my kingdom?', the great officers will say, 'What is to be done to profit our families?' and the inferior officers and the common people will say, 'What is to be done to profit our persons?' Superiors and inferiors will try to snatch this profit the one from the other, and the kingdom will be endangered.

【赵甄陶英译】

If Your Majesty says, 'How can I profit my state?' the high officials will say 'How can we profit our fiefs?' and the intellectuals and the commoners will say, 'How can we profit ourselves?' If those above and those below strive to snatch profit one from the other, the state will be endangered.

【赏析重点】

（1）对比分析文化关键词"士庶人""交征利"的翻译用词。

（2）分析“上下交征利而国危矣”的逻辑结构和翻译方法。

【原典 4】

万乘之国，弑其君者，必千乘之家；千乘之国，弑其君者，必百乘之家。

【今译】

在一个拥有数万兵车的国家里，杀害国君的，一定是拥有千辆兵车的大夫；在一个拥有千辆兵车的国家里，杀害国君的，一定是拥有百辆兵车的大夫。

【理雅各英译】

In the kingdom of ten thousand chariots, the murderer of his sovereign shall be the chief of a family of a thousand chariots. In a kingdom of a thousand chariots, the murderer of his prince shall be the chief of a family of a hundred chariots.

【赵甄陶英译】

In the state of ten thousand chariots, the killer of the ruler must be the chief of a fief of a thousand chariots and in a state of a thousand chariots the killer of the ruler must be the chief of a fief of a hundred chariots.

【赏析重点】

（1）对比分析文化关键词“乘”“弑”的翻译用词。

（2）分析“必千乘之家”的逻辑结构特点和翻译方法。

【原典 5】

万取千焉，千取百焉，不为不多矣。苟为后义而先利，不夺不餍。

【今译】

这些大夫在拥有万辆兵车的国家中就拥有千辆，在千辆兵车的国家中就拥有百辆，他们的拥有不算不多。可是，如果轻义重利，他们不夺取国君的地位是永远不会满足的。

【理雅各英译】

To have a thousand in ten thousand, and a hundred in a thousand, cannot be said not to be a large allotment, but if righteousness be put last, and profit be put first, they will not be satisfied without snatching all.

【赵甄陶英译】

To have a fief of a thousand chariots in a state of ten thousand chariots or a fief of a hundred chariots in a state of a thousand chariots can not be regarded as a small allotment. But if profit comes first and righteousness second, the killers will not be satisfied without seizing possession of whatever they covet.

【赏析重点】

（1）对比分析文化关键词“后义”“先利”“餍”的翻译用词。

（2）分析“不夺不餍”的逻辑结构特点和翻译方法。

拓展训练 | Extension Training

1. 思考练习

（1）用英文简要介绍《大学》《中庸》《论语》《孟子》主要内容。

（2）对比总结中外译者的翻译风格和翻译策略。

2. 文化外宣汉英翻译

（1）儒家，是诸子百家中最为重要的一个学派，同时也是中国历史上最有影响力的学派之一。“儒”早在春秋以前就已经出现了，最初是指专门从事殡丧礼仪的职业者，也称“儒者”。随着时代的发展，儒者渐渐成为专门从事礼仪的人。经过几百年的发展，西周时期（前 1046—前 771）礼乐被提升到了新的高度，儒者的社会地位也相应上升。在此基础上，孔子对儒家进行了总结和创新，创立了正统的儒学。孟子又在孔子思想的基础上进行了继承和发展。后来，荀子又对儒家的方法论进行了创新和完善。

（2）儒家思想的核心是“仁”。孔子将其作为世间最高的道德标准和理想，并发展出系统的道德范畴，即仁、义、礼、智、信、恕、忠、孝、悌。“仁”就是爱人，主张人与人之间应该友爱。“义”的意思是行为要公正、合理。孔子将“义”放在了行事的首位。而孟子对“义”又进行了进一步的阐述，将“义”提升到道德核心的地位。“礼”是指周礼，孔子最先提出了“克己复礼”的主张，希望恢复周朝的礼制。荀子对“礼”又进行了进一步的深化，认为只有“礼治”才能使人民顺从、国家稳定。“智”即智慧、知识，儒家将“智”的标准明确为博学、审问、慎思、明辨、笃行。儒家认为只有有知识、有智慧才能最终实现“仁政”，因此应特别注重人才的培养和教育。“信”是指诚实、讲信用，主张人们应该遵守信用、言行一致。“恕”是指宽恕、包容，不能将自己的意志强加于别人。“忠”是忠诚。孔子主张要尽力帮助别人，对待朋友要忠厚、忠实。孟子则将“忠”引申为要尽心尽力地教导别人。“孝”是对父母要尽孝。“悌”是对兄弟要有爱。

（3）在政治上，孔子渴望建立“天下为公”的大同社会，主张推行“仁政”，强调君主应该用宽厚的态度对待人民，用道德准则来治理国家，使人民真心归顺，接受君主的统治。对待百姓，君主要采取“德治”，即对待人民要宽厚，减轻徭役，让人民安居乐业。反对用刑法管理人民，主张用道德去教化人民，从而维护社会的稳定和发展。在经济方面，孔子系统地探讨了财富与道德之间的关系。在他看来，“君子爱财，取之有道”。要将道德放在首位，将财富放在道德的后面。孔子还倡导富民的思想，认为只有人民富足了，国家才能富足。在美学方面，孔子注重美和善的统一，即内容与形式的和谐。此外，他还提倡“诗教”，即通过文学艺术来改变社会和政治风貌。

第二章　道家经典英译

Translation of Taoist Classics

一、学习目标

（1）用英文介绍道家思想基本内容。

（2）掌握道家文化核心概念汉英翻译。

（3）鉴赏道家代表性典籍汉英翻译方法。

二、文化背景

道教不仅是宗教，还是一种哲学。“道”基本是难以定义的，它是指事物自然发展的顺序，是一种生活“方式”，是流经每个人、生物和非生物以及整个宇宙的力量。道教由与孔子同时代的人物老子（约前571—约前471）创立，并由庄子（前369—前286）加以发展。道教开始是建立在心理学和哲学基础之上的，但在公元前440年演变成了宗教信仰而被当作国教。当时老子成为被普遍崇拜的神。道教与佛教和儒家思想一起成为中国传统文化的三大支柱。

Taoism is a religion as well as a philosophy. Tao is basically indefinable. It is the natural order of things. It refers to a “Way”of life, the power that flows through every sentient being living and non-living, and through the entire universe as well. Taoism was founded by Laozi (571 BC–471 BC), a contemporary of Confucius, and was developed by Zhuangzi (369 BC–286 BC). Taoism started as a combination of psychology and philosophy but evolved into a religious faith in 440 BC when it was adopted as a state religion. At that time Laozi became popularly venerated as a deity. Taoism, along with Buddhism and Confucianism, became one of the three foundations of Chinese traditional culture.

道教的代表性哲学家有老子、庄子、王弼、郭象、嵇康等。中国人常说“内圣外王”（人的内部世界应像圣人一样；外部世界应像国王一样）。它实际上可分为两个部分：儒家思想的社会标准——外表做一个有很高的道德和才能以及道家精神修养的国王；内在做一个有非凡理解力，可以看清社会世界和自然真理的圣人。总之，道教倾向于个人的内在和精神，外表表现为个性和人品；儒家倾向于整个社会的管理和发展，体现民族实力和社会和谐。

The representative philosophers of Taoism are Laozi, Zhuangzi, Wang Bi, Guo Xiang, Ji Kang and so on. Chinese people often say Nei Sheng Wai Wang (Persons Interior World like a Saint's and Exterior World like a King's). It is actually divided into two segments of Confucianism's social criteria: to be an exterior King or Emperor with high morality and talents as well as Taoism's self-cultivation in spirit: to be an interior Saint with extraordinary understanding to see the social world and natural truth. In a word, Taoism is apt to the individual's internality and spirituality which are characterized of personality and humanity revealed outside; Confucianism focuses on the whole society's administration and development which are featured with the national power and social harmony.

道家首先摆脱儒家的思路，用自己的独立和客观的方式来探索人与自然的统一和物质与精神的和谐。它的这种方式，世界上大多数主宰者都不可能接受。它只注重天和人的本性。但另一方面，它深刻地影响了中国绘画、中国书法、中国哲学和中国人的生活方式。道教也是人与自然和谐共处的完美倡导者，道家是环保主义者。在他们的经典著作中，自然被视为人类之母!

Taoism firstly gets rid of the road that Confucianism goes along and has its own independent and objective way to explore the oneness of human and nature and the harmony of spirituality and materiality. In this way, it is impossibly accepted by majority of dominators in the world. It just pays attention to the heaven's nature and human's nature. But on the other hand, it has the predominant influence on Chinese painting, Chinese calligraphy, Chinese philosophy and Chinese people's lifestyle. Taoism is also a perfect advocator of harmonious co-existence of human and nature.Taoists are environmentalists anyway. In their classics, nature is regarded as the mother of human beings.

道教在长期的发展过程中积累了卷帙浩繁的经籍书文，其内容包罗万象，不仅记录了道教的教理教义、教规教戒、修炼方术、斋醮科仪，还保留了中国古代哲学、文学、医药学、养生学、化学、音乐等诸多方面的珍贵资料。

During the long process of its development, the religion of Taoism has accumulated a voluminous collection of scriptures and books. The contents of these scripture and books are all-inclusive. They not only record the teachings, doctrines, canons, rules cultivation, immortal practice of alchemy, rituals and ceremonies of the Taoism, but also preserve such valuable materials of ancient Chinese philosophy, literature medicine, regimen, chemistry, music, and many others.

三、文化关键词

无为 Wuwei (non-action)
慈俭朴 compassion, thrift and simplicity
阴阳五行 Yin Yang and Five Elements
柔弱不争 non-contentious suppleness
性命双修 dual cultivation of innate nature and physical life
物极必反 When a thing reaches one extreme, it reverts from it.
去甚，去奢，去泰 discarding extremes, extravagance and excess
《道德经》 *Tao Te Ching*
《庄子》 *Zhuangzi*

第一节 《道德经》

Tao Te Ching

一、典籍简介

《道德经》是春秋时期老子的哲学作品，又称《老子》，是中国古代先秦诸子分家前的一部著作，其具体成书时间仍有待考量。《道德经》与《庄子》并称为道家思想的奠基石。该书对法家、儒家等学说影响深远，包括佛教起初被引入中国时，也运用了许多道家术语与观念。《道德经》为许多诗人、书法家、园林学家等中国艺术家提供了灵感，被翻译成多种语言，影响着东亚乃至整个世界。

Tao Te Ching also translated as *The Classic of the Way's Virtue(s)*, is a Chinese classic text traditionally credited to the 6th-century BC sage Laozi. The text's authorship, date of composition and date of compilation are debated. *Tao Te Ching*, along with the *Zhuangzi*, is a fundamental text for both philosophical and religious Taoism. It also strongly influenced other schools of Chinese philosophy and religion, including Legalism, Confucianism, and Buddhism, which was largely interpreted through the use of Taoist words and concepts when it was originally introduced to China. Many Chinese artists, including poets, painters, calligraphers, and gardeners, have used *Tao Te Ching* as a source of inspiration. Its influence has spread widely outside East Asia and it is among the most translated works in world literature.

在《道德经》一书中，老子认为：宇宙由天空、地球、人类和他所谓的“原则”或“道”组成。道是宇宙的第一成因，宇宙中其他所有东西都是由道派生出来的。而且，宇宙中存在相互对立的平衡，这可以从最常见的道教神学图加以说明，即阴阳图。阴（阴暗面、负面）形成地球之气。阳（阳面、正面）形成天之气。他认为所有事物都受相互矛盾、相互依存的客观自然规律支配。有时坏事可以变成好事，反之亦然。

Laozi stated in *Tao Te Ching* that the universe consisted of sky, earth, humanity and what he called “principles” or “ways”, for which he coined the term Tao. Tao was the first cause of the universe, from which everything else in the universe was derived. What's more, there was the balance of opposites in the universe, which can be illustrated by the most common graphic representation of Taoist theology—the circular Yin Yang figure, Yin (dark side, negative form) is the breath that formed the earth. Yang (light side positive form) is the breath that formed the heaven. He believed that all things are equally governed by objective natural laws that are contradictions, and yet depend on each other. Sometimes bad things could turn into good things and vice versa.

二、作者简介

老子，中国古代哲学家、作家，姓李名耳，字伯阳，号曰聃，作《道德经》（即《老子》），道家学派创始人和主要代表人物，春秋末期人，生卒年不详。他出生于楚国，比孔子早几十年。他是周朝皇室管理藏书的史官。业余主要研究哲学，一生试图寻找可以避免无休止的封建战争和其他扰乱社会冲突的方法。

Laozi (literally: Old Master) was an ancient Chinese philosopher and writer. In traditional accounts, Laozi's personal name is usually given as Li Er, and his courtesy name as Boyang. A prominent posthumous name was Li Dan. He is the reputed author of *Tao Te Ching*, the founder of philosophical Taoism, and a deity in religious Taoism and traditional Chinese religions. Some modern historians consider him to have lived during the Warring States period of the 4th century BC. He was born in the State of Chu before Confucius by scores of years. He had been a low ranking official in the palace of the Zhou dynasty. Working in the library, he was engaged in philosophical studies, searching for a way that would avoid the constant feudal warfare and other conflicts that disrupted society during his lifetime.

老子被唐朝帝王追认为李姓始祖。老子崇尚“无为”，主张顺其自然，合乎天理。在政治上，老子主张无为而治、不言之教。在权术上，老子讲究物极必反之理。在修身方面，老子是道家性命双修的始祖，讲究虚心实腹、不与人争的修持。他的思想既对法家学派影响深远，又被起义运动的支持者所广泛接受。

Laozi is claimed by both the emperors of the Tang dynasty and modern people of the Li surname as a founder of their lineage. Laozi’s work has been embraced by both Chinese Legalism and various anti-authoritarian movements. The core concept of his work is Wu wei, it can mean “not forcing” “acting spontaneously” and “flowing with the moment.”

三、典籍英译赏析

【原典】

道可道，非常道。

名可名，非常名。

无名，天地之始。

有名，万物之母。

故常无欲以观其妙。

常有欲以观其徼。

此两者同出而异名，同谓之玄。

玄之又玄，众妙之门。

【今译】

可以言说的“道”，并非真正的、恒常不变的“道”。可以用文辞说出来的“名”，都不是永恒、终极的“名”。“无”可以用来表述天地混沌未开之际的状况；而“有”，则是宇宙万物产生之本原的命名。因此，要常从“无”中去观察领悟“道”的奥妙；要常从“有”中去观察体会“道”的端倪。无与有这两者来源相同而名称相异，都可以称之为玄妙、深远。它们不是一般的玄妙、深奥，而是玄妙又玄妙、深远又深远，是宇宙天地万物之奥妙的总门。

【理雅各英译】

The Tao that can be trodden is not the enduring and unchanging Tao.

The name that can be named is not the enduring and unchanging name.

(Conceived of as) having no name, it is the Originator of heaven and earth;

(Conceived of as) having a name, it is the Mother of all things.

Always without desire we must be found, if its deep mystery we would sound;

But if desire always within us be, its outer fringe is all that we shall see.

Under these two aspects, it is really the same; but as development takes place, it receives the different names. Together we call them the Mystery.

Together we call them the Mystery. Where the Mystery is the deepest is the gate of all that is subtle and wonderful.

【林语堂英译】

The Tao that can be told of
Is not the Absolute Tao;
The Names that can be given
Are not Absolute Names.
The Nameless is the origin of Heaven and Earth;
The Named is the Mother of All Things.
Therefore:
Oftentimes, one strips oneself of passion
In order to see the Secret of Life;
Oftentimes, one regards life with passion,
In order to see its manifest forms.
These two (the Secret and its manifestations)
Are (in their nature) the same;
They are given different names
When they become manifest.
They may both be called the Cosmic Mystery:
Reaching from the Mystery into the Deeper Mystery
Is the Gate to the Secret of All Life.

【赏析重点】

（1）对比分析文化关键词“道”“名”“无名”“有名”的理解和译法。

（2）对比分析译文的句式逻辑结构转换。

第二节 《庄子》

Zhuangzi

一、典籍简介

《庄子》一书在先秦时期便有流传，荀子就读过这本书并对它有所评论。秦朝初年吕不韦所著的《吕氏春秋》中也引用过《庄子》。最早记载《庄子》的是司马迁的《史记》，但只说“其书十万余言”，没有说明章数，更没有内篇、外篇和杂篇之分。《庄子》在汉朝流传的是 52 篇，但是在秦汉期间并不太流行，直到魏晋南北朝时出现了何晏、王弼、向秀、郭象、李颐等多种注本，其中以郭象的 33 卷本最为流行，成为通行本。一直流传至今。

The book *Zhuangzi* began to be circulated before the Qin dynasty. The famous scholar Xunzi once read the book and made some comments on it. Lü Buwei in the early years of the Qin dynasty quoted from *Zhuangzi* in his *Lü's History of China*. In Sima Qian's *The Records of the Historian*, the earliest book to mention *Zhuangzi* the man and his book. It is said that the book contains over 100,000 words without mentioning the division of “inner chapters”, “outer chapters” and “miscellaneous chapters”. The book *Zhuangzi* that was circulated in the Han dynasty was composed of 52 chapters, but it was not popular until the dynasties of Wei and Jin when such annotated editions as by He Yan, Wang Bi, Xiang Xiu, Guo Xiang, and Li Yi. Guo Xiang's edition which is composed of 33 chapters was the most popular one, which has been handed down up to the present day.

《庄子》本来跟宗教没有什么关系，道教孕育于东汉末年（公元 2 世纪），在魏晋时期，一些出身士族的道士尊崇庄子，把他当作偶像，使庄子跟道教发生了联系。唐朝时，《庄子》是被正式列为道教经典，称作《南华真经》。现存的《庄子》33 章，分为内篇、外篇和杂篇三个部分，其中内篇 7 章、外篇 15 章、杂篇 11 章。

The book *Zhuangzi* originally had nothing to do with religion at all. The Taoist religion came into being at the end of the eastern Han dynasty (2nd century A.D). Some Taoists from noble families in the dynasties of Wei and Jin held Zhuangzi in high esteem, took him as an idol and thus linked him with Taoism. It was in the Tang dynasty that Zhuangzi was assigned as a Taoist classic, entitled *The Holy Canon of Nanhua*. The extant

33 chapters in *Zhuangzi* can be divided into three pars: " Inner Chapters" (7) , "Outer Chapters" (15) and "Miscellaneous Chapters" (11).

二、作者简介

庄子（约前 369—前 286）姓庄名周，字子休，是战国中期宋国蒙（位于现在的河南省商丘市附近）地的一位学者。庄子一生大部分日子里，都跟社会下层的农夫、渔夫、樵夫、隐者甚至残疾人相处在一起，经常穿着破衣服，由于营养不良而形容枯槁。然而，他安贫乐道，周游列国，在贫苦的生活中寻求精神解脱，执教乡里，著书立说，撰有《庄子》一书流传于世。庄子的思想体系是博大精深的，概括起来可以包括"以道为本""万物齐一""自然无为""逍遥而游"四个方面。

Little is known as to the life of Zhuangzi (369 BC–286 BC) from the historical records. We only get to know from the historical records that Zhuangzi was Zhuang by family name and Zhou by personal name, with the courtesy name Zixiu. He was a scholar in the region of Meng in the state of Song (now somewhere near Shangqiu, Henan Province) during the period of Warring States. For the most part of his life he mixed himself with farmers, fishermen, woodmen, hermits and even the disabled. In ragged clothes, he looked languid as a result of undernourishment. However, he took pride in his honest poverty and made tours to various states, seeking spiritual freedom from his wretched life. Later, he taught in his village and wrote his works, now known as *The Complete Works of Zhuangzi* or *Zhuangzi*. Zhuangzi's profound philosophy can be summarized in four phrases "Tao as the source of the world" "uniformity of things" "non-action in face of nature" and "absolute freedom".

三、典籍英译赏析

【原典 1】

且夫水之积也不厚，则其负大舟也无力。覆杯水于坳堂之上，则芥为之舟。置杯焉则胶，水浅而舟大也。

【今译】

如果聚集的水不深，那么它就没有负载一艘大船的力量了。在堂前低洼的地方倒上一杯水，一棵小草就能被当作是一艘船。放一个杯子在上面就会被粘住，这是水浅而船却大的原因。

【翟理斯英译】

If there is not sufficient depth, water will not float large ships. Upset a cupful into a small hole and a mustard-seed will be your boat. Try to float the cup, and it will stick, from the disproportion between water and vessel.

【冯友兰英译】

Without sufficient depth, the water would not be able to float a large boat. Upset a cup of water into a small hole and a mustard seed will be the boat. Try to float the cup, and it will stick, because the water is shallow and the vessel is large.

【赏析重点】

（1）对比分析“且夫”句式逻辑结构的转换。

（2）对比分析关键词“覆”“坳堂”“芥”翻译用词。

【原典2】

风之积也不厚，则其负大翼也无力。故九万里则风斯在下矣；而后乃今培风，背负青天而莫之夭阏者，而后乃今将图南。

【今译】

如果聚集的风不够强大的话，那么负载一个巨大的翅膀也就没有力量了。因此，鹏在九万里的高空飞行，风就在它的身下了；凭借着风力，背负着青天毫无阻挡，然后才开始朝南飞。

【翟理斯英译】

So with air. If there is not a sufficient depth it cannot support large birds. And for this bird a depth of ninety thousand *li* is necessary, and then with nothing save the clear sky above, and no obstacle in the way, it starts upon its journey to the south.

【冯友兰英译】

Without sufficient density, the wind would not be able to support the large wings. Therefore, when the peng ascends to the height of ninety thousand *li*, the wind is all beneath it. Then, with the blue sky above, and no obstacle on the way, it mounts upon the wind and starts for the south.

【赏析重点】

（1）对比分析“风之积也不厚，则其负大翼也无力”译文的逻辑结构转换。

（2）对比分析关键词“培风”“夭阏”“图南”的理解和翻译。

【原典 3】

小知不及大知，小年不及大年。奚以知其然也？朝菌不知晦朔，蟪蛄不知春秋，此小年也。

【今译】

小智比不上大智，短命比不上长寿。怎么知道是这样的呢？朝生暮死的菌类不知道是一天。春生夏死、夏生秋死的寒蝉，不知道一年的时光，这就是短命。

【翟理斯英译】

Small knowledge has not the compass of great knowledge any more than a short year has the length of a long year. How can we tell that this is so? The mushroom of a morning knows not the alternation of day and night. The chrysalis knows not the alternation of spring and autumn. Theirs are short years.

【冯友兰英译】

Small knowledge is not to be compared with the great nor a short life to a long one. How do we know that this is so? The morning mushroom knows not the end and the beginning of a month. The chrysalis knows not the alternation of spring and autumn. These are instances of short life.

【赏析重点】

（1）分析文化关键词“小知”“大知”“小年”“大年”的理解和翻译方法。

（2）对比分析关键词“晦朔”“春秋”的理解和翻译方法。

【原典 4】

楚之南有冥灵者，以五百岁为春，五百岁为秋；上古有大椿者，以八千岁为春，八千岁为秋，此大年也。而彭祖乃今以久特闻，众人匹之，不亦悲乎！

【今译】

楚国的南方有一种大树（灵龟），它把五百年当作一个春季，五百年当作一个秋季。上古时代有一种树叫作大椿，它把八千年当作一个春季，八千年当作一个秋季，这就是长寿。可是彭祖到如今还是以年寿长久而闻名于世，人们与他攀比，岂不可悲可叹！

【翟理斯英译】

But in the State of Chu there is a tortoise whose spring and autumn are each of five hundred years' duration. And in former days there was a large tree which had a spring and autumn each of eight thousand years' duration. Yet, Peng Tsu is still as an object of envy to all.

【冯友兰英译】

In the south of the Chu state, there is Ming-ling, whose spring is five hundred years, and whose autumn is equally long. In high antiquity, there was Ta-chun, whose spring was eight hundred years, and whose autumn was equally long. Peng Tsu was the one specially renowned until the present day for his length of life. If all men were to match him, would they not be miserable?

【赏析重点】

（1）对比分析关键词“冥灵”“大椿”的理解和翻译用词。

（2）对比分析“不亦悲乎”的句式特点和翻译方法。

拓展训练 | Extension Training

1. 思考练习

（1）用英文简要介绍《庄子》主要内容。

（2）对比分析中外译者的翻译方法和翻译策略。

2. 文化外宣汉英翻译

（1）老子思想的核心是“道”，“道”是宇宙的本原、本体和法则。老子认为，“道”派生了天地万物，是宇宙存在的依据；“道”的基本运动形式是“反者道之动”，即矛盾的对立面各向其相反的方面转化；“道”的基本性质是自然无为的。“道”的学说，是老子思想的理论基础。老子的人生观是消极退隐的，主张宿命静观、以柔克刚、以退为进、以弱胜强。

（2）道家以“有为”与“无为”相对。所谓“有为”，一般是指统治者把自身的意志强加给他人或世界，不尊重或不顺应万物的本性。“无为”的意义与之相反，包含三个要点：其一，权力通过自我节制的方式遏制自己的干涉欲望；其二，顺应万物或百姓的本性；其三，发挥万物或者百姓的自主性。“无为”并不是不作为，而是更智慧的作为方式，通过无为来达到无不为的结果。

（3）老子用“道”来说明宇宙万物的产生和演变，他告诉人们在思想和行为上也要遵循“道”的特点和规律，顺应自然，要以柔克刚，因为表面脆弱的东西往往本质坚强。后来的庄子继承和发展了老子的思想。庄子在他的著作《庄子》中，继承和发展了老子“道法自然”的观点，主张将外在的万物与自我等同起来，将生与死等同起来，庄子追求的是精神世界的超越和逍遥。因为老子和庄子的思想有很多相似性，所以后人习惯以“老庄”并称。

第二篇 历史军事篇

History and Millitary

第三章　编年史书英译

Translation of Chronicle Books

一、学习目标

（1）用英文介绍中国古代治国思想和军事思想。

（2）掌握中国历史军事相关文化概念汉英翻译。

（3）鉴赏《史记》《尚书》《孙子兵法》的汉英翻译方法。

二、文化背景

我国的史学传统极其古老。商代甲骨文中称史官为“史”“作册”“尹史”。西周的史官，沿用商代的称号，周代史官的人数大大增加，《周礼·春官·宗伯》有大史、小史、内史、外史、御史之称。春秋以后，不仅王室有史官，各诸侯国也有史官的设置，《左传》里就记载了许多史官的活动和言论。夏、商、周三代的史官，负有双重使命，一方面，他们掌管天文历法、祈祷、祭享、贞卜等活动；另一方面，他们又负责记录时事、起草文书、保管典籍等工作。这种现象一直延续到西汉，司马迁撰写《史记》时，仍兼管着天象星历、祭祷等事项。

China has a long history of historiography tradition. In the oracle bone inscriptions of the Shang dynasty, historians are called “shi”, “zuo ce”, or “yin shi”, which were still used by the historians of the Western Zhou dynasty. The number of historians of the Zhou dynasty increased so greatly that they were classified into Dashi (Great Historian), Xiaoshi (Minor Historian), Neishi (Historian of Domestic Affairs), Waishi (Historian of Foreign Affairs), Yushi (Royal Historian) as recorded in *Zhou Li* (Rites of the Zhou). After the Spring and Autumn period, there were historians not only in the royal family, but also in the vassal states. In *Zuo Zhuan* were recorded many historians’ activities and remarks. The historians of Xia, Shang and Zhou dynasties had dual missions. On the one hand, they were in charge of astronomy and calendar, prayer, sacrifice and divination; on the other hand, they were also responsible for recording state affairs, drafting documents and keeping ancient books. Such tradition was kept until the Western Han dynasty. For example, Sima Qian, the writer of *Shi Ji* (The Records of the Historian), was also in charge of celestial observation and sacrificial activity.

中国史籍的编纂形式主要分为三大类：按年月编排史事的编年体；以人物为记载中心的纪传体；以记事为主的纪事本末体。

The methodology of historiography falls into three categories in China: Biannianti (chronological style), Jizhuanti (biographical style) and Jishi Benmoti (historical events-thematic style)

编年体按时间顺序记载史实，是编写历史最早、最基本的手段。孔子编写的《春秋》是我国现存的第一部史学著作，也是我国现存最早的编年体史籍。《春秋》一书是孔子在春秋末期依据鲁国国史——《鲁春秋》，兼采列国史料，以鲁国十二位君主世系为序整理编纂而成的，所以它不单纯是鲁国一国的历史，而是把春秋一代天下大势的演变做了全面记载。继《春秋》之后出现的编年体史著是流传于战国中后期的《左传》，全称《春秋左氏传》。编年史这种古老的史体在宋代由司马光的《资治通鉴》（简称《通鉴》）达到又一个发展高峰。《通鉴》全书二百九十四卷，记载周威烈王二十三年（前 403 年）至五代周世宗显德六年（959 年）的历史。它是我国一部成熟完备的编年体通史，可与纪传体通史《史记》相媲美，因此后人将两书的作者司马迁和司马光并称“史学二司马”。

The Biannianti, or chronological style is a literary type in Chinese historiography in which history is dealt with strictly chronologically. The prototypes of this style of historiography are the *Chunqiu* (Spring and Autumn Annals) of the state of Lu, and the *Zhushu Jinian* (Bamboo Annals). The style was revived in *Sima Guang's Zizhi Tongjian*. The book *Spring and Autumn* was compiled by Confucius at the end of the Spring and Autumn period. Although it was based on the history of the state of Lu, the book also collected the historical materials of other countries as a comprehensive record of the historical development during the Spring and Autumn period. The chronological historical works following the *Spring and Autumn Annals* is *Zuo Zhuan*, or *Zuo's Spring and Autumn Annals*, which spread in the middle and late Warring States period. Sima Guang's *Zizhi Tongjian* represented another peak of chronological historiography in the Song dynasty. The book with 294 volumes records the history from the 23rd year of King Weilie of Zhou dynasty (403 BC) to the sixth year of Xiande of emperor Shizong of Zhou dynasty (959). As a mature and complete chronological historiography in China, it can be comparable to the

Shi Ji. Therefore, the authors of the two books Sima Qian and Sima Guang are called "The Top Two Sima of Historiography".

纪传体史书以人物为记载中心，是继编年体而兴的史书体裁。这种综合布局的史书体裁覆盖面广，历史内容丰富，被视为"正史"。从体裁的形式上看，纪传体包括本纪、世家、列传、书志、史表五种类型。纪传体是由西汉杰出的史学家司马迁编撰《史记》所创造的。《史记》一书，共一百三十篇，记载了上起黄帝，下至汉武帝时期，长达三千年左右的历史。《史记》问世以后，纪传体史籍得到了连续不断地发展，首先是东汉班固，他继承《史记》的体例，进一步完成了纪传体的正统化和规范化。《汉书》一百卷，专记汉代历史。纪传体史籍被定为"正史"，自唐代开始，官修断代纪传史成为改朝换代后的一项重要任务，历代继作，前后相续，形成了一套系列纪传史丛书——"二十四史"，包括由《史记》至《明史》等二十四部纪传体史籍。

The Jizhuanti (biographical style) is a literary type in Chinese historiography in which history is dealt with in biographies and thematic treatises. The standard histories written in this historiographic type are the official dynastic histories (zhengshi 正史). In terms of genres, Jizhuanti can be classified into three types of biographies and two types of treatises: Benji (biographies of prominent rulers); Shijia (biographies of duckes and princes); Liezhuan (biographies of important figures); ShuZhi (treatises about state rituals, courtly etiquette, calendar and astronomy, penal law, the military, literature, and also diplomatic relations); ShiBiao (lists of genealogy, important figures and events). The Jizhuanti was created by Sima Qian, an outstanding historian in the Western Han dynasty who wrote *Shiji* (The Records of Historian), a total of 130 articles, covering about 3000 years of history from the Yellow Emperor to Emperor Wu of Han. After Sima Qian's *Shiji*, Ban Gu of the Eastern Han dynasty further developed the orthodoxy and standardization of Jizhuanti by completing *Hanshu* (Book of Han) in one hundred volumes which recorded the history of the Han dynasty. Since the Tang dynasty, it has become an important task for officials to review and collect the chronicle history after the change of dynasties. Successive dynasties have produced a series of chronicle history books—"Twenty Four Books of History", including twenty-four chronicle historical books from *Shiji* to *Mingshi* (History of the Ming).

纪事本末体是继编年、纪传体之后出现的第三大史书体裁。它以南宋袁枢的《通鉴纪事本末》为起端，是一种以记事为主，每事一篇，独立标题，自具首尾的编纂形式。因为它专记一事，始末了然，故称之为"纪事本末"。袁枢创造的纪事本末体，正是以记事为特长，解决了编年体将一事分载数年而纪传体则在本纪、列传、书志中反复叙述一事的缺陷。纪事本末体史书为我国史籍的多样性、连续性特征增加了新的内容，是继编年、纪传体史籍以后的一大流派。

Jishi Benmoti is the third methodology of historiography appearing after Biannianti and Jizhuanti. It started with the *Tongjian Jishibenmo* by Yuan Shu of the Southern Song dynasty. It is a compilation form based on historical events, with each event given a title and complete plot structure. This type of historiography is featured by recording the clear beginning and end of event, so it is called "Jishi Benmo" (Recording beginning and end of events). Yuan Shu's Jishi Benmo type of historiography solves the Biannianti's defect of dividing an event into different years, and the Jizhuanti's disadvantage of repeatedly narrating an event in different sections (benji, liezhuan, shuzhi) of the book. Jishi Benmoti promotes the diversity and continuity of China's historiography.

三、文化关键词

编年　chronological order

本纪　biographies of prominent rulers

世家　biographies of dukes and princes

列传　biographies of important figures

六经　Six Classics

纪传体　biographical style

《周礼》 *Zhou Li* (*Rites of the Zhou*)

《史记》 *Shi Ji* (*The Records of the Historian*)

《虞夏书》 *Yuxiashu* (*Books of Yu and Xia*)

《尚书》 *Shangshu* (*Books of Shang*)

《周书》 *Zhoushu* (*Books of Zhou*)

《汉书》 *Hanshu* (*Books of Han*)

《春秋》 *Chunqiu* (*Spring and Autumn Annals*)

《左传》 *Zuo Zhuan* (*Zuo's Spring and Autumn Annals*)

第一节 《史记》

The Records of the Historian

一、典籍简介

《史记》原名《太史公书》，西汉时多沿用此称，大约到东汉桓灵年间（147—189），才更名为《史记》。《史记》流传到今天的两千多年间，出现了众多的写本和刻本。目前两汉的旧本已无存，魏晋南北朝至隋唐的抄本也仅存断简残篇，今天所能看到的宋代以来的各种刻本约有 60 种。在中国传统文化典籍中，《史记》堪称精品，司马迁以崇高的人格、坚强的毅力和卓越的史才，完成了《史记》这部体系完整、规模宏大、见识超群的历史巨著，《史记》的伟大思精使它堪称古代的百科全书。它有着取之不尽的思想源泉，具有无限的凝聚力，生命之树常青。

The Records of the Historian was originally named the *Grand Astrologer's Book*, and kept that name until the Han dynasty moved its capital from Chang'an to Luoyang, ushering in the Eastern Han dynasty (25–220). The book was then renamed Records of the Historian. No copies of the book dating from the Western or Eastern Han dynasties are extant, and only a few damaged copies date from the Wei (220–265), Jin (265–420), Northern and Southern dynasties (420–589), Sui (581–618) and Tang (618–907) dynasties. Around 60 different block-printed copies dating from the Song dynasty (960–1279) and beyond are preserved. Among the classics of China's culture, *The Records of the Historian* is a masterpiece. Sima Qian's lofty personality, dogged perseverance and outstanding insights into history shine through the pages of this original and ground-breaking work. The book is an inexhaustible source of information and ideas.

《史记》是中国"二十四史"中的第一部，也是中国史书中最具典范性、最优秀的一部。它是以纪传体的形式写出的一部从中国的五帝时期到汉武帝后期（约公元前 100 年）的上下三千年的历史。司马迁首创纪传体体例，《史记》全书 130 篇，由五部分组成，即十二本纪、十表、八书、三十世家和七十列传。"十二本纪"用编年的形式来记载帝王的言行，反映朝代变迁的大势，是全书的纲领所载。"十表"是联系纪传的桥梁，用表格的形式把纷繁的历史内容纳入尺幅之中，用寓繁于简的形式，勾勒出历史的轮廓及发展的主要线索。"八书"则是从礼、乐、律、历、天官、封禅、河渠、平准八个方面，分专题载述司马迁认为的经国大政，是按专题叙述发展及源流的文化专史。“三十世家”也是像本纪一样按年月编年记事，主要是给诸侯王作传。“七十列传”则是以专传、合传、类传、附传等形式给上至公卿大臣下至平民百姓的社会各阶层的人士作传。

The Records of the Historian stands first among the Twenty-four Histories, official chronicles of China from remote antiquity to the Ming dynasty (1368–1644). It is regarded as the most representative and outstanding of all history books in the Chinese tradition. In the form of a series of biographies, the book records the history of China from the Five Legendary Rulers Period (c 30 century–c. 21 century BC) to around 100 BC, under the reign of Emperor Wu of the Western Han dynasty (206 BC–25 AD). *The Records of the Historian* was the first general history in the form of a series of biographies to appear in China, recording all that was known at that time of historical events from Huangdi in prehistoric times to the reign of Emperor Wu of the Han dynasty. The 130 chapters are divided into five categories:12 chapters of Benji (biographies of prominent rulers), ten chapters of Biao (timelines of events), eight chapters of Shu (governance and cultural records), 30 chapters of Shijia (biographies of dukes and princes) and 70 chapters of Liezhuan (biographies of important figures). The Benji record the words and deeds of kings and emperors in chronological order reflecting the trends of dynastic changes. The Biao give the historical and developmental outlines in tabular form. The Shu record the development of what Sima Qian considered important governance in eight aspects, including rituals, music, law and the calendar. The Shijia are mainly biographies of dukes or princes in chronological order. The Liezhuan are accounts of people of different social strata, from ministers and officials to commoners, in the forms of special biography, joint biography, categorized biography and attached biography.

二、作者简介

司马迁，西汉左冯翊夏阳（今陕西韩城）人，生活在西汉景帝（前 156—前 140 在位）到武帝（前 140—前 86 在位）时期。司马迁幼年耕读于故里，19 岁随家徙茂陵，入京师长安。汉武帝元朔三年（前 126），司马迁 20 岁，正当盛壮之年，他走出书斋，进行了一次足迹遍布大江南北的全国漫游，在实地考察中追寻前代先贤的足迹，考察风俗。汉武帝元封三年（前 108）司马迁继父职任太史令。西汉太史令司天官之职，掌管图籍和宫中档案，并参与重大制度的兴革及各种典礼仪节，这给司马迁修史提供了有利的条件。

The Records of the Historian was written by Sima Qian who was born in Xiayang (present-day Hancheng, Shaanxi Province) in the Western Han dynasty. He lived in the reigns of Emperor Jing (156 BC–140 BC) and Emperor Wu (140 BC–86 BC). Sima Qian studied in his hometown in his childhood, moved to Maoling with his family at the age of 19, and then moved to Chang'an, capital of the Han dynasty. In 126 BC, when Sima Qian was 20 years old, he started a nationwide tour, following in the footsteps of wise men of previous dynasties. He examined local customs and collected anecdotes from around the country. In 108 BC, Sima Qian inherited his fathers position as the grand Astrologer. In the Western Han dynasty this official, apart from his other duties, was in charge of the palace archives, and so sima Qian was in an ideal position to compile his history.

三、典籍英译赏析

秦始皇本纪

【原典 1】

分天下以为三十六郡，郡置守、尉、监。更名民曰“黔首”。大酺。收天下兵，聚之咸阳，销以为钟鐻，金人十二，重各千石，置廷宫中。

【今译】

把天下分为三十六个郡，每郡设置守、尉、监。改称百姓为“黔首”。天下狂欢饮酒庆祝。把全国的武器收集起来，集中到咸阳，熔化后铸成钟，十二个铜人，各重千石，放在宫廷中。

【杨宪益英译】

So the empire was divided into thirty-six provinces, each with a governor, an army commander and an inspector. The common people were renamed the Black-Headed People. There were great celebrations. All the weapons were collected and brought to the capital Xianyang where they were melted down to make bronze bells and twelve bronze statues of giants, each weighing two hundred and forty thousand catties and these were placed in the courts and palaces.

【倪豪士英译】

He divided the world into thirty-six commanderies, each with a governor, a commandant, and a superintendent. He [officially] used the term “the black-haired” to replace “the people”. They celebrated a great bacchanal. He confiscated the weapons of the world, collected them together in Hsien-yang, and smelted them into bells and bell-racks, as well as twelve bronze statues, weighing one-thousand tan each, to be placed in the courtyard of the palace.

【赏析重点】

（1）对比分析文化关键词“郡”“黔首”英译的用词差异。

（2）对比分析两译文的句式特点。

【原典 2】

一法度衡石丈尺。车同轨。书同文字。地东至海暨朝鲜，西至临洮、羌中，南至北向户，北据河为塞，并阴山至辽东。

【今译】

统法制和度量衡。车辆统一轨宽。书写用同一种文字。领土东到大海和朝鲜，西到临洮、羌中，南到北向户，北面占据黄河要塞，沿阴山直到辽东。

【杨宪益英译】

All weights and measures were standardized, all carriages had gauges of the same size. The script was also standardized. The empire extended in the east to the ocean and the land of Chaoxian, in the west to Lintao and Qiangzhong, in the south to Beixianghu, in the north to the fortresses by the Yellow River and along Mount Yinshan to Liaodong.

【倪豪士英译】

He unified the measurements of capacity, weight, and length. Carts all had the same width between wheels, and writings all used the same characters. His territory reached the seas and Ch'ao-hsien in the east, Lin-t'ao and the heartland of the Ch'iang in the west, so far south that houses were built facing north, and so far north that, holding to the Ho, he built fortifications (i.e. the Great Wall), encompassing the Yin Mountains, up to Liao-tung.

【赏析重点】

（1）对比分析文化关键词“轨”“文字”的译文用词差异。

（2）对比分析“南至北向户”译文的语义差异。

廉颇蔺相如列传

【原典 1】

既罢归国，以相如功大，拜为上卿，位在廉颇之右。廉颇曰：“我为赵将，有攻城野战之大功，而蔺相如徒以口舌为劳，而位居我上，且相如素贱人，吾羞，不忍为之下。”宣言曰：“我见相如，必辱之。”

【今译】

渑池会结束以后回到赵国，由于蔺相如功劳大，被封为上卿，官位在廉颇之上。廉颇说：“作为赵国的将军，我有攻战城池作战旷野的大功劳，而蔺相如只不过靠能说会道立了点功，可是他的地位却在我之上，况且蔺相如本来就出身卑贱，我感到羞耻，无法容忍在他的下面。”并且扬言说：“我遇见蔺相如，一定要羞辱他一番。”

【杨宪益英译】

Upon their return to Zhao after this meeting, Lin Xiangru was appointed a chief minister for his outstanding service, taking precedence over Lian Po. Lian Po protested, “As a general of Zhao I have served the state well in the field and stormed many cities. All Lin Xiangru can do is wag his tongue, yet now he is above me. I'd think shame to work under such a base-born fellow.” He swore, “When I meet Lin Xiangru I shall humiliate him!”

【倪豪士英译】

After concluding the meeting and returning home, Hsiang-ju was appointed Senior Excellency because his merit was great. His seat was to the right of Lien Po's. Lien P'o said, “I have served as Chao's commander; I have earned great merit attacking walled cities and fighting in the fields. Lin Hsiang-ju has labored only with his tongue and mouth, and his seat is in front of mine. Moreover this Hsiang-ju was once a commoner! I am shamed; I cannot bear to be a subordinate to him.”

He announced [to all], “When I see Hsiang-ju, I will be sure to insult him.”

【赏析重点】

（1）对比分析“上卿”“位在廉颇之右”的文化要素翻译方法。

（2）分析“贱人”的语义特点和翻译方法。

【原典 2】

相如闻，不肯与会。相如每朝时，常称病，不欲与廉颇争列。已而相如出，望见廉颇，相如引车避匿。

【今译】

蔺相如听到这话后，不愿意和廉颇相会。每到上朝时，蔺相如常常声称有病，不愿和廉颇去争位次的先后。没过多久，蔺相如外出，远远看到廉颇，蔺相如就掉转车子回避。

【杨宪益英译】

When Lin Xiangru got word of this, he kept out of Lian po's way and absented himself from court on grounds of illness, not wanting to compete for precedence. Once when he caught sight of Lian Po in the distance on the road he drove his carriage another way.

【倪豪士英译】

Hsiang-ju heard this and was unwilling to meet with him. Whenever court was held, Hsiang-ju always claimed illness, since he did not want to argue over ranking with Lien P'o. A short while after, Hsiang-ju came out [of his house] and saw Lien P'o in the distance. Hsiang-ju turned his cart aside and hid.

【赏析重点】

对比分析"引车避匿"的翻译方法。

【原典3】

于是舍人相与谏曰:"臣所以去亲戚而事君者,徒慕君之高义也。今君与廉颇同列,廉君宣恶言而君畏匿之,恐惧殊甚,且庸人尚羞之,况於将相乎!臣等不肖,请辞去。"

【今译】

于是蔺相如的门客就一起来向蔺相如抗议说:"我们之所以离开亲人来侍奉您,是仰慕您高尚的节义呀。如今您与廉颇官位相同,廉颇传出坏话,而您却害怕躲避着他,胆怯得也太过分了,一般人尚且感到羞耻,更何况是身为将相的人呢!我们这些人没有出息,请让我们辞去吧!"

【杨宪益英译】

His stewards reproached him saying, "We left our kinsmen to serve you because we admired your lofty character, sir. Now you have the same rank as Lian Po, but when he insults you in public you try to avoid him and look abjectly afraid. This would disgrace even a common citizen, let alone generals and ministers! We are afraid we must beg to resign."

【倪豪士英译】

At this, his retainers protested, "The only reason your servants left their families and took service with your lordship is because we admired your high principles. Now your lordship holds the same rank as Lien P'o, but Lord Lien openly utters insults and you timidly hide from him, palpitating in fear! Even the commonest of men would be ashamed to do this, how much more a commander or minister? Your servants are unworthy, allow us to take leave and depart."

【赏析重点】

（1）对比"高义"的翻译用词特点。

（2）学习"况於将相乎"的翻译句式。

【原典 4】

蔺相如固止之，曰："公之视廉将军孰与秦王？"曰："不若也。"

【今译】

蔺相如坚决地挽留他们，说："诸位认为廉将军和秦王相比谁更厉害？"众人都说："廉将军比不上秦王。"

【杨宪益英译】

Lin Xiangru stopped them, asking, "Is General Lian Po as powerful in your eyes as the king of Qin?" "Of course not," they replied.

【倪豪士英译】

Hsiang-ju detained them, "How do you gentlemen think General Lien compares with the King of Ch'in?" "He is not his equal."

【赏析重点】

分析"公之视廉将军孰与秦王"的结构特点和翻译方法。

【原典 5】

相如曰："夫以秦王之威，而相如廷叱之，辱其群臣，相如虽驽，独畏廉将军哉？顾吾念之，彊秦之所以不敢加兵于赵者，徒以吾两人在也。今两虎共斗，其势不俱生。吾所以为此者，以先国家之急而后私仇也。"

【今译】

蔺相如说："以秦王的威势，而我尚敢在朝廷上呵斥他，羞辱他的群臣，我蔺相如虽然无能，难道会害怕廉将军吗！但是我想到，强大的秦国之所以不敢对赵国用兵，就是因为有我们两人在呀。如今我们俩相斗，就如同两猛虎争斗一般，势必不能同时生存。我之所以这样忍让，就是将国家的危难放在前面，而将个人的私怨搁在后面罢了！"

【杨宪益英译】

"If, useless as I am, I lashed out at the mighty king of Qin in his court and insulted his ministers, why should I be afraid of General Lian Po? To my mind, however, were it not for the two of us, powerful Qin would not hesitate to invade Zhao. When two tigers fight, one must perish. I behave as I do because I put our country's fate before private feuds."

【倪豪士英译】

"As awesome as the King of Ch'in was, I shouted at him in his own court, and insulted his assembled vassals. I may be a plug, but would I fear a mere General Lien? But I thought this: the sole reason mighty Ch'in does not dare to bring its arms to bear against Chao is the presence of the pair of us. When a pair of tigers fight, the circumstances are such that one of them cannot live. The reason I acted as I have is because I place the needs of my state and house first and my private grudges last."

【赏析重点】

（1）对比分析"独畏廉将军哉？"的译文句式差异。

（2）对比分析"徒以吾两人在也"的翻译方法。

（3）对比分析"先国家之急而后私仇"的译文句式差异。

第二节　《尚书》

Book of Shang

一、典籍简介

历史上，《诗》《书》《礼》《易》《春秋》《乐》总称为"六经"。到汉代才将"书"尊称为《尚书》，"尚，上也，言久远也"，被尊奉为儒家"六经"中最重要的一经，其间出现了今文、古文不同本子。由此，它和《左传》《周礼》一起引起了学术史上长期的今古文之争。到晋代又出现了伪古文《尚书》，纠葛更多。其所记载的历史，上起传说中的尧舜禹时代，下至东周春秋中期的历史约1500多年。作为我国最早的一部历史文献汇编，《尚书》涉及先秦时代的政治、军事天文、地理、哲学思想、教育、刑法和典章制度等，保存了我国古代丰富的人文科学和自然科学的各种重要资料，对于研究我国上古史而言是不可替代的。

Originally, the *Six Classics* of Confucius were briefly called Shi (*Book of Poetry*), Shu (*Book of Documents*), Li(*Book of Rites*), Yi (*Book of Changes*), Chunqiu(*Annals of the Spring and Autumn Period*) and Yue (*Book of Music*). However, in the Han dynasty, Shu was considered to be the most important one of the Six Classics and got the name of *The Shangshu* (*Book of Shang*), that is, history of ancient generations. Like the two Chinese books *Zuo Zhuan* (Commentary to Annals of the Spring and Autumn Period) and *Rites of Zhou* (one of three ancient ritual texts listed among the Confucian Canons) the book also caused a long-term dispute in the academic field over the two versions of New Text and Old Text. This dispute was even more severe and presented to the imperial court of the Eastern Jin dynasty. The book is arranged in chronological order that extends 1,500 from the legendary emperors Yao, Shun and Yu to the Eastern Zhou and the middle of the Spring and Autumn Period. As the earliest collection of the history, it covered a wide range of subjects such as politics, military, astronomy geography, philosophy, education, criminal law, ancient laws and regulations and some others of the Pre-Qin times, and preserved various valuable materials on humanities and natural sciences. Thus it is of great importance to the research of ancient Chinese history.

《尚书》按文体可分为诰、训、谟、誓、命、典六种。“诰”，有晓喻的意思。凡以言语、文字告人，具有告诫、慰勉之意的，便称为“诰”。为晓谕民众、祭告宗庙神祇、劝告君王、君戒臣属、同官相诰之意，如《大诰》就是平定管蔡、武庚之乱时周公告诫属下的话。“训”指的是说教、训诫的言辞。大凡贤臣告诫君主的言辞，便称为“训”，类似于现代的建议书、倡议书，如《伊训》《太甲》等便是此类篇章。“谟”，就是谋议、计划之意。君臣一起谋划事情，君有“典”，臣有“谟”，有施政方案，如《皋陶谟》就是大禹、皋陶、伯益向虞舜陈述的嘉言。“誓”是君主誓众之词，多为军事行动的誓词，用于告诫将士或约束敌人，类似于现代的条约，如《甘誓》《汤誓》等篇均为此类篇章。“命”即命令，是国君对臣下颁布的命令，类似于现代的下发公文，如《顾命》就是成王将崩，有所托付之遗“命”。“典”就是常法、常典之意，记载了重要史事经过或某项专题史实，如《尧典》《舜典》就记载了唐尧、虞舜的嘉言善政。除此之外，还有以人名标题的，如《盘庚》《微子》；以事标题的，如《高宗肜日》《西伯戡黎》；以内容标题的，如《禹贡》《洪范》《无逸》等。

Those chapters can be divided into six types of speeches: gao (诰) , xun (训) ,

mo（谟）, shi（誓）, ming（命）and dian（典）. "Gao" means the words or speeches contain warnings, comforts or encouragements, which might be instructions from the monarch to the subjects, or to the people, or the advice between subjects. For example, "The Great Announcement" is a collection of Zhougong's(or Duke Zhou's) instructions to his subordinates when quelling the Guancai-Wugeng Rebellion. "Xun" refers to the speeches of sermonizing and admonishing. All the advice from the subjects to the monarch is called "xun", similar to the modern proposals or recommendations, "The Instructions of "Yi" and "The Taijia" are examples. "Mo" means consultations between the subjects on state affairs, and the subjects reach the governance program under the monarch's canon. "*The Counsels of Gao-yao*" is the good words that emperors Yu, Gao-yao and Bo-yi advised to emperor Shun. "Shi" means the Kings declarations mostly for the military actions, which is used to warn the soldiers or to pin down the enemy, somewhat similar to modern treaties "The Speech at Gan" and "The Speech of Tang" are of this category. "Ming" is commands issued by the monarch to the subjects, similar to today's official documents. "The Testamentary Charge" is Emperor Cheng's will made on his deathbed. "Dian" means canons of important historical records or a specific historical event. For example, "The Canon of Emperor Yao" and " The Canon of Emperor Shun" record emperors Yao and Shun's good words and governance. Besides, there are also some chapters named after a person, like "King pan-geng" and "The Count of Wei". "The day of the Supplementary Sacrifice to Gao Zong" and "The Chief of the Wests Conquest of Li" are named after the events, while "The Tribute of Yu", "The Great Plan and Wu Yi" are named after the contents.

二、典籍英译赏析

【原典 1】

任贤勿贰，去邪勿疑。

《尚书 · 虞书 · 大禹谟》

【今译】

任用贤人不可怀有二心，铲除恶人不可犹豫不决。

【英译】

In your employment of men of worth, let none come between you and them. Put away evil with out hesitation.

The Counsels of the Great Yu

【赏析重点】

分析译文的句式结构转换。

【原典 2】

汝惟不矜，天下莫与汝争能；汝惟不伐，天下莫与汝争功。

《尚书·虞书·大禹谟》

【今译】

如果你不去自夸自傲，那么天下便没有人能与你一争高下；如果你不自高自大，那么天下便没有与你争功劳的人。

【英译】

You are without any prideful assumption, but no one under heaven can contest with you the palm of ability; you make no boasting, but no one under heaven can contest with you the palm of merit.

The Counsels of the Great Yu

【赏析重点】

学习译文的句式和用词特点。

【原典 3】

克勤于邦，克俭于家。

《尚书·虞书·大禹谟》

【今译】

治理国家要勤恳；管理家庭要节俭。

【英译】

Full of toilsome earnestness in the service of the country, and sparing in your expenditure on your family.

The Counsels of the Great Yu

【赏析重点】

学习文化关键词"勤""俭"的翻译用词。

【原典 4】

好问则裕，自用则小。

《尚书·商书·仲虺之诰》

【今译】

遇事多问的人就会不断丰富自己的知识，自以为是、刚愎自用的人会使自己知识贫乏。

【英译】

He who likes to put questions, becomes enlarged; he who uses only his own views, becomes smaller (than he was).

The Announcement of Zhonghui

【赏析重点】

学习文化关键词“裕”“小”的翻译用词。

【原典5】

民可近，不可下。民惟邦本，本固邦宁。

《尚书·虞书·五子之歌》

【今译】

百姓可以亲近，而不可看轻。百姓是国家的根本基础，百姓安居乐业，国家就能太平。

【英译】

The people should be cherished,
And not looked down upon.
The people are the root of a country;
The root firm, the country is tranquil.

The Songs of the Five Sons

【赏析重点】

分析“本固邦宁”的翻译方法。

【原典6】

不矜细行，终累大德。为山九仞，功亏一篑。

《尚书·周书·旅獒》

【今译】

不注重细行，终究会损害大德，比如筑九仞高的土山，工作未完只在于一筐土。

【英译】

If you do not attend jealously to your small actions, the result will be to affect your virtue in great matters; In raising a mound of nine fathoms, the work may be unfinished for want of one basket (of earth).

The Hounds of Lü

【赏析重点】

分析“功亏一篑”译文的句式结构转换。

【原典 7】

虑善以动，动惟厥时。有其善，丧其善；矜其能，丧其功。惟事事，乃其有备，有备无患。

《尚书·商书·说命中》

【今译】

考虑妥善而后行动，行动又当适合时机。自恃自己有善行，就会失掉善行；夸自己有能力，就会失去成功。做事情，要有准备，有准备才没有后患。

【英译】

Anxious thought about what will be best should precede your movements, which also should be taken at the time proper for them. Indulging the consciousness of being good is the way to lose that goodness; being vain of one's ability is the way to lose the merit it might produce. For all affairs let there be adequate preparation; with preparation there will be no calamitous issue.

The Charge to Yue（Ⅱ）

【赏析重点】

对比分析“有其善”“有备无患”中“有”的翻译用词差异。

【原典 8】

满招损，谦受益。

《尚书·虞书·大禹谟》

【今译】

自满招致损害，谦虚获得益处。

【英译】

Pride brings loss, and humility receives increase.

The Counsels of the Great Yu

【赏析重点】

分析“受益”的翻译用词特点。

【原典 9】

人心惟危，道心惟危，惟精惟一，允执厥中。

《尚书·虞书·大禹谟》

【今译】

人心是危险难测的，天理又是精微难明的，最好的办法是全心全意地治理天下，执行中庸的原则。

【英译】

The mind of man is restless, prone to error; its affinity to what is right is small. Be discriminating, be uniform (in the pursuit of what is right), that you may sincerely hold fast the mean.

The Counsels of the Great Yu

【赏析重点】

学习文化关键词“精”“一”的语义特点和翻译用词。

【原典 10】

居上克明，为下克忠。

《尚书·商书·伊训》

【今译】

在上位的人要能查是非，在下位的人要尽忠职守。

【英译】

Occupying the highest position, he displayed intelligence; occupying an inferior position, he displayed his loyalty.

The Instructions of Yi

【赏析重点】

学习文化关键词“明”“忠”的翻译用词。

第三节 《群书治要》

The Compilation of Books and Writings on the Important Governing Principles

一、典籍简介

《群书治要》(以下简称《治要》)是我国古代治政书籍的选辑。唐初著名谏官魏征及虞世南、褚遂良等在贞观初年受命于唐太宗李世民(599—649),以辑录前人著述作谏书,为唐太宗"偃武修文""治国安邦",创建"贞观之治"提供警示的匡政巨著。《治要》取材于六经、四史、诸子百家,"上始五帝,下迄晋年",以"务乎政术,存乎劝戒"为宗旨,从一万四千多部、八万九千多卷古籍中"采摭群书,剪截淫放",呕心沥血数年,于贞观五年(631)编辑成书,计六十五部约五十余万言。

Qunshu Zhiyao, or *The Compilation of Books and Writings on the Important Governing Principles*, is a compilation containing advice, methods, and historical notes on the successes and failures of the imperial government of China. At the beginning of the Zhenguan Era, Emperor Taizong (599–649) of the Tang dynasty decreed that *Qunshu Zhiyao* (The Compilation of Books and Writings on the Important Governing Principles) be compiled. Taizong ordered two advisors, the honorable Wei Zheng and Yu Shinan, to comb through all the historical records on imperial governing principles from the Six Classics, the Four Collections of History and the Hundreds of Schools, and to extract the most important lessons related to the cultivation of oneself, management of family, good government, and ways to bring about peace in the world. The result was a collection, titled Qunshu Zhiyao, carefully excerpted from 14,000 books and 89,000 scrolls of ancient writings–500,000 words in all, and covering sixty-five book categories–dating from the era of the Five Legendary Emperors to the Jin dynasty.

《群书治要》虽然诞生于一千三百多年以前,但是,书中的治国思想实为中国古圣先王治国教民之集大成,其治国平天下之智慧、理念、方法、经验与成效,均是历经几千年考验所累积的宝藏结晶。《群书治要》理所当然地成为唐太宗之后,历代君王乃至辅臣和各级官吏修身、治国、平天下的教科书。

This compilation takes us through thousands of years of Chinese political thinking, and offers us some valuable leadership principles which not only helped the great Tang

Emperor Taizong to establish the glorious Reign of Zhenguan, but which will also prove valid as points of reference for contemporary leaders. As for the general public, this compilation is a great source of inspiration for self-improvement, family management and human relations.

二、作者简介

魏徵（580—643），字玄成，唐朝杰出的政治家、思想家、文学家和史学家。曾任谏议大夫、左光禄大夫，封郑国公，谥文贞，魏徵参与修撰《群书治要》及《隋书》等，其言论多见《贞观政要》。

Wei Zheng (580–643), courtesy name Xuancheng, posthumously known as Duke Wenzhen of Zheng, was a Chinese politician and historian. He served as a chancellor of the Tang dynasty for about 13 years during the reign of Emperor Taizong. He was also the lead editor of the official history of the Sui dynasty, the *Book of Sui*, which was composed in 636.

三、典籍英译赏析

【原典 1】

夫物速成则疾亡，晚就则善终。朝华之草，夕而零落；松柏之茂，隆寒不衰。是以大雅君子恶速成。

（卷二十六·魏志下）

【今译】

大凡事物发展过快则衰亡也快，缓慢稳定地发展则容易有圆满的成果。早晨开花的草，到了傍晚就凋落了；茂盛的松柏，即使在非常寒冷的冬天也不会枯萎。所以，德高才大的君子忌讳速成。

【英译】

In general, anything that develops too fast will fall apart just as quickly, whereas a slow and steady development is more assured of yielding favorable results. Plants that unravel into full bloom in early morning may wither and fall by the evening, but the slow-growing pine trees will not wither even in the extreme winter cold. Hence, a superior person does not hasten to achieve results.

Scroll 26: *Wei Zhi*, Vol. 2

【赏析重点】

（1）学习“善终”的语义特点和翻译方法。

（2）分析“松柏之茂，隆寒不衰”译文的句式结构转换。

【原典 2】

古之人曰：“一夫不耕，或受之饥；一女不织，或受之寒。”生之有时，而用之无度，则物力必屈。古之治天下，至纤至悉也，故其蓄积足恃。

（卷十四·汉书二）

【今译】

古人说：“一个农夫不耕种，就有人要挨饿；一个妇女不织布，就有人会受冻。”万物生长是有时节的，但使用却没有节制，这样物资势必会用尽。古代治理天下，达到非常细致周详的地步，所以国家有足够的积蓄可以依靠。

【英译】

The ancients said, “If a farmer refuses to work, some people will starve. If a woman refuses to weave, some people will suffer in the cold.” When the growth of all things is limited by seasons but we consume them as if they will be available without limitation, the resources will sooner or later be depleted. The ancients governed and planned meticulously and they would have had the foresight to ensure the treasury had enough reserves to sustain the nation.

Scroll 14: *Han Shu*, Vol. 2

【赏析重点】

分析“生之有时，而用之无度”的语义特点和翻译方法。

【原典 3】

子贡曰：“君子之过也，如日月之食焉。过也，人皆见之；更也，人皆仰之。”

（卷九·论语）

【今译】

子贡说：“君子的过错，就像日蚀、月蚀一样。所犯的错，人人都看得见；改正了，像日月蚀后重现光明那样，人人都敬仰他。”

【英译】

Zigong said, “The faults of a superior person are analogous to the eclipses of the sun and the moon. When he is at fault, everyone can see his faults clearly. But when he corrects his faults, everyone will look up to him with respect."

Scroll 9: *The Analects*

【赏析重点】

学习"日月之食""人皆仰之"的翻译用词。

【原典 4】

帝王之于亲戚，爱虽隆，必示之以威；体虽贵，必禁之以度。

（卷二十四·后汉书四）

【今译】

君主对于亲属，爱护虽然深厚，但一定要有威严，否则亲属就会傲慢；亲属的身份虽然尊贵，但一定要用法度来制约，否则亲属会横行无忌。

【英译】

Although a leader may love his relatives deeply, he should maintain his authority over them or they will become arrogant and disrespectful. The status of the relatives may be privileged but they must be held accountable by law in order to restrain them from behaving wildly and uncontrollably.

Scroll 24: *Hou Han Shu*, Vol. 4

【赏析重点】

分析"必示之以威""必禁之以度"的翻译方法。

【原典 5】

金玉满堂，莫之能守，富贵而骄，还自遗咎。功成名遂身退，天之道也。

（卷三十四·老子）

【今译】

金玉满堂、丰富的物质生活，很难长久的保有；富贵时生活骄纵奢侈，就会给自己种下祸根。功成名就之后，懂得不居功贪位，适时退下，才符合大自然的运行之道。

【英译】

A house full of gold and jade cannot be safely kept forever. When wealth and honor leads to arrogance, it sows the seeds of one's own downfall. To retire at the height of one's own merit and fame, is in accord with the law of nature.

Scroll 34: *Tao Te Ching*

【赏析重点】

分析“还自遗咎”的语义特点和翻译方法。

【原典 6】

子曰：“侍于君子有三愆：言未及之而言，谓之躁；言及之而不言，谓之隐；未见颜色而言，谓之瞽 [gǔ]。”

（卷九 · 论语）

【今译】

孔子说：“随侍君子时容易犯三种过失：话没到该说时就说，这就是心浮气躁；话当说而不说，这就是隐匿之过；没有观察君子的神色就说话，这就是不懂言语分寸。”

【英译】

Confucius said, “For the ones who serve the lords may make the following three errors: To speak when it is not necessary is being rash; not to speak when it is necessary is being evasive; to speak without observing the lord’s facial expression is being blind.”

Scroll 9: *The Analects*

【赏析重点】

（1）学习关键词“躁”“隐”“瞽”的翻译用词。

（2）学习“颜色”的语义特点和翻译方法。

【原典 7】

故君子之接如水，小人之接如醴；君子淡以成，小人甘以坏。

（卷七 · 礼记）

【今译】

君子之间的交往淡如清水，小人之间的交情蜜如甜酒；君子之交虽平淡却能互相成就，小人之交虽亲密却易互相败坏。

【英译】

The friendship offered by a superior person is plain like water; the friendship offered by a petty person is pleasing like sweet wine. Being friends with a superior person may not be exciting but the interactions are nevertheless beneficial to both sides. Being friends with a petty person may be exciting but may hurt in the end when no more selfish gains are to be made from it.

Scroll 7: *The Books of Rites*

【赏析重点】

（1）分析“故君子之接如水，小人之接如醴”的翻译方法。

（2）分析“君子淡以成，小人甘以坏”的句式逻辑特点和翻译方法。

【原典8】

孔子曰：“导之以政，齐之以刑，民免而无一耻。导之以德，齐之以礼，有耻且格。”老氏称：“法令滋章，盗贼多有。”

（卷十二·史记下）

【今译】

孔子说：“用政治来教化人民，用刑罚来管理人民，这样做，人民只想到如何免于刑罚，不会想到是不是可耻。但是用德行来教化人民，用礼义来管理人民，人民不但守法知耻而且能改过向善。”老子说：“法律政令愈繁复苛刻，走法律漏洞的盗贼反而愈来愈多。”

【英译】

Confucius said, “Guide the people with policies and align them with punishment, and people will evade capture and gain no personal sense of shame. Guide them with virtues and align them with propriety, and they will gain their own sense of shame and thus correct themselves.” Laozi said, “As law and orders are increasingly written, loopholes and thievery will become increasingly common.”

Scroll 12: *The Records of the Historian*, Vol. 2

【赏析重点】

（1）分析“民免而无一耻”的语义特点和翻译方法。

（2）分析“法令滋章，盗贼多有”的句法特点和翻译方法。

拓展训练 | Extension Training

1. 思考练习

（1）用英文简要介绍《史记》《尚书》《群书治要》主要内容。

（2）总结历史典籍语言特点和翻译策略。

2. 文化外宣汉英翻译

（1）唐朝贞观年间（627—649）是唐太宗李世民统治的鼎盛时期，史家称誉为“贞观之治”。到李世民的曾孙唐玄宗李隆基开元年间（713—741），唐朝达到繁荣昌盛的顶峰，史称“开元盛世”。唐太宗深知“为政之要，惟在得人”，以政治家的胆识，不拘一格，不记恩仇，网罗了大批精干的人才。贞观年间的宰相班子汇集了天下最杰出的精英：房玄龄善于谋划，杜如晦长于决断，魏徵犯颜直谏，李靖出将入相，为开创开元新局面奠定了基础。

（2）战国末期的思想家荀子曾经说过：“君者，舟也；庶人者，水也。水则载舟，水则覆舟。”意思是：君主如船，百姓如水，水既能使船安稳地航行，也能使船沉没。唐太宗以史为镜，对荀子的这一观点十分赞赏，在与君臣讨论国家的治理问题时，多次引用和发挥了这一观点。他在《论政体》一文中说：“君，舟也；人，水也；水能载舟，亦能覆舟。”

唐太宗长期以来坚持以民为本、不夺农时的治理策略。他曾对自己的幕僚讲：这样做不只是“忧怜百姓”，也是为了“长守富贵”。基于这样的目的，他在位时期，以国家稳定为政策要务，以稳定求发展，居安思危，终使隋末天下大乱的局面得到了大治。

（3）养育人民，包括满足人民的生活需要和对人民进行教育。《尚书·大禹谟》将其作为“善政”（良好政治）的目的：为了实现这一目的，治国者必须治理协调好“六府三事”。“六府”是指金、木、水、火、土、谷，即人民生活所需的各种物质资料；“三事”是指“正德”（端正人民品德）、“利用”（使物质资料为百姓所用）、“厚生”（使人民生活充裕）。这是一种以民为本、物质文明和精神文明兼顾并举的治国理念。

第四章　兵法典籍英译

Translation of Art of War Classics

一、学习目标

（1）学会用英文介绍中国古代主要兵法思想。

（2）掌握中国古代军事兵法文化概念汉英翻译。

（3）鉴赏兵法典籍的汉英翻译策略。

二、文化背景

兵书是中国古代军事著作的总称，是对古代军事斗争经验的总结。兵书和其他社会事物一样，是社会发展到一定阶段的产物。在正式的兵书诞生之前，甲骨文、金文中便有了许多关于中国古代战争的记载。在此基础上，春秋战国时期产生了中国历史上最早的兵书《军志》和《军政》。

The books on the art of war is a general term of ancient Chinese military canons, also the conclusion of the experience on ancient military battles. Similar to other social matters, its origin is the product of the development of society. Before the birth of formal books on the art of war, there were many inscriptions on bones tortoise shells or bronze that recorded. Based on that, the earliest relevant books, *Military Strategy* and *Military Theory* appeared in the spring and Autumn Period (770 BC–476 BC) and Warring States Period (475 BC –221 BC).

中国古代兵书的内容十分丰富，种类繁多。虽然哪一本是最早的兵书目前尚不能确定，但还是能够从春秋战国（前 770—前 221）以来的《左传》《孙子兵法》等文献中找到一些早期兵书的内容。《军志》和《军政》一直被认为是中国最早的兵书，但是这两部兵书早已失传，只是在后来的史籍中还保留着一些片段。据研究，这两部兵书大致是西周晚期的作品。《军志》和《军政》的内容丰富，不仅仅有对军事活动的简单记载，还总结和概括了一些军事活动的经验，并在一定程度上揭示了战争和军事活动中的某些规律。

The content of books on the art of war in ancient China is rich and diversified. Although the first book on the art of war can not be confirmed yet, several records about the early books on the art of war still can be found in the literatures, such as *The Commentary of Zuo* and *Sun Tzu's Art of War* written since the Spring and Autumn Period (770 BC–476 BC). *Military Strategy* and *Military Theory* have been considered as the earliest works. However, they had been long gone. Only some fragments of record can prove its existence. According to the research, the two books were approximately written in the late Western Zhou dynasty (1046 BC–771 BC). They have ample content and not only are the simple record on military activities but also conclude the relevant experience and reveal some regular patterns in these activities.

自春秋末期至清朝末年的2500多年中，中华民族涌现出了许多杰出的军事家和兵书著述家。他们所著的兵书浩如烟海，构成了中国古代军事文化的重要内容，成为人们研究中国古代军事思想的文献宝库。

Within the 2,500 years of history from the late Spring and Autumn Period (770 BC–476 BC) and to the late Qing dynasty (1644–1911), there appeared numerous outstanding strategists and writers of the books on the art of war. These countless canons and masterpieces constitute an important part of ancient Chinese military culture and have become the treasury of the references for people's study on ancient Chinese military theories.

三、文化关键词

三十六计 Thirty-Six Stratagems

围魏救赵 Besiege Wei to Rescue Zhao

声东击西 Clamor in the East, Attack in the West

隔岸观火 Observe the Fire on the Opposite Shore

李代桃僵 Sacrifice the Plum Tree in Place of the Peach

顺手牵羊 Seize the Opportunity to Lead a Sheep Away

调虎离山 Lure the Tiger Down the Mountain

欲擒故纵 To Catch Something, First Let It Go

《孙子兵法》 *Sun Tzu's Art of War*

《吴子兵法》 *Wu Tzu's Art of War*

第一节　《孙子兵法》

Sun Tzu's Art of War

一、典籍简介

《孙子兵法》是中国古代最著名的军事著作，是中华民族的优秀文化遗产，也是世界上最古老的兵书。有人认为，普鲁士的克劳塞维兹（1780—1831）的《战争论》可以和《孙子兵法》相比，但是克劳塞维兹的《战争论》比《孙子兵法》晚了两千多年。可见，《孙子兵法》是历史上影响最深远的军事论著。

Sun Tzu's Art of War is the most famous work on military operations in ancient China. Being the oldest military treatise in the world, it is one of the greatest cultural legacies of the Chinese nation. Only the Prussian Clausewitz's *On War* may compare with it. But *On War* was written more than 2,000 years later. Therefore, *Sun Tzu's Art of War* is a classic on military operations and the most influential in the world today.

《孙子兵法》之所以负有盛名，因为在两千多年前就提出了一些用兵的重要原则。如“不战而屈人之兵，善之善者也”。战争的目的不是多杀人，如果能不战而取胜，才是用兵的上策。《孙子兵法》又强调在战争中要学会利用优势，“攻其无备，出其不意”；在战争时要懂得“兵贵胜不贵久”；军事领袖们应对敌方人员有深入了解，因为“知彼知己，百战不殆”。所有这些原则对现今世界的军事实践都有重大的意义。

In this well-known book, Sun Tzu puts forward many important principles in military operations. He says, winning a victory and subduing the enemy without fighting is the highest excellence. “War is not for slaughter, if you win without fighting, the way you can do so is the greatest military strategy.” Sun Tzu in his book stresses, “To attack where the enemy is unprepared and hit when it is unexpected” is another wise observation. “Military operations should aim at speedy victory and not prolonged campaigns.” “Know both the enemy and yourself, you will fight a hundred battles without danger of defeat.” All these principles are, unquestionably, significant even in military strategies in the world today.

《孙子兵法》共十三篇，是一部有系统而全面的军事著作。虽然每篇只讲一个问题，但十三篇却是一个有机的整体。所以，在研究十三篇时，不能把每篇割裂开来，战争是一个整体，作战的理论也同样是一个整体。本书把十三篇分成一百段，并不意味每一段都是独立的，而只是为了使读者能更细致地了解每一段的含义。

The thirteen military essays in *The Art of War* form a systematic military work. Each essay discusses one problem, but thirteen essays constitute an organic whole, which can never be taken separately. In this book the original thirteen chapters are divided into one hundred topics for easy reading and comprehension. It does not mean that each topic is an independent one. It will be advantageous for the readers to understand the text, know the relation of its parts and grasp its essence in its entirety.

二、作者简介

孙子，名孙武，春秋末期军事家。后人尊称其为孙子、孙武子、兵圣、百世兵家之师、东方兵学的鼻祖。著有《孙子兵法》。主要成就包括论兵、论政的篇章，代表作品有《计篇》《作战篇》《谋攻篇》《形篇》《势篇》《虚实篇》。

Sun Tzu, also known as Sun Wu, was a military strategist in the late Spring and Autumn Period. He was respectfully titled by future generations as Sun Tzu, SunWu zi, Soldier Saint, The Master of Soldiers for Generations and the Originator of Oriental Strategy. He is said to have authored *The Art of War*. Major achievements: quite a few important articles about the art of war and the theory of politics. Representative works: *Laying Plans*, *Waging War*, *Attack by Stratagem*, *Tactical Dispositions*, *Energy* and *Weak Points and Strong Points*.

三、典籍英译赏析

【原典 1】

孙子曰：兵者，国之大事，死生之地，存亡之道，不可不察也。

【今译】

孙子说：战争，是国家的大事，是军队生死的所在，国家存亡的途径，不能不认真考察。

【林戊荪英译】

Sunzi said: War is a question of vital importance to the state, a matter of life and death, the road to survival or ruin. Hence, it is a subject which calls for careful study.

【安乐哲英译】

Master Sun said: War is a vital matter of state. It is the field on which life or death is determined and the road that leads to either survival or ruin, and must be examined with the greatest care.

【赏析重点】

对比分析“死生之地”的语义特点和翻译方法。

【原典2】

故经之以五事，校之以计，而索其情，一曰道，二曰天，三曰地，四曰将，五曰法。

【今译】

所以，要从五个方面进行分析，比较敌我双方的各种条件，以探索战争的情势：一是道，二是天，三是地，四是将，五是法。

【林戊荪英译】

To assess the outcome of a war, we need to examine the belligerent parties and compare them in terms of the following five fundamental factors. The first is the way（*dao* 道）; the second, heaven（*tian* 天）; the third, earth（*di* 地）; the fourth, command（*jiang* 将）; and the fifth, rules and regulations（*fa* 法）.

【安乐哲英译】

Therefore, to gauge the outcome of war we must appraise the situation on the basis of the following five criteria, and compare the two sides by assessing their relative strengths. The first of the five criteria is the way (*tao*), the second is climate, the third is terrain, the fourth is command, and the fifth is regulation.

【赏析重点】

对比分析文化关键词“天”“地”的翻译用词特点。

【原典3】

故校之以计，而索其情，曰：主孰有道？将孰有能？天地孰得？法令孰行？兵众孰强？士卒孰练？赏罚孰明？吾以此知胜负矣。

【今译】

所以，要通过对双方情况的比较来探索战争的情势。就是说：哪一方君主更贤明？哪一方将帅更有才能？哪一方天时地理有利？哪一方法令能贯彻执行？哪一方武器装备精良？哪一方兵卒训练有素？哪一方赏罚严明？我根据这些就可以判断谁胜谁负了。

【林戊荪英译】

Therefore when assessing the outcome of a war, compare the two sides in terms of the above factors and appraise the situation accordingly. Find out which sovereign possesses more moral influence, which general is more capable, which side has the advantages of heaven and earth, which army is better disciplined, whose troops are better armed and trained, which command is more impartial in meting out rewards and punishments, and I will be able to forecast which side will be victorious.

【安乐哲英译】

Therefore, to gauge the outcome of war we must compare the two sides by assessing their relative strengths. This is to ask the following questions:

Which ruler has the way (*tao*)?

Which commander has the greater ability?

Which side has the advantages of climate and terrain?

Which army follows regulations and obeys orders more strictly?

Which army has superior strength?

Whose officers and men are better trained?

Which side is more strict and impartial in meting out rewards and punishments?

On the basis of this comparison I know who will win and who will lose.

【赏析重点】

分析“天地孰得”“法令孰行”的语义特点和翻译方法。

【原典 4】

将听吾计，用之必胜，留之；将不听吾计，用之必败，去之。计利以听，乃为之势，以佐其外。势者，因利而制权也。

【今译】

如果君上听从我的计策，用计作战定能胜利，我就留下；如果君上不听我的计策行事，用计必然失败，我就离开。分析利害得失的意见已被采纳，然后就要造成有利的态势，作为外在的辅助条件。所谓有利的态势，就是根据对自己有利的情况，掌握作战主动权。

【林戊荪英译】

The general who employs my assessment methods is bound to win; I shall therefore stay with him. The general who does not heed my words will certainly lose; I shall leave him.

Having paid heed to my assessment of the relative advantages and disadvantages, the general must create a favourable strategic situation which will help bring the victory to fruition. By this I mean being flexible and making the most of the advantages to gain the initiative in war.

【安乐哲英译】

If you heed my assessments, dispatching troops into battle would mean certain victory, and I will stay. If you do not heed them, dispatching troops would mean certain defeat, and I will leave.

Having heard what can be gained from my assessments, shape a strategic advantage (*shih*) from them to strengthen our position. By "strategic advantage" I mean making the most of favorable conditions (in)and tilting the scales in our favor.

【赏析重点】

对比分析"势者，因利而制权也"的语义特点和翻译方法。

【原典5】

兵者，诡道也。故能而示之不能，用而示之不用，近而示之远，远而示之近。利而诱之，乱而取之，实而备之，强而避之，怒而挠之，卑而骄之，佚而劳之，亲而离之，攻其无备，出其不意。此兵家之胜，不可先传也。

【今译】

用兵应以诡诈为原则。所以，能打而装作不能打，要打而装作不要打，向近处而装作向远处，向远处而装作向近处。敌人贪利，就引诱它；敌人混乱，就攻取它；敌人力量充实，就要防备它；敌人兵力强大，就要避开它；敌人气势汹汹，就要屈挠它；敌人辞卑慎行，就要骄纵它；敌人休整得好，就要劳累它；敌人内部团结，就要离间它。在敌人毫无防备之处发动进攻，在敌人意料不到之时采取行动。这是军事家指挥的奥妙，是不能预先呆板规定的。

【林戊荪英译】

War is a game of deception. Therefore, feign incapability when in fact capable; feign inactivity when ready to strike; appear to be far away when actually nearby, and vice versa. When the enemy is greedy for gains, hand out a bait to lure him; when he is in disorder, attack and overcome him; when he boasts substantial strength, be doubly prepared against him; and when he is formidable, evade him. If he is given to anger, provoke him. If he is timid and careful, encourage his arrogance. If his forces are rested, wear them down. If he is united as one, divide him. Attack where he is least prepared. Take action when he least expects you. Herein lies a strategist's subtlety of command which is impossible to codify in hard and fast rules beforehand.

【安乐哲英译】

Warfare is the art (*tao*) of deceit. Therefore, when able, seem to be unable; when ready, seem unready; when nearby, seem far away; and when far away, seem near. If the enemy seeks some advantage, entice him with it. If he is in disorder, attack him and take him. If he is formidable, prepare against him. If he is strong, evade him. If he is incensed, provoke him. If he is humble, encourage his arrogance. If he is rested, wear him down. If he is internally harmonious, sow divisiveness in his ranks. Attack where he is not prepared, go by way of places where it would never occur to him you would go. These are the military strategists calculations for victory, they cannot be settled in advance.

【赏析重点】

（1）分析“利而诱之”“乱而取之”的语义逻辑特点和翻译方法。

（2）对比“攻其无备”“出其不意”的翻译方法。

第二节 《尉缭子》

Wei Liao Zi

一、典籍简介

《尉缭子》是一部系统的军事战略学著作，继承并发展了《孙子兵法》《吴子兵法》等兵书的军事思想，受到中国乃至世界兵法研究者的推崇。该兵书成书于战国中后期，今存 24 篇，按内容可分为两部分：前 12 篇主要论述了作者的战争观和政治观，后 12 篇主要论述了军令和军制。《尉缭子》的军事理论以治国、富国为基础，对强兵、用兵的问题进行了广泛而深刻的研究。《尉缭子》是最早流传至国外的兵书之一，在日本、朝鲜和西方国家广为流传。该兵书的传播对于扩大中国古代军事文化的影响产生了重要的作用。

Wei Liao Zi, a systematical canon on military strategies, which inherited and developed the theories in *Master Sun's Art of War* and *Master Wu's Art of War* has been praised by researchers of military strategy in China and even across the world. This book was written in the middle and late period of the Warring States Period (475 BC–221 BC), now existing 24 chapters. According to the content, it can be divided into two parts: the first half (1–12 chapters) is mainly about the concept of the war and politics and the second half (13–24 chapters) is mainly about the military disciplines and organization. The military theory in *Wei Ligo Zi* is based on the national governance and development. It gives detailed research on the issues of military enhancement and operation. It was also one of the military books which were introduced to foreign countries, including Japan, Korea and the western countries. The spread of this book exerted a great influence on the expansion of ancient Chinese military culture.

《尉缭子》以朴素的唯物主义思想为其军事理论奠定了坚实的哲学基础；认为正确的政治策略和经济措施，是军事胜利的先决条件和根本保证；在战争指导上，认为培养和激励己方士气，削弱和瓦解敌方的士气，是最高明的制胜韬略；认为战争有三种取胜方式："道胜""威胜""力胜"；在军队管理上，强调"明正赏罚"，依法治军；详尽地讨论了军事训练的方法内容及其意义。

Wei Liao Zi with its naive materialist thinking has laid a solid philosophical foundation for its military theory. It holds that correct political tactics and economic measures are a prerequisite and basic guarantee for military victory. With regard to the conduct of war, it holds that building up and boosting the morale of one's own side, and dampening and destroying the enemy's morale were the most intelligent tactic to win victory. It maintains that a war can be won by three ways: "by Dao (Right Way)", "by awesomeness" and "by strength". With regard to managing the army, it stresses "fair and strict in meting out punishments", and running military affairs according to law. It also elaborates the ways and means as well as the contents and significance of military training.

本书不仅为中国历代论兵者所重，也对其他国家产生较大影响。日本关于它的研究著作多达 30 余种，朝鲜很早就有了《尉缭子》刊本。18 世纪，传入西方。

The book not only has drawn attention from military scholars of various periods in China, but also has exerted great influence in other countries. In Japan there are well over thirty research works on *Wei Liao Zi*, and in Korea there were printed editions of the book in earlier time. The book was circulated to the west in the 18th century.

二、作者简介

尉缭，生卒年不详，战国时期兵家。古人对所尊敬的人一般称“子”，故称其“尉缭子”。尉缭曾在魏国为臣，为振兴魏国付出了巨大努力，《尉缭子》一书就是他与魏王谈论军事学的记录。

Wei Liao, unknown dates of birth and death, was a military strategist in the Warring States Period (475 BC–221 BC). Ancient people liked to add the character Zi behind the respected scholar's name, hence the name Wei Liao Zi. Wei Liao once served in the State Wei and contributed a lot for its prosperity. The book *Wei Liao Zi* is the conversation record about military strategy between him and the king of the Wei.

三、典籍英译赏析

【原典 1】

量土地肥挠而立邑。建城称地，以城称人，以人称粟。三相称，则内可以固守，外可以战胜。战胜于外，备生于内，胜备相应，犹合符节，无异故也。

【今译】

应该根据土地的肥瘠来确定设置都邑。都邑的兴建要与土地的广狭相称，都邑的大小要与人口的多少相称，人口的多少要与粮食的产量相称。三者相称，那么自卫时就可以稳固防守，进攻时就可以取得胜利。能在国外战胜敌人，在于国内有充分的准备。胜利和准备的相互对应，就像符节的两半相吻合一样，是由于没有差异呀。

【英译】

Survey the fertility and sterility of the soil and then erect cities and towns. The establishment of a city must be commensurate to the size of the surveyed land. The area of the city must be commensurate to the number of the population and the number of the population must be commensurate to the quantities of food supplies. When these three are in conformity with each other, then internally one can set up a solid defense, and externally gain victory in battle. Moreover, the external victory is gained on the basis of the internal preparations. Hence victory is closely connected with preparation, and they are like the halves of a tally exactly matching each other.

【赏析重点】

（1）分析“建城称地，以城称人，以人称粟”的语义逻辑特点和翻译方法。

（2）分析“战胜于外，备生于内”的句法结构和翻译方法。

【原典2】

治兵者，若秘于地，若邃于天，生于无。故开之，大不窕，小不恢。明乎禁舍开塞，民流者亲之，地不任者任之。夫土广而任则国富，民众而制则国治。富治者，民（车）不发轫，车不暴出（甲不出橐），而威制天下。故曰：“兵胜于朝廷。”不暴甲而胜者，主胜也。陈而胜者，将胜也。

【今译】

统兵的将帅（指挥部队），犹如深藏于大地，犹如运行于高天，产生于无形之中。所以用兵作战时，战斗规模再大也不会感到兵力不足，规模再小也不会感到兵力过多。明了禁绝坏事、赦免小错、广开财源、杜绝浪费之术，人民流离失所的招徕亲抚他们，土地荒芜闲置的开垦利用起来。土地广阔而能利用，国家就富庶；人民众多而管理有序，国家就安定。富庶安定的国家，战车不必出动，盔甲不必启封，就能凭威势而制服天下。所以说：“军事的胜利取决于朝廷的决策。”不动用军队而获胜，是君主的胜利；两军对阵而后取胜，是将领的胜利。

【英译】

Controlling the army is as secretive as the deep recesses of Earth, as remote as the topmost space of Heaven, and derives from the invisible nonexistence. Hence it must be opened to apply in military operations. When the troops disperse in the field, they will not be out of control for its vastness, and when they concentrate they will not be congested for its narrowness. All measures of prohibitions, pardons, enlightenments and putting an end to extravagance must be taken in public. The displaced persons should be treated kindly, and the unworked lands be cultivated. When land is vast and under cultivation the state will be prosperous; when the people are in great numbers and well ordered, the state will be governed in good condition. When a state is well governed and moreover wealthy, even though it does not remove the blocks from the chariots, nor is the armor taken out from the bags, its awesomeness will cause All Under Heaven to submit. Therefore, it is said: “Militar victory depends upon the court.” When one is victorious without using the army, it is the sovereigns victory; when victory comes after deploying the army to confront the enemy, it is a general’s victory.

【赏析重点】

（1）分析“禁舍开塞”的语义特点和翻译方法。

（2）分析“夫土广而任则国富，民众而制则国治”的语义逻辑特点和翻译方法。

【原典3】

兵起，非可以忿也。见胜则与（兴），不见胜则止。患在百里之内，不起一日之师；患在千里之内，不起一月之师；患在四海之内，不起一岁之师。

【今译】

出兵作战，不可只凭一时的意气。有取胜的把握就出兵，没有取胜的把握就不要出兵。祸患在百里之内，部队不可只作一天的准备；祸患在千里之内，部队不可只作一个月的准备；祸患在遥远的区域，部队不可只做一年的准备。

【英译】

The army cannot be deployed to engage in war by an enraged general. If it is sure in winning, the army will be mobilized; if not, the mobilization of the army will be stopped. If trouble arises within a hundred *li*, do not make just one day's preparation. If trouble arises within a thousand *li*, do not make merely a month's preparation. If trouble lies within the Four Seas, do not make only one year's preparation.

【赏析重点】

（1）分析“兵起，非可以忿也”的结构特点和翻译方法。

（2）分析“患在百里之内，不起一日之师”英译中的句式转换。

【原典4】

兵之所及，羊肠亦胜，锯齿亦胜，缘山亦胜，入谷亦胜，方亦胜，圆亦胜。重者如山如林，如江如河；轻者如炮如燔，如垣压之，如云覆之。令之聚不得以散，散不得以聚，左不得以右，右不得以左。（兵）如总木，弩如羊角。人人无不腾陵张胆，绝乎疑虑，堂堂决而去。

【今译】

军队所到之处，在羊肠小道上能取胜，在崎岖的山路上也能取胜；攀山而上能取胜，深入狭谷也能取胜；设置方阵能取胜，设置圆阵也能取胜。部队稳重时就像高山深林、长江大河，轻捷时就像煨烤的袅袅文火、渗泄的涓涓细流。要像城垣倒塌那样将敌人压倒，像乌云蔽日那样将敌人吞没。使敌人集结时无法分散，分散时又无法集中；左边的部队无法调到右边，右边的部队也无法调到左边。我军刀枪并举如丛林，弓弩齐发如旋风，人人无不奋发踊跃、放胆直前，毫不犹豫，勇敢果决地冲向敌人。

【英译】

Wherever the army maneuvers, it will be victorious along the narrow winding trails, and it will be victorious too along the most rugged paths. Its venture to climb mountains and step down to valleys will be victorious, and it deployment in square formation or round formation will be victorious too. When the heavy army attacks, it is like mountains, like forests, like rivers and great streams. When the light troops attack, it is like blazing flames, like the collapse of city walls pressing upon the enemy and like clouds covering him. They cause the enemy to be unable to disperse out of concentration, nor to be concentrated from dispersal. The enemy troops on the left are unable to rescue the right, and those on the right unable to rescue the left, the massive weapons are like forests, and catapulting crossbows are like whirlwinds. Every man without exception plucks up in high spirit. Casting off all doubts, they press forward decisively with an indomitable will.

【赏析重点】

（1）分析“方亦胜，圆亦胜”中的文化增译方法。

（2）分析“左不得以右，右不得以左”的语义特点和翻译方法。

第三节 《三十六计》

Thirty-Six Stratagems

一、典籍简介

《三十六计》是集历代韬略、诡道之大成的一部通俗易懂的兵书。该书分为两大部分，一部分是以优胜劣的作战计谋，包括“胜战计”“敌战计”“攻战计”三套；另一部分是以劣胜优的作战计谋，包括“混战计”“并战计”“败战计”三套。每一套计谋各又分为六计，共三十六计。《三十六计》中，每一计都是众所周知的成语，易记易理解，因此能在群众中广为流传。《三十六计》中所蕴含的道理是对于中国古代社会政治、经济、军事等活动的规律与方法的集中分析阐释，在当今社会的各个领域也得到了广泛的应用。

Thirty-Six Stratagems, is a popular strategic book which includes the tactics and schemes raised by former masters. It has two parts: one is about the tactics for the advantaged side, including winning tactic, enemy tactic and attack tactic (total three sets); the other is about the tactics for the disadvantaged side, including wild tactic, joint tactic and defeat tactic (total three sets). And each set also includes six stratagems, totally 36 stratagems. In the book, each stratagem is written in popular idiom, which is convenient to remember and understand. Therefore, it can be widely spread among the people. The theories implied in the *Thirty-Six Stratagems* explain the rules and principles of the social politics, economy and military activity in ancient China, which are still broadly applied in various domains nowadays

《三十六计》强调，善于用兵的人，一定要避开敌军旺盛的士气，不采取直接进攻的战略，而是坚守阵地，消磨敌军的士气，使敌军势力损耗，当敌军疲于奔命时再出击。同时，将领应选用一直驻守此地的士兵来攻打远道而来的敌军，用休整完好的士兵来攻打疲惫不堪的敌军，用饱食的士兵来攻打饥饿的敌军，这才是从实力上战胜敌人的最好方法。这便是胜战计中的“以逸待劳”。

Thirty-Six Stratagems emphasizes that the man who excels in military operation knows to avoid the enemy with high morale and defense the position instead of the direct attack to consume the enemy's fighting will. While the opponent becomes exhausted, then launch a strike. Meanwhile, the local stationed soldier can be selected to attack the hostile army who comes from distant lace. The rested soldiers can be selected to confront with the exhausted enemy. The satiated soldiers can be selected to deal with the hungry enemy. These are the good methods to triumph over the enemy, which are referred in the winning tactic as waiting at one's ease for an exhausted enemy.

二、作者简介

《三十六计》究竟为何人所著、何年撰写，至今尚未有定论，但有不少学者认为该书为南北朝时期檀道济所著，明清之际流传开来。檀道济（？—436），南朝著名将领，戎马一生，智勇兼备，战绩卓著。

The author and exact finishing time of the book *Thirty-Six Stratagems* haven't been confirmed yet. Many scholars assume this book was written by Tan Daoji in the Southern and Norther dynasties (420–589) and was widely spread in the Ming dynasty (1368–1644) and Qing dynasty (1644–1911). Tan Daoji (?–436) was a famous general in the Southern Dynasties, who dedicated his whole life to protect his country. He was brave and also very resourceful, which helped him achieve several great accomplishments.

三、典籍英译赏析

【原典 1】

第一计 瞒天过海

备周则意怠；常见则不疑。阴在阳之内，不在阳之对。太阳，太阴。

【今译】

防备十分周全的，往往容易斗志松懈；习以为常的事情，就不会产生怀疑。秘密常潜藏在公开的事物里，而不是在公开暴露的事物之外。非常公开的事情里，往往就蕴藏着最隐秘的秘密。

【英译】

Strategy 1 Fool the Emperor to Cross the Sea

Moving about in the darkness and shadows, occupying isolated places, or hiding behind screens will only attract suspicious attention. To lower an enemy's guard you must act in the open, hiding your true intentions under the guise of common every day activities.

【赏析重点】

（1）分析"常见则不疑"的翻译思路。

（2）分析"阴""阳"概念的语义所指和翻译方法。

【原典 2】

第二计 围魏救赵

共敌不如分敌；敌阳不如敌阴。

【今译】

进攻兵力集中的敌人，不如攻打兵力分散的敌人；攻击气势旺盛的敌人，不如打击气势不旺盛的敌人。

【英译】

Strategy 2 Besiege Wei to Rescue Zhao

When the enemy is too strong to attack directly, then attack something he holds dear. Know that in all things he cannot be superior. Somewhere there is a gap in the armour, a weakness that can be attacked instead.

【赏析重点】

（1）分析"共敌""分敌"的翻译思路。

（2）分析“敌阳不如敌阴”的逻辑结构和翻译方法。

【原典 3】

第四计　以逸待劳

困敌之势，不以战；损刚益柔。

【今译】

迫使敌人处于困难的境地，不一定要出兵直接攻打；可以采取“损刚益柔”的办法，使敌人由盛转衰，由强变弱。

【英译】

Strategy 4 Await the Exhausted Enemy at Your Ease

It is an advantage to choose the time and place for battle. In this way you know when and where the battle will take place, while your enemy does not. Encourage your enemy to expend his energy in futile quests while you conserve your strength. When he is exhausted and confused, you attack with energy and purpose.

【赏析重点】

（1）分析本句的阐释翻译方法。

（2）分析“损刚益柔”的语义特点和翻译方法。

【原典 4】

第六计　声东击西

敌志乱萃，不虞，坤下兑上之象。利其不自主而取之。

【今译】

使敌人处于心迷神惑、行为紊乱、意志混沌的状况，不能判明和应对突发事件的发生，这是出现意想不到的变化的一种征兆，这时就要利用敌人心智混乱、无主张的时机将其消灭。

【英译】

Strategy 6 Clamor in the East, Attack in the West

In any battle the element of surprise can provide an overwhelming advantage. Even when face to face with an enemy, surprise can still be employed by attacking where he least expects it. To do this you must create an expectation in the enemy's mind through the use of a feint.

【赏析重点】

分析“坤下兑上”的文化语义和翻译方法。

【原典 5】

第七计 无中生有

诳也，非诳也，实其所诳也。少阴，太阴，太阳。

【今译】

运用假象欺骗对方，但并非全部都是假的，而是让对方把假象当成真相。这就是要巧妙地用阴阳转化之理，把小假象发展到大假象，在极端虚假之后，再采用真实的行动。

【英译】

Strategy 7 Create Something From Nothing

You use the same feint twice. Having reacted to the first and often the second feint as well, the enemy will be hesitant to react to a third feint. Therefore the third feint is the actual attack catching your enemy with his guard down.

【赏析重点】

分析本句的文化阐释翻译方法。

拓展训练 | Extension Training

1. 思考练习

（1）用英文简要介绍《孙子兵法》《三十六计》主要内容。

（2）总结兵法典籍语言特点和翻译策略。

2. 文化外宣汉英翻译

（1）孙武提出了“兵者国之大事”的思想，认为军事关系到国家民众的存亡生死，统治者应从政治的高度去处理军事问题，军事是实现政治目的的工具。他认为在军事中有五种因素最重要，即“道”“天”“地”“将”“法”。“道”是争取民众对战争的支持的方略，“天”是自然的变化，“地”是地形状况，“将”是军事指挥者的素质，“法”是制度规范。其中，特别强调“道“和“将”的作用，认为“将帅”要“知道”，即从政治的高度去处理军事、做出决策。

（2）《孙子兵法》中充满了辩证思想，孙武强调“将”“天”“地”三者之间的互制互动，提出了综合天地人为一体的系统论思想。他说：“知彼知己，胜乃不殆；知天知地，胜乃可全。”再如，他强调变化，他说：“夫兵形象水……故兵无常势，水无常形，能因敌变化而取胜者谓之神。”此外，他认为“兵者，诡道也”，揭示了军事的特殊规律，即“兵以诈立，以利动”，表现出功利主义的价值取向。

（3）中国古典名著《三国演义》中的“火烧赤壁”是书中最为著名的片断之一，所描述的内容是中国古代历史上著名的战争——赤壁之战。赤壁之战发生于东汉建安十三年（208），孙权和刘备联军在长江的赤壁一带与曹操军队展开决战，这场战役是对《孙子兵法》的完美运用。孙刘联军在敌强我弱、敌众我寡的形势下，利用我方熟悉水战的优势，避实击虚，采取火攻的计策，烧毁曹军战船，从而大破曹军。

第三篇 文学艺术篇

Literature and Arts

第五章　先秦诗歌英译

Translation of the Pre-Qin Poetry

一、学习目标

（1）用英文介绍先秦时期诗歌特点。

（2）掌握《诗经》《楚辞》作品中的文化关键词英译。

（3）对比鉴赏中外译者翻译方法。

二、文化背景

在中国，最早的诗歌总集是《诗经》，它收集了公元前六世纪以前的、以四言为主的诗歌三百多首，有的是较早的舞歌、祭歌，有的是稍晚的叙事诗、讽刺诗，还有不少反映广大人民的生活、思想情感的各地民歌。

The Book of Poetry is the earliest anthology of poetry in China and one of her greatest treasures. It contains more than three hundred songs composed before the sixth century B. C., most of them with four characters to a line. Some are ancient songs for dances and sacrifices others narrative poetry and satire belonging to a later period, yet others folk-songs from different districts reflecting the life and thoughts of the common people.

《诗经》这部书，特别是其中的民歌，在我们祖国的文学史上，是有崇高的位置的。它们大都能够忠实地反映周代的现实生活，能够表达出社会生活中本质的东西，使读者能形象地看到统治阶级的丑恶，看到劳动人民的苦难，他们的坚决反抗和优良品质。字句虽然可能经过统治者的改变，但仍然透露出这些民间诗人们的创作的才华来。

The Book of Poetry, especially its section of folk-songs holds a very high position in Chinese literature. Though feudal commentators distorted the meaning of many of the poems, for over two thousand years this collection has been dear to innumerable Chinese readers. These beautiful lyries with their graphic images and simple evocative language give a true picture of life in the Chou dynasty and laid the foundations of the fine tradition of realism in Chinese poetry.

战国时期的文学中，最重要的就是《楚辞》。《楚辞》是用楚国人民的语言和楚国特有的音调来创作的诗篇。其中最早的是“九歌”共十一篇，是春秋末年与战国初年的楚国各地的民间祭歌。这里边所祭祀的大都是与生产有关的自然神祇，如日神、云神、山神、水神等。

The most outstanding literature of the Spring and Autumn Period is *The Verse of Chu*, the poetry of the kingdom of Chu. These poems were written in the dialect of Chu and set to Chu music. The earliest are the *Nine Odes* actually eleven in numberused in sacrifices in the kingdom of Chu at the end of the Spring and Autumn Period and the beginning of the Warring States Period. The deities and spirits to whom sacrifices were made were for the most gods and goddesses related to agriculture: the sun god, the cloud god, or mountain and water goddesses.

“九歌”以后不久，就出现了伟大的诗人屈原。屈原的杰作当推“离骚”，这是一篇长达三百七十多句，两千五百多字的自叙性的抒情诗。它的结构很完整，句法有很多变化，语言有浓厚的南方色彩。它的主题思想很明确，就是一方面深切地表达自己对于祖国的热爱，对于人民的关怀；另一方面无情地抨击国王的昏庸，奸臣的贪诈。他虽然为腐朽势力所排挤而死，但他这种爱祖国、爱人民的伟大精神，却通过他的不朽诗篇永远留在读者的心上。屈原死后，继之而起的有唐勒、景差、宋玉等人，但只有宋玉的作品流传下来。传说宋玉是屈原的学生，做过楚国的大夫，屈宋两人可以代表晚周诗歌发展较高的一个阶段。

Soon after the *Nine Odes* were composed lived the brilliant poet Qu Yuan, a noble of the kingdom of Chu. His masterpiece is the *Li Sao*, a poem of more than three hundred and seventy lines, which sets forth his aspirations and emotions. It is beautifully constructed with considerable variety in the sentence structure and magnificent imagery. The theme of the poem is clear. Qu Yuan expresses his sincere love for his country and concern for his countrymen, ruthlessly exposing the king's folly and the treachery of evil ministers. Though he was hounded to his death, his immortal poems will always live on to inspire fresh generations of patriots. Qu Yuan was succeeded by the poets Tang Leh, Ching Chai and Sung Yu, but only Sung Yu's work remains today. Sung Yu is said to have been Qu Yuan's student and to have served in the court of Chu. These two men are the greatest poets of the later Chou.

三、文化关键词

赋　Fu (narration)

比　Bi (comparison)

兴　Xing (stimulation)

《风》 *Regional Songs*

《雅》 *Odes*

《颂》 *Hymns*

《诗经》 *The Book of Poetry*

《楚辞》 *The Verse of Chu, the Songs of the South, Poetry of the South*

《离骚》 *Sadness of Separation, Tales of Woe*

《天问》 *Inquiries into the Universe*

第一节　《诗经》

The Book of Poetry

一、典籍简介

《诗经》是中国第一部诗歌总集，共收入自西周初期（公元前 11 世纪）至春秋中叶（公元前 6 世纪）500 余年间的诗歌 305 篇，另有 6 篇笙诗，有目无辞，不计在内。《诗经》最初称《诗》《诗三百》，被汉代儒者奉为经典，于是称《诗经》。

The Book of Poetry is the first comprehensive anthology of poems in China, including altogether 305 poems composed from the early stage of the Western Zhou dynasty (the 11th century B.C.) to the middle stage of the Spring and Autumn Period (the 6th century B.C.). In addition, six more poems are usually excluded since they contain no words but the titles. *The Book of Poetry* was originally called *Shi* (*Poems*) or *Shi Sanbai* (*Three Hundred Poems*). As the Confucian scholars in the Han dynasty honoured it as one of their classics, it started to be called *The Book of Poetry*.

“赋”“比”“兴”是《诗经》的重要艺术特征，简言之，“赋”就是铺陈直叙，即诗人把思想感情及其有关的事物平铺直叙地表达出来。“比”就是比方，分为比喻和比拟。“比”的特点是以彼物写此物，诗中所描写的事物并不是诗人真正要歌咏的对象，而是借用打比方的方法，来表达诗人的思想感情。“兴”，即“起兴”，由于客观事物触发了诗人的情感，激发诗人歌唱，所以在大多数情况下出现在一首诗的开头或一个诗章的开头。

“Fu”, “Bi” and “Xing” are important artistic features of *The Book of Poetry*, heralding the poetic compositions in ancient China. In short, “Fu” means to narrate in detail and in a simple and direct way. That is, the poet should express his own thoughts, feelings and other related things as they are. “Bi” means to make comparison, including metaphors and similes. That is, the poet should write about one object by comparing it to another. In other words, the object that the poet depicts in the poem is not what he really means to sing of. He only makes a comparison to convey his thoughts and feelings. “Xing” means “to stimulate”. That is, the poet is prompted to sing when certain objective things arouse his emotions. Therefore, it usually appears at the beginning of a poem or a stanza within a poem.

二、作者简介

《诗经》的作者成分很复杂，包括从贵族到平民的社会各个阶层人士，除了少数诗篇署有作者姓名，绝大部分已经不可考证。大体上说，由于《风》为来自各地的地方民歌，其中保存的大量作品来自劳动人民的口头创作。西周后期的《雅》诗中也有少数劳动人民的作品。《雅》诗中的大部分诗篇为统治阶级内部的人物所作，其中《大雅》的作者主要是上层贵族；《小雅》的作者既包括上层贵族也包括下层贵族。

The composition of the authors of *The Book of Poetry* is very complex, consisting of people from all walks of life, from aristocrats to civilians. Except that a small proportion of the poems bear the authors' names, most of the authors' identity cannot be put to textual research. Generally speaking, *Regional Songs* contains a great number of poems created by the laboring people orally as they are folk songs from different regions. A very small proportion of *The Odes* made in the last years of the Western Zhou dynasty are also the works of the working people, while most of *The Odes* are the products of the ruling class: the authors of *Major Odes* are mainly aristocrats of high status; those of *Minor Odes* include aristocrats of both high and low status.

三、典籍英译赏析

国风·周南

【原典1】

关雎

关关雎鸠，在河之洲。

窈窕淑女，君子好逑。

【今译】

雎鸠关关相对唱，双栖河里小岛上。

纯洁美丽好姑娘，真是我的好对象。

【理雅各英译】

Kwan ts'eu

Kwan-kwan go the ospreys,

On the islet in the river.

The modest, retiring, virtuous, young lady:

For our prince a good mate she.

【赏析重点】

（1）对比分析叠词“关关”和叠韵词“窈窕”的翻译方法。

（2）对比分析“君子好逑”的翻译方法。

【原典2】

参差荇菜，左右流之。

窈窕淑女，寤寐求之。

【今译】

长长短短鲜荇菜，左手右手顺流采。

纯洁美丽好姑娘，醒着相思梦里爱。

【理雅各英译】

Here long, there short, is the duckweed,

To the left, to the right, borne about by the current.

The modest, retiring, virtuous, young lady:

Waking and sleeping, he sought her.

【许渊冲英译】

Water flows left and right.

Of cress long here short there:

The youth yearns day and night.

For the good maiden fair.

【赏析重点】

对比分析文化关键词“参差”“寤寐”的用词特点和翻译方法。

【原典 3】

求之不得，寤寐思服。

悠哉悠哉，辗转反侧。

【今译】

追求姑娘难实现，醒来梦里意常牵。

一片深情悠悠长，翻来覆去难成眠。

【理雅各英译】

He sought her and found her not,

And waking and sleeping he thought about her.

Long he thought; oh! Long and anxiously;

On his side, on his back, he turned, and back again.

【许渊冲英译】

His yearning grows so strong.

He cannot fall asleep,

But tosses all night long,

So deep in love, so deep!

【赏析重点】

（1）对比分析叠词“悠哉悠哉”的理解和翻译方法。

（2）对比分析“辗转反侧”的不同翻译方法。

【原典 4】

参差荇菜，左右采之。

窈窕淑女，琴瑟友之。

【今译】

长长短短荇菜鲜，左手采来右手拣。

纯洁美丽好姑娘，弹琴奏瑟来亲近。

【理雅各英译】

Here long, there short, is the duckweed;

On the left, on the right, we gather it.

The modest, retiring, virtuous, young lady:

— With lutes, small and large, let us give her friendly welcome.

【许渊冲英译】

Now gather left and right

Cress long or short and tender!

O lute, play music bright

For the bride sweet and slender!

【赏析重点】

（1）对比分析文化关键词“友”的理解和翻译方法。

（2）对比分析“左右”“琴瑟”的不同翻译方法。

【原典 5】

参差荇菜，左右芼之。

窈窕淑女，钟鼓乐之。

【今译】

长长短短鲜荇菜，左手右手拣拣。

纯洁美丽好姑娘，敲起钟鼓来取悦。

【理雅各英译】

Here long, there short, is the duckweed;

On the left, on the right, we cook and present it.

The modest, retiring, virtuous, young lady:

— With bells and drums let us show our delight in her.

【许渊冲英译】

Feast Friends at left and right

On cress cooked till tender

O bells and drums, delight

The bride so sweet and slender!

【赏析重点】

对比分析文化关键词“乐”的理解和翻译方法。

第二节 《楚辞》

The Verse of Chu

一、典籍简介

与《诗经》一样，产生于2000多年前的《楚辞》是中国诗歌乃至中国文化的源头之一。刘向编订的《楚辞》16卷原本已佚，今存最早的《楚辞》注本是东汉王逸的《楚辞章句》。《楚辞章句》以刘向《楚辞》为底本，除了对《楚辞》做了较完整的训释之外，还提供了有关原本的情况。南宋洪兴祖在《楚辞章句》的基础上作了《楚辞补注》，南宋朱熹著有《楚辞集注》，清初王夫之撰有《楚辞通释》，清代蒋骥有《山带阁注楚辞》等。当代学者也有不少《楚辞》研究方面的著作。

The Verse of Chu, like *The Book of Poetry*, is one of the sources of Chinese poetry and in a broader sense, of Chinese culture. The sixteen-volume edition compiled by Liu Xiang of the Western Han dynasty has already been lost. The earliest edition extant today is *The Verse of Chu with Notes and Commentary* compiled by Wang Yi of the Eastern Han dynasty, which supplies us with information of the sixteen-volume edition and rather detailed textual interpretations. In the Southern Song dynasty, Hong Xingzu compiled *The Verse of Chu with Supplementary Notes and Commentary* on the basis of *The Verse of Chu with Notes and Commentary* and Zhu Xi put out his *Variorum Edition of The Verse of Chu*. In the Qing dynasty, Wang Fuzhi and Jiang Ji respectively published *The Verse of Chu with Verified Explanations* and *The Shandai Pavillion Edition of The Verse of Chu*.

屈原流传下来的作品共26篇。《离骚》是屈原的代表作，也是中国古代文学史上最长的一首浪漫主义政治抒情诗。《天问》提出了170多个问题，涉及天文、地理、历史、社会、伦理、文学（神话、传说）、哲学等许多领域，表现了诗人对传统观念的大胆怀疑和追求真理的科学精神。《楚辞》突破了《诗经》的表现形式，极大地丰富了诗歌的表现力，对汉赋的形成和后代的诗歌创作产生了深刻影响，为中国的诗歌创作开辟了一片新天地。屈原是我国文学之父、骚人墨客百世不祧之祖；《楚辞》融入了华夏文化，丰富了中国语言，是世界的文化瑰宝。

Handed down are twenty-six pieces composed by Qu Yuan, the representative writer of *The Verse of Chu*. These include *Tales of Woe*, his masterpiece, which is the longest romantic political lyric in the history of Chinese literature, *The Nine Hymns*, eleven poems adapted from elegiac songs, *Inquiries into the Universe*, which gives expression to the poet's critical mind about the convention and to his scientific spirit of seeking the truth by raising more than 170 questions concerning such fields as astronomy, geography, history, sociology, ethics, literature (mythology and legendry), and philosophy. *The Verse of Chu*, having broken through the forms of expression of *The Book of Poetry*, has enhanced the expressiveness of poetry and produced a great impact on the formation of Fu (a literary form of descriptive prose interspersed with verse) of the Han dynasty, and has opened up a new horizon for the development of Chinese poetry.

二、作者简介

屈原（约前 339—前 278），名平，出生于战国时期楚国的丹阳（今湖北秭归），是我国历史上杰出的政治家和第一位伟大的爱国诗人。他明于治乱，娴于辞令，在担任三闾大夫、左徒期间坚决主张联齐抗秦，积极辅佐怀王变法图强，使楚国一度出现国富兵强、威震诸侯的局面，成为“合纵”抗秦的重要力量。公元前 278 年（顷襄王二十年），秦将白起攻破郢都，屈原在极度悲愤中自沉汨罗江。

Qu Yuan (approx. 339 BC–278 BC), other name Qu Ping, was born during the Warring States Period in Danyang（the now Zigui of Hubei）. He was a distinguished statesman and the first great poet in the history of China. Astute and eloquent, he advocated the alliance with the State of Qi in resistance to the aggression of Qin and helped King Huai of Chu in the reforms for the strengthening of Chu when he was in the positions of Lord of the Three Clans and Senior Councilor of Statutes. As a result Chu became so powerful that it became a mighty force in the vertical Alliance against Qin. In 278 BC (the 21th year of King Qingxiang's reign), the Qin forces under the command of Bai Qi captured the capital Ying. In his great sorrow and indignation Qu Yuan drowned himself in the River of Miluo.

屈原的崇高精神和伟大人格，动天地而泣鬼神。司马迁（前 145—？）评价说，屈原“虽与日月争光可也”（《史记屈原列传》）。据《续齐谐记》和《隋书·地理志》

载，屈原投江的时间是农历五月五日。中国民间五月五端午节包粽子、赛龙舟的习俗就源于人们对屈原的景仰。1953 年，屈原被列为世界四大文化名人之一，受到世界和平理事会和全世界人民的隆重纪念。

The lofty personality of Qu Yuan, whose glory, as Sima Qian (145 BC–?) says, can be compared to the sun and the moon, is most touching and inspiring. According to *Sequel of the History of Qi* and *Geography in the History of the Sui dynasty*, Qu Yuan took his own life on the 5th day of the 5th month in the lunar calendar. It is customary of the Chinese people to make zongzi (a cone-shaped dumpling of glutinous rice wrapped in reed leaves) and observe the Dragon Festival on the very day to pay homage to the great poet. In 1953, Qu Yuan was acknowledged as one of the Four Most Renowned Cultural Figures in the World, since which people all over the world, as well as the World Council of Peace, cherish their memory of Qu Yuan every year.

三、典籍英译赏析

【原典 1】

亦余心之所善兮，虽九死其犹未悔。

——《离骚》

【今译】

我真心爱好修身洁行，就是死多次也不会后悔。

【许渊冲英译】

My heart tells me it's good and meet, oh!

I won't regret to die nine times.

【杨宪益英译】

But since my heart did love such purity,

I'd not regret a thousand deaths to die.

【赏析重点】

对比分析文化关键词“九死”的翻译用词。

【原典 2】

路漫漫其修远兮，吾将上下而求索。

——《离骚》

【今译】

道路远又长，我将上天下地地求索（理想）。

【许渊冲英译】

My way ahead is a long, long one, oh!
I'll seek my beauty high and low.

【杨宪益英译】

The way was long, and wrapped in gloom did seem,
As I urged on to seek my vanished dream.

【赏析重点】

对比分析文化关键词“上下”的翻译用词。

【原典 3】

不吾知其亦已兮，苟余情其信芳。

——《离骚》

【今译】

人们不了解我也罢了，只要我内心确实是美好的。

【许渊冲英译】

Unknown, I care not if it grieves, oh!
My heart will shed fragrance and light.

【杨宪益英译】

Why should I grieve to go unrecognized?
Since in my heart fragrance was truly prized?

【赏析重点】

对比分析“不吾知其亦已兮”的语法结构转换。

【原典 4】

悲莫悲兮生别离，乐莫乐兮新相知。

——《九歌·少司命》

【今译】

人生最大的悲痛啊莫过于生生地别离，人生最大的欢喜啊莫过于遇到了新相识。

【许渊冲英译】

None is so sad, oh! as those who part;

Nor so happy, oh! as new sweetheart.

【杨宪益英译】

For Life to part, no Grief more Pain can move.

No Joy excels the Rapture of first Love.

【赏析重点】

对比分析“悲莫悲兮”“乐莫乐兮”的语义理解和翻译用词。

【原典 5】

与天地兮同寿，与日月兮齐光。

——《九章·涉江》

【今译】

和天地一样长寿，同日月一样永放光芒。

【许渊冲英译】

I'd live as long, oh! as earth and sky.

I would outshine, oh! sun and moon on high.

【杨宪益英译】

My Life should thus outlast the Universe,

With Sun and Moon supreme.

【赏析重点】

对比分析文化关键词“同寿”“齐光”的翻译方法。

【原典 6】

苟余心之端直兮，虽僻远其何伤。

——《九章·涉江》

【今译】

只要我的心志还端直啊！即便放逐远方又有何悲伤。

【许渊冲英译】

But since my heart is true and straight, oh!

What if I'm in a distant state?

【杨宪益英译】

Since I am upright, and my Conscience clear,

Why should I grieve to leave?

【赏析重点】

对比分析文化关键词“端直”的翻译用词。

【原典7】

夫尺有所短，寸有所长；物有所不足，智有所不明；数有所不逮，神有所不通。

——《卜居》

【今译】

尺有它不足的地方，寸有它的长处；物有它不足的地方，智者有它不能明白的问题；卦有它算不到的事，神有它无法显灵的地方。

【许渊冲英译】

A foot may be too short for something long;
For something weak an inch is strong.
Everything has its weak points;
Sometimes a wise man disappoints.
There's something which to fate we must resign.
And other things beyond the power divine.

【杨宪益英译】

Some simple Problem the most Skilled defies,
Some Knowledge is kept hidden from the Wise.
To point your Way I cannot undertake,
Nor conjure up the spirits for your sake.

【赏析重点】

对比分析译文的逻辑语义转换。

【原典8】

举世皆浊我独清，众人皆醉我独醒。

——《渔夫》

【今译】

世界都是浑浊的而只有我是清白的，所有人都醉了只有我是清醒的。

【许渊冲英译】

When all the world in mud has sunk,
Alone I'm clean.

When all the people are drunk,
Sober I'm seen.

【杨宪益英译】

"The crowd is dirty," said Chu Yuan, "I alone am clean. The crowd is drunk. I alone am sober. So I was banished."

【赏析重点】

对比分析译文的句式结构转换。

拓展训练 | Extension Training

1. 思考练习

（1）用英文简要介绍《诗经》《楚辞》主要内容。

（2）对比分析《诗经》《楚辞》不同译本的翻译风格和翻译策略。

2. 文化外宣汉英翻译

（1）《诗经》中依体裁与音乐对诗歌所分出的类型，“风”（国风）是不同地区的音乐，大部分是民歌：“雅”是宫廷宴享或朝会时的乐歌，分为“大雅”与“小雅”，大部分是贵族文人的作品：“颂”是宗庙祭祀用的舞曲歌辞，内容多是歌颂祖先的功业。“雅”“颂”指雅正之音，而“国风”系民间乐歌，因此“风雅颂”既是《诗经》的体裁，同时也有高雅纯正的含义。“风雅”后来一般指典雅与高雅的事物。

（2）《诗经》创作的三种表现手法：“赋”是铺陈事物直接叙述；“比”是类比；“兴”是先言他物以引出所咏之词，有两层含义，一是即兴感发，二是在感发时借客观景物婉转地表达出某种思想感情。“赋比兴”为汉代儒家所总结和提出，后来演变为中国古代文学创作的基本原则和方法。

第六章　汉魏晋诗英译

Translation of the Poetry of Han, Wei and Jin Dynasties

一、学习目标

（1）用英文介绍汉魏晋时期诗歌特点。

（2）掌握曹操、陶渊明代表性诗歌和乐府诗作品中的文化关键词英译。

（3）对比鉴赏中外译者翻译方法。

二、文化背景

从刘邦建立汉朝到隋朝灭亡的800多年中，历经两汉（西汉、东汉）、三国（魏、蜀、吴）、两晋（西晋、东晋）、南北朝和隋朝等多个朝代，其中有过稳定统一的时期，也有过动荡分裂的时期。这个时期的诗歌继承和发扬了《诗经》和《楚辞》的优良传统，广泛生动地反映了当时的社会生活，并在体裁和样式上进行了有益的探索和尝试，实现了由四言诗向五言诗和七言诗的转变，为我国诗歌在唐代更大的繁荣和发展奠定了基础。

During the 800 years from the founding of the Han dynasty and the fall of the Sui dynasty, there were the periods of two Hans (the Western Han dynasty and the Eastern Han dynasty), the Three Kingdoms (Wei, Shu and Wu), two Jins (the Western Jin dynasty and the Eastern Jin dynasty), the Southern and Northern Dynasties, and the Sui dynasty. There were periods of stability and unification, and periods of riot and disintegration. The poems during this period inherited and developed the fine tradition of *The Book of Poetry* and *The Songs of Chu*. Truthful reflections of the social life of the time and beneficial experiments in genres and forms, these poems shifted from four-syllabic to five-syllabic and seven-syllabic and thus laid a solid foundation for the further development of Chinese poetry in the Tang dynasty.

（一）汉诗（前 206—220）

两汉时期 400 余年中的诗歌，作者和作品的数量都比较少，可以分为乐府诗和文人诗两个部分。所谓“乐府”，是古代掌管音乐歌舞的官府，最早出现于秦代。西汉建立之初，这一官署被沿袭下来。乐府诗是这一官署收集和配制音乐演唱的歌辞，汉代乐府中最优秀的作品是采自民间的歌辞，也就是两汉的民歌。乐府民歌的内容多为爱情婚姻、战争徭役、孤儿病妇，感时伤世。如项籍的《垓下歌》和刘邦的《大风歌》，一个是失败者的怨叹，另一个是胜利后的感慨。

The Han Poems (206 BC–220 AD)

The poems in the 400 years of the Western Han dynasty and the Eastern Han dynasty are small in the number of poets and works. They can be divided into two categories: the yuefu ballads and the literary poems. The yuefu, an ancient office in charge of music, songs and dance, which first emerged in the Qin dynasty, was kept when the Western Han dynasty was founded. The yuefu ballads are words collected and set to music by the office. The best yuefu ballads are folk songs collected from among the people in the two Hans. Most of the yuefu ballads deal with love and marriage, war and conscript labour, orphans and sick women, and lamentations over the world. Xiang Ji's *Song of Gaixia* is a grievous song of the defeated while Liu Bang's *Song of Strong Winds* is a victorious song of the conqueror.

（二）魏诗（220—280）

三国时期，吴国和蜀国的诗歌比较没落，而魏国的诗歌繁荣昌盛，因此以魏代称三国。魏诗起自东汉末年汉献帝建安年间，以曹氏父子曹操、曹丕和曹植为首，另有王粲、刘桢、徐干、陈琳等建安七子，以及繁钦等诸多才士。曹操在政治、军事和文学上都有成就，他现存诗歌 24 首，全都是用乐府旧调旧题来写现实的新内容和抒发个人的情怀。曹丕的《燕歌行》是第一首由文人创作的成熟的七言诗。曹植的近 80 首诗歌代表了建安文学的最高成就，他的《白马篇》《赠白马王彪》《七步诗》等都是不朽的名篇。

The Wei Poems（220–280）

During the period of Three Kingdoms, there were not many distinguished poems in Wu and Shu while there were many distinguished poems in Wei. Therefore, the term Wei poems is used instead of the poems of the Three Kingdoms. The Wei poems, which originated in the Jian'an period of Emperor Xian of Han, are poems written by Cao Cao and his sons Cao Pi and Cao Zhi, the Seven Jian'an Scholars of Wang Can, Xu

Gan, Chen Lin and so on, and such scholars as Po Qin. Cao Cao distinguishes himself in politics, military and literature. All of his 24 extant poems employ the old yuefu tunes and titles to depict the new social reality and to vent his personal feelings. Cao Pi's *A Song from Yan* is the first mature seven-syllabic poem written by a man of letters. The nearly 80 poems written by Cao Zhi are incarnations of the highest achievement of the Jian'an literature, including such masterpieces as *A White Steed*, *To Cao Biao, Prince of Baima* and *An Off-hand Poem*.

（三）晋诗（265—420）

两晋150余年的历史，经过短暂的统一之后，就陷入了连年的战乱。在前期较为安定的20年中，出现了三张（张华、张载、张协）和傅玄、潘岳、左思、陆机等一批重要的诗人，在这些诗人中除了左思清劲豪放的《咏史》诗表达了他的建功立业的政治理想以外，余者多为“儿女情多，风云气少”，在语言上注重雕饰。例如，潘岳的《悼亡诗》悼念亡妻，写得婉转凄恻、一往情深，也是千古流传的名篇。后期晋诗的巅峰之作则是田园诗人陶渊明朴实淳美的诗篇。他的诗篇总共流传下来126首，《归园田居》《饮酒》和《桃花源记》等描绘了一幅幅美丽的自然图画，“羁鸟恋旧林，池鱼思故渊”“种豆南山下，草盛豆苗稀”“采菊东篱下，悠然见南山”等佳句脍炙人口。

The Jin Poems（265–420）

In the 150 odd years of the Western Jin dynasty and the Eastern Jin dynasty, the country suffered years of war and disturbance after a short period of unification. In the early years of comparative stability, there appeared such important poets as three Zhangs (Zhang Hua, Zhang Zai and Zhang Xie), Fu Xuan, Pan Yue, Zuo Si and Lu Ji. With the exception of Zuo Si, whose vigorous poems entitled *On History* express political ideals, the other poets are marked by their indulgence in family life and lack of political aspirations. Their poems are noted for flowery diction, e.g. Pan Yue's *Elegies* have been known through the ages for their genuine emotion. The peak of late Jin poems is reached by the pastoral poet Tao Yuanming's unsophisticated and beautiful verse. Among his 126 extant poems *Back to Country Life*, *Drinking Wine* and *Peach-Blossom Springs* offer pictures of natural beauty, with famous lines like "Birds in the cage would long for wooded hills, Fish in the pond would yearn for flowing spills", "When I plant beans at the foot of Southern Hill, Bean shoots were few but rank grass grows at will" and "I pluck hedge-side chrysanthemums with pleasure, And see the tranquil Southern Mount in leisure".

三、文化关键词

乐府诗　yuefu ballads

五言诗　five-syllabic poem

建安七子　Seven Jian'an Scholars

建安文学　Literature of Jian'an

田园诗人　pastoral poet

第一节　曹操

Cao Cao

一、诗人简介

曹操，字孟德，小字阿瞒，一名吉利，汉族，沛国谯（今安徽亳州）人。中国东汉末年著名的军事家、政治家和诗人，三国时代魏国的奠基人和主要缔造者。其子曹丕称帝后，追尊他为魏武帝。曹操一生征战，为使全国尽快统一，在北方广泛屯田，兴修水利，这也对当时的农业生产恢复有一定作用；其次，他用人唯才，打破世族门第观念，抑制豪强，所统治的地区社会经济得到恢复和发展。此外，他还精于兵法，著《孙子略解》《兵书接要》《孟德新书》等书。作为一代枭雄，他精通音律，善作诗歌，抒发政治抱负，并反映汉末人民苦难生活。

Cao Cao, Han nationality and native of Qiao, the State of Pei (now Bozhou, Anhui province), was a prominent military strategist, statesman and poet in the late Eastern Han dynasty of ancient China, as well as the founder and main builder of the State of Wei during the Three Kingdoms Period. His courtesy name was Mengde and infant names were Aman and Jili. He was posthumously titled Emperor Wu of Wei by his son Cao Pi following Pei's succession. He devoted his life to waging military campaigns. In order to unify the country as early as possible, he began a series of agricultural programs in the north. Refugees were recruited and given wasteland to cultivate, a policy conducive to the recovery of agricultural production to some extent; secondly, he adopted any talented people regardless of their family backgrounds and revoked the privileges of the wealthy and the strong, a policy conducive to the economic recovery and development of his districts. In addition, he was skilled in the art of war, authoring books, including *Sun Zi Lue Jie* (Annotation of *Sun Zi*), *Bing Shu Jie Yao* (*Essence of the War*) and *New Book of Mengde*. As an ambitious person, he also had a way with rhythms and poetry, where he expressed his political ambitions and talked about the hardship of people's lives in the late Han Period.

曹操对文学、书法、音乐等都有精深的造诣。他写的诗歌虽不多，但气魄宏伟，慷慨悲壮。由于曹操对文学的重视和推崇，使建安时期的文学在战乱中仍得到蓬勃的发展，出现了曹丕、曹植、蔡琰、孔融等一大批优秀的文学家，这一时期的诗歌文学作品也因其特有的慷慨悲凉、直面现实的风格而被称为“建安文学”。

Cao Cao was of great attainments in literature, calligraphy, music, and so on. His poems, though not in a great number, are full of grandeur and solemn fervour. Since Cao Cao paid great attention to and had a great esteem for literature, the literature developed flourshingly during the Jian'an period despite the chaos caused by war. There emerged large numbers of excellent writers, such as Cao Pi, Cao Zhi, Cai Yan and Kong Rong. The poems and works of literature of this period are called "Literature of Jian'an" for their unique characteristics.

二、典籍英译赏析

观沧海

东临碣石，以观沧海。
水何澹澹，山岛竦峙。
树木丛生，百草丰茂。
秋风萧瑟，洪波涌起。
日月之行，若出其中；
星汉灿烂，若出其里。
幸甚至哉，歌以咏志。

【许渊冲英译】

The Sea

I come to view the boundless ocean, From Stony Hill on eastern shore.
Its water rolls in rhythmic motion, And islands stand amid its roar.
Tree on tree grows from peak to peak; Grass on grass looks lush far and high.

The autumn wind blows drear and bleak; The monstrous billows surge up high.
The sun by day, the moon by night, Appear to rise up from the deep.
The Milky Way with stars so bright, Sinks down into the sea in sleep.
How happy I feel at this sight! I croon this poem in delight.

【汪榕培英译】

Viewing the Sea

When I climb atop the rocky hill, I view the vast east sea at will.
The waters quietly ebb and flow; The island mountains skyward go.
The trees are growing dense and green; The grass is sprouting lush and clean.
When autumn winds sweep o'er the shore, Huge waves and billows surge and roar.
The sun and the moon on their way, Seem to rise there from day to day.
The stars that shine bright in the sky, Seem to grow there far and nigh.
In such a happy mood I am, That I sing it as an epigram.

【赏析重点】

（1）对比句式结构转换、押韵手法。

（2）分析描写词汇“澹澹”“竦峙”“萧瑟”的翻译方法。

短歌行

对酒当歌，人生几何？
譬如朝露，去日苦多。
慨当以慷，忧思难忘。
何以解忧，唯有杜康。
青青子衿，悠悠我心。
但为君故，沉吟至今。
呦呦鹿鸣，食野之苹。
我有嘉宾，鼓瑟吹笙。
明明如月，何时可掇。
忧从中来，不可断绝。
越陌度阡，枉用相存。
契阔谈宴，心念旧恩。
月明星稀，乌鹊南飞。
绕树三匝，何枝可依？

山不厌高，海不厌深。
周公吐哺，天下归心。

【许渊冲英译】

A Short Song

We should sing before wine. For how long can life last?
Like dew on morning fine, So many days have passed.
How can we be unbound, By grief which weighed us down?
Grief can only be drowned, In wine of good renown.
Talents with collars blue, For you I pine away.
So much I long for you, My heart aches night and day.
How gaily call the deer, While grazing in the shade!
When I have talents here, Let lute and lyre be played!
Bright as the moon on high, How can I bring it down?
Grief from within comes nigh; Ceaselessly it flows on.
Across the fields and lanes, You are kind to come here.
Talking of far-off plains, You cherish friendship dear.
The moon's bright and stars nice, The crows in southward flight.
They circle the trees thrice; There's no branch to alight.
With crags high mountains rise; With water the sea's deep.
With the help of the wise, An ordered world we'll keep.

【汪榕培英译】

A Short Song

When I drink, I'll sing a song, As life can by no means last long.
Life is like the morning dew; The bygone days come not anew.
I sigh and sigh, for life is short; I'm always haunted by the thought.
How can I relieve my pang? Nothing but the wine Dukang.
The collar of your coat is blue; This colour brings back thought of you.
As you remain far, far away, I sing this famous song today.
The bleating deer can oft be seen, Nibbling there on wormwood green.
In the heaven it is strewn. To renowned guests I pay salute,
With music of the lute and flute. Bright, oh bright is the moon;
Over this I always grieve; My lasting sorrows never leave.
However, you've come all the way; To offer service here you stay.
We chatter freely as old friends; Our deep affections never ends.

The moon and stars shine in the sky; Toward the south the songbirds fly.
When birds are circling round the birch, On which branch are they to perch?
The mountain needs more rocks to grow; The ocean needs more water to flow.
The Duke of Zhou accepts the wise, And so his state expands in size.

【赏析重点】

（1）对比分析“青青子衿，悠悠我心”句式结构转换、节奏处理。

（2）对比分析“我有嘉宾，鼓瑟吹笙”逻辑结构处理。

（3）分析分析“山不厌高，海不厌深”中“厌”字的语义和翻译方法。

第二节　陶渊明

Tao Yuanming

一、诗人简介

陶潜（365—427），江西浔阳（今九江）人，也叫陶渊明，字元亮。中国最伟大的诗人之一，著名隐士。陶潜出生在一个落魄贵族家庭。20 多岁时为了养活年迈的双亲，陶潜做了个小官。陶潜在那个职位上干了大约 10 年，又做了短期的县令之后辞职，因为他厌恶官场的繁文缛节和普遍的腐败。陶潜和妻子、孩子一起隐退在长江以南的一个农庄。尽管农民生活非常辛苦，并且经常要忍饥挨饿，但是陶潜可以饮酒（他的诗中常见的主题）、作诗、养菊（与他的诗歌有着不可分割的联系），他的内心是满足的。由于与陶潜同时代的人喜欢“富艳难踪”的文章，所以他平淡自然的诗篇直到唐朝（618—907）才得到充分的重视。作为写五言诗的大师，陶潜被称为第一个伟大的田园诗（与当时盛行的山水诗相对）人。尽管从本质上来说陶潜持的是道教的生死观，但是他还自由地采用了儒家学说和佛教的思想元素。最被陶潜吸引的是佛教。

Tao Qian (365–427), born in Xunyang (Jiujiang, Jiangxi Province), also called Tao Yuanming, courtesy name Yuanliang, was one of China's greatest poets and a noted recluse. Born into an impoverished aristocratic family, Tao Qian took a minor official post while in his 20s in order to support his aged parents. After about 10 years at that post and a brief term as county magistrate, he resigned from official life, repelled by its excessive formality and widespread corruption. With his wife and children he retired to a farming village south of the Yangtze River. Despite the hardships of a farmer's life and frequent food shortages, Tao was contented, writing poetry, cultivating the chrysanthemums that became inseparably associated with his poetry, and drinking wine, also a common subject of his verse. Because the taste of Tao's contemporaries was for an elaborate and artificial style, his simple and straight forward poetry was not fully appreciated until the Tang dynasty (618–907). A master of the five-word line, Tao has been described as the first great poet of tianyuan ("fields and gardens"), landscape poetry inspired by pastoral scenes (as opposed to the then-fashionable shanshui "mountains and rivers" poetry). Essentially a Daoist in his philosophical outlook on life and death, he also freely adopted the elements of Confucianism and Buddhism that most appealed to him.

在中国诗歌史上，陶渊明已被公认为是继屈原之后，李白、杜甫之前最杰出的诗人。陶渊明的作品，现存诗歌 120 余首，散文、辞赋等 10 多篇。他的诗歌，或叹行役之劳，或抒厌仕之感，或写田园之美，或记闲居之趣，或咏务农之乐，或述贫困之苦，或发人生之感慨，或言自然之理趣，或缅怀远古之盛世淳风，或赞赏历朝之高人雅上，莫不真情流露，使人回味无穷。其中描写田园风光的诗歌，历来最为人们所称道。陶渊明诗歌在当时的诗坛上独树一帜，艺术上有着极高的欣赏价值。陶诗最显著的，被公认的艺术特色就是平淡自然、质朴无华。

In the history of Chinese poetry, Tao Yuanming has been considered as the great poet after Qu Yuan and before Li Bai and Du Fu. Among Tao Yuanming's works extant, there are 120 poems and a dozen prose essay. All his poems are full of emotion and everlasting pleasure, whether they deal with the dreariness of official duties, the disgust for an official career, the beauty of country life, the fun of a leisurely life, the pleasure of farming, the inflictions of poverty, the meditation on human existence, the lessons drawn from nature, the nostalgia for ancient simplicity, or the eulogy of hermits and recluses. His nature poems are especially praiseworthy. With a distinguished style, Tao Yuanming's poems have been enjoyed through the ages for their artistic merits. The most distinguished style of these poems is plainness and simplicity.

二、典籍英译赏析

桃花源记

【原典 1】

晋太元中，武陵人捕鱼为业。缘溪行，忘路之远近。忽逢桃花林，夹岸数百步，中无杂树，芳草鲜美，落英缤纷。渔人甚异之。复前行，欲穷其林。

【林语堂英译】

The Peach Colony

During the reign of Taiyuan of Chin, there was a fisherman of Wuling. One day he was walking along a bank. After having gone a certain distance, he suddenly came upon a peach grove which extended along the bank for about a hundred yards. He noticed with surprise that the grove had a magic effect, so singularly free from the usual mingling of brushwood, while the beautifully grassy ground was covered with its rose petals.

【戴维斯（A. R. Davis）英译】

Peach-Blossom Source

During the Taiyuan period (376–396) of Jin, a man of Wuling, who made his living as a fisherman, ascended a stream, forgetful of the distance he traveled. Suddenly he came upon a grove of peach trees in blossom. They lined the banks for several hundred paces: among them were no other kinds of tree. The fragrant herbage was fresh and beautiful; fallen blossom lay in profusion. The fisherman, in extreme wonder, again went forward, wishing to go to the end of the grove.

【赏析重点】

（1）对比分析"夹岸数百步"的语义理解和翻译方法。

（2）对比分析"芳草鲜美，落英缤纷"的翻译方法。

【原典 2】

林尽水源，便得一山。山有小口，仿佛若有光。便舍船，从口入。初极狭，才通人。复行数十步，豁然开朗。土地平旷，屋舍俨然，有良田美池桑竹之属。阡陌交通，鸡犬相闻。其中往来种作，男女衣着，悉如外人。黄发垂髫，并怡然自乐。

【林语堂英译】

He went further to explore, and when he came to the end of the grove, he saw a spring which came from a cave in the hill. Having noticed that there seemed to be a weak light in the cave, he tied up his boat and decided to go in and explore. At first the opening was very narrow, barely wide enough for one person to go in. After a dozen steps, it opened into a flood of light. He saw before his eyes a wide, level valley, with houses and fields and farms. There were bamboos and mulberries; farmers were working and dogs and chickens were running about. The dresses of the men and women were like those of the outside world, and the old men and children appeared very happy and contented.

【戴维斯（A. R. Davis）英译】

At first it was very narrow, barely allowing a man to pass, but as he went on for some tens of paces, it came out into the open air, upon lands level and wide with houses of a stately appearance. There were fine fields and beautiful pools, clumps of mulberries and bamboo. The field dykes intersected; cocks crowed and dogs barked to each other. The clothes of the men and women who came and went, planted and worked among them were entirely like those of people outside. The white-haired and the children with their hair in tufts happily enjoyed themselves.

【赏析重点】

（1）对比分析“初极狭，才通人”译文的句式结构转换。

（2）对比分析“阡陌交通，鸡犬相闻”译文的语义重组。

【原典 3】

见渔人，乃大惊，问所从来。具答之。便要还家，设酒杀鸡作食。村中闻有此人，咸来问讯。自云先世避秦时乱，率妻子邑人来此绝境，不复出焉，遂与外人间隔。问今是何世，乃不知有汉，无论魏晋。此人一一为具言所闻，皆叹惋。余人各复延至其家，皆出酒食。停数日，辞去。此中人语云：“不足为外人道也！”

【林语堂英译】

They were greatly astonished to see the fisherman and asked him where he had come from. The fisherman told them and was invited to their homes, where wine was served and chicken was killed for dinner to entertain him. The villagers hearing of his coming all came to see him and to talk. They said that their ancestors had come here as refugees to escape from the tyranny of Tsin Shih-huang (builder of the Great Wall) some six hundred years ago, and they had never left it. They were thus completely cut off from the world, and asked what was the ruling dynasty now. They had not even heard of the Han dynasty (two centuries before to two centuries after Christ), not to speak of the Wei (third century ad) and the Chin (third and fourth centuries). The fisherman told them, which they heard with great amazement. Many of the other villagers then began to invite him to their homes by turn and feed him dinner and wine. After a few days, he took leave of them and left. The villagers begged him not to tell the people outside about their colony.

【戴维斯（A. R. Davis）英译】

When they saw the fisherman, they were greatly surprised and asked from what place he had come. When he had answered all their questions, they invited him to come back to their homes, where they set out wine, killed a chicken and make a meal. When the villagers heard of this man, they all come to pay their respects. They told him that their ancestors, fleeing from the troubles during the Qin period (221 BC–208 BC), had brought their wives and children and neighbors to this inaccessible spot and had never gone out again. Thus they became cut off from people outside. They asked what dynasty it was now: they did not know that there had been Han (206 BC–220ad), nor of course Wei (220–265) or Jin. The fisherman told them all he knew, item by item, and at everything they sighed with grief. The others in turn also invited him to their homes, and all set out wine and food. He stayed for several days and then took leave of them. The people of this place said to him: "You should not speak of this to those outside."

【赏析重点】

（1）对比分析"设酒杀鸡作食"的结构处理。

（2）对比分析历史朝代翻译方法。

【原典 4】

既出，得其船，便扶向路，处处志之。及郡下，诣太守，说此。太守即遣人随其往，寻向所志，遂迷，不复得路。南阳刘子骥，高尚士也，闻之，欣然规往。未果，寻病终。后遂无问津者。

【林语堂英译】

The man found his boat and came back, marking with signs the route he had followed. He went to the magistrate's office and told the magistrate about it. The latter sent someone to go with him and find the place. They looked for the signs but got lost and could never find it again. Liu Tsechi of Nanyang was a great idealist. He heard of this story, and planned to go and find it, but was taken ill and died before he could fulfill his wish. Since then, no one has gone in search of this place.

【戴维斯（A. R. Davis）英译】

When he had gone out, he found his boat and followed the route by which he had come: everywhere he noted the way. When he reached the commandery, he called on the prefect and told him this story. The prefect immediately sent a man to go with him and seek out the places he had previously noted, but they went astray and could not find the way again. Liu Ziji of Nanyang, who was a scholar of lofty ideals heard of it and joyfully planned to go. Soon after, before he had carried out his plan, he fell and died. Afterwards there was no one who "sought the ford".

【赏析重点】

对比分析"南阳刘子骥，高尚士也，闻之，欣然规往"译文的结构重组。

第三节　乐府诗

Yuefu Poetry

一、文化背景

乐府诗在我国文学史上，继往开来，承前启后，魅力令人称绝。"乐府"一名始于秦，秦及西汉惠帝时均设有"乐府令"。乐府这一古代音乐官署的名称，后来演变成为一种诗体，被称为乐府，或乐府诗。中国诗歌起源最早可以追溯到夏、商、周时期，早在那时，我们的祖先就在从事生产劳动的过程中创造了集音乐、舞蹈和诗歌为一体的艺术形式。周代设立的专司礼乐的机关——大司乐，就是乐府这一官署的雏形，而我国第一部诗歌总集《诗经》，事实上就是周代"乐府诗"的缩影。

Yuefu poetry performed an irreplaceable function in the history of Chinese literature. It inherited the past and ushered the future with its excellent charm. The name "Yuefu" originated from the Qin dynasty. Yuefuling was set up then as well as in the Western Han dynasty reined by Emperor Hui. Yuefu was originally a name of a government office in charge of music in ancient China and it later evolved into a referent to a verse form. Poems of this form were called Yuefu or Yuefu poetry. Its origin can be traced back to the three ancient Chinese dynasties of Xia, Shang and Zhou. Early at that time, our ancestors had created an artistic form which integrated music, dance and poetry in the process of laboring. In the Zhou dynasty, there was a special institution called "Dasiyue" which was the embryo of the Yuefu office. *The Book of Poetry*, the first general poetic collection in China, was actually a miniature of the Yuefu poetry in the Zhou Dynasty.

乐府诗，最初主要是指自两汉至魏晋南北朝时由乐府机关采集编制的用来入乐的诗歌，然而随着乐府诗的发展，其所涵盖的范围也不断扩大，很多文人的仿作也被包含在内。这些仿作主要包括三类：一是根据乐府旧曲，创作新辞入乐。二是沿用乐府旧题，仿照其思想和艺术风格撰写新辞，多不入乐。三是另创新题新意作辞，并不入乐，被称为“新乐府”。这三类仿作中，当数第二类最为普遍。建安时期的“三曹”就多以旧题作诗咏志。

The Yuefu poetry originally referred to those singable poems collected by the Yuefu office during the period from the two Han Dynasties through Wei and Jin to the Southern and Northern Dynasties. Later, with the development of this genre, its scope was enlarged and many literary men's imitation works were included. They imitated the Yuefu poetry in mainly three ways: first, writing new lines to the old yuefu tunes; second, following the old theme and writing similar non-musical lines; third, creating new themes and writing new non-musical lines which were also called the New Yuefu. Among these three ways, the most commonly practiced was the second type. The "Three Caos" of the Jian'an Period were good at writing new poems with old themes.

汉乐府诗是继《诗经》《楚辞》之后出现的第一个重要发展阶段。汉武帝设乐府，目的之一就是考察民风，因此汉乐府诗多为民歌，其音乐性尤为突出。在汉乐府诗中我们常会遇到“解”“乱”“艳”“趋”之类的音乐名词。

Yuefu in the Han Dynasties turned out to be a significant stage after *The Book of Poetry* and *The Verse of Chu* in its development. One of Emperor Wu's intentions in establishing the Yuefu office was to observe the real conditions of the people. So most of the Yuefu poems in the Han Dynasties were folk songs, with a strong musical characteristics. In the Han Yuefu poetry, we often come across the musical terms such as "Jie"（解）, "Luan"（乱）, "Yamn"（艳）and "Qu"（趋）.

南北朝乐府诗是继周民歌和汉乐府民歌之后出现的又一批人民的口头创作，是我国诗歌历史上又一新发展。它不仅反映了新的社会现实，而且创造了新的艺术形式和风格。一般来说，南北朝的乐府诗篇幅短小，抒情多于叙事。南北朝时期的乐府诗呈现出民间乐府诗繁盛的局面。在体制上南北朝时期的乐府诗多为五言四句的短篇，这种体制早在汉代就已经存在，但真正被发扬光大则是在南北朝时期。此类乐府诗的流行为南北朝乐府诗的发展开辟出一条抒情小诗的新道路，尤其适合在民间流传。

Mostly created orally, the Yuefu poetry of the Southern and Northern Dynasties showed another tide of the folk Yuefu after the folk songs of the Zhou dynasty and the folk Yuefu of the Han Dynasties. They not only reflected the new social realities but also were endowed with new artistic forms and styles. Generally speaking, the Yuefu poems of this period were much shorter and there were more lyrics than narratives. The creation of the folk Yuefu was prosperous in the Southern and Northern Dynasties. Most of the works were short five-character quatrains. This form had existed since the Han Dynasties, but it flourished in this period. The prevailing of this kind of Yuefu opened a new way of lyrics for the development of the Yuefu in the Southern and Northern Dynasties, and they spread quickly among the common people.

二、诗歌汉英翻译赏析

敕勒歌

敕勒川，
阴山下。
天似穹庐，
笼盖四野。
天苍苍，
野茫茫。
风吹草低见牛羊。

【杨宪益英译】

A Shepherd's Song

By the side of the rill,
At the foot of the hill
The grassland stretches under the firmament tranquil.
The boundless grassland lies
Under the boundless skies.
When the winds blow
And grass bends low,
My sheep and cattle will emerge before your eyes.

【赏析重点】

（1）分析“天似穹庐，笼盖四野”译文的逻辑重组。

（2）赏析“天苍苍，野茫茫”修辞手法的翻译方法。

长歌行

汉乐府（两汉）

青青园中葵，
朝露待日晞。
阳春布德泽，
万物生光辉。
常恐秋节至，
焜黄华叶衰。
百川东到海，
何时复西归？
少壮不努力，
老大徒伤悲！

【杨宪益英译】

A Song in Slow Time

Green the mallow in the garden,
Waiting for sunlight to dry the morning dew;
Bright spring diffuses virtue,
Adding fresh lustre to all living things.
Yet I dread the coming of autumn
When leaves turn yellow and the flowers fade.
A hundred streams flow eastwards to the ocean,
Nevermore to turn west again;
And one who mis-spends his youth
In old age will grieve in vain.

【赏析重点】

赏析“少壮不努力，老大徒伤悲”的翻译方法。

木兰辞（节选）

唧唧复唧唧，
木兰当户织。
不闻机杼声，
唯闻女叹息。

问女何所思，
问女何所忆。
女亦无所思，
女亦无所忆。
昨夜见军帖，
可汗大点兵，
军书十二卷，
卷卷有爷名。
阿爷无大儿，
木兰无长兄，
愿为市鞍马，
从此替爷征。

【杨宪益英译】

The Song of Mulan

One sigh after another,
Mulan sat opposite the door weaving;
But no sound of the shuttle was heard,
Except the sighs of the girl.
When asked what she was pondering over,
When asked what she had called to mind,
Nothing special the girl was pondering over,
Nothing special the girl had called to mind.
Last night I saw the draft dispatch,
The Khan is mustering a mighty army;
The roster consists of many muster rolls,
And every roll has father's name on it.
Father has no grown son,
Nor Mulan an elder brother;
I want to buy a saddle and a horse,
And from now on fight in place of my father.

【赏析重点】

（1）赏析“唧唧复唧唧”修辞手法的翻译方法。

（2）对比分析中文英文句式特点。

拓展训练 | Extension Training

1. 思考题

（1）用英文介绍汉魏晋时期代表性诗人。

（2）总结乐府诗英译方法。

2. 文化外宣汉英翻译

（1）“乐府”本是秦以后由朝廷设立用来训练乐工、采集民歌并配器作曲的专门官署，后专指由乐府机关所采集、配乐并由乐工演唱的民歌。乐府诗是继《诗经》之后古代民歌的一次创造，是与《诗经》《楚辞》并列的诗歌形态。至今保存的汉乐府民歌有五六十首，大都真实反映了当时社会生活的各个方面，表现出纯真质朴的思想感情，并由此形成反映普通民众声音与情感的文学创作传统。其中最有特色与成就的是描写女性生活的作品。汉代以后将可以入乐的诗歌及仿乐府古题而写的诗歌统称为乐府。

（2）“建安风骨”又称“汉魏风骨”。指汉献帝建安年间（196—220）至魏初这一时期的文学作品中由刚健悲慨的思想感情与清朗遒劲的文辞凝结而成的时代精神和总体风格。汉末政治动荡，战乱频繁，人民流离失所。这一时期的代表作家“三曹”（曹操、曹丕、曹植）、“七子”（孔融、陈琳、王粲、徐干、阮瑀、应玚、刘桢）和女诗人蔡琰等人，继承了汉乐府民歌的现实主义传统，在创作中多直面社会动乱，反映民生疾苦及个人抱负，抒发了建功立业的理想和积极进取的精神，表现出刚健、向上的抱负和豪迈、悲慨的情怀。“建安文学”的总体风格是悲凉慷慨、风骨遒劲、华美壮阔，具有鲜明的时代特征和个性特征，形成了文学史上独特的“建安风骨”，从而被后人尊为典范，其中又以诗歌成就最为突出。

（3）意境指文艺作品所描绘的景象与所表现的思想情感高度融合而形成的审美境界。“境”本指疆界、边界，汉末魏晋时期佛教传入中国，认为现实世界皆为空幻，唯有心灵感知才是真实的存在，“境”被认为是人的心灵感知所能达到的界域，作为文艺术语，“境”有多重含义。“意境”由唐代著名诗人王昌龄提出，侧重指文艺作品中主观感知到的物象与精神蕴涵相统一所达到的审美高度，其特点是“取意造境”“思与境偕”。相对于“意象”，“意境”更突出文艺作品的精神蕴涵与美感的高级形态，它拓展了作品情与景、虚与实、心与物等概念的应用，提升了文艺作品及审美活动的层次。后经过历代丰富发展，“意境”成为评价文艺作品水准的重要概念，是历代经典作品层累的结果，也是优秀文艺作品必须具备的重要特征。“意境”这一术语也是外来思想文化与中华本土思想融合的典范。

第七章　唐诗英译

Translation of the Tang Poetry

一、学习目标

（1）用英文介绍唐诗分类和特点。
（2）掌握唐诗文化关键词英译。
（3）对比鉴赏代表性唐诗中外译者翻译方法。

二、文化背景

唐诗代表着中国诗歌的最高水平。国家的强大富足和政治开明、以诗取仕的选拔制度，以及文人对诗歌创作技巧的不懈探索，造就了唐诗的辉煌成就，使之成为中国文化宝库里永不褪色的瑰宝。在经历其后一千多年的沧桑巨变之后，保存至今的唐诗数量仍有将近五万首。唐诗的最大特色在于它内在的灵魂和气魄。唐朝是中国历史上最强大的封建帝国，唐诗的整体特征正反映出唐人气壮山河的自信与雄浑豪迈的激情，这种心胸气概在唐诗里就表现为“盛唐气象”。

The poetry of the Tang dynasty represents the highest level of Chinese poetry. The mighty and prosperous country, the liberal politics, the official selection system upon writing poems, and the constant exploration of the writing skills accomplished the glorious achievement of the Tang poetry and made it an everlasting treasure in Chinese literature. After the great changes in the more than one thousand years, there are nearly fifty thousand poems preserved until now. The biggest feature of Tang poetry is its internal soul and spirit. It was born in the most powerful Chinese feudalist empire. Its main character was to reflect the confidence and passion of the people in that age, which was called “Blooming Tang Grandeur” in Tang poetry.

（一）唐诗的发展 Stages of Tang Poetry

唐诗的发展与唐王朝的命运息息相关，虽然起伏的曲线跟政治上的分期不完全吻合，但大致走向是一致的，所以后世文学史都以初唐、盛唐、中唐和晚唐为唐诗发展的分期。

The development of the Tang dynasty was closely related with the fate of the Tang Empire. Though the fluctuating curve didn't exactly fit with the political stages, the rough tendency was the same. So the history of literature of the later generation divided the development of the Tang poetry into early Tang (618–712), blooming Tang (713–765), middle Tang (766–835) and late Tang (836–907).

唐朝初建时百废待兴，新王朝的朝气初露，前朝诗歌并不完善，有待发展，此为初唐。初唐时期的代表诗人是“初唐四杰”——王勃（650—676）、杨炯（650—？）、卢照邻（约 630—680 后）、骆宾王（约 638—？），还有“诗骨”陈子昂（659—700）。他们的创作为唐诗后来的发展奠定了良好的基础。

In the early Tang dynasty, the leftover was waiting to be rebuilt and the new empire just unveiled its vitality. The poetry of the former dynasties also needed to be improved. This is the early Tang. The representative poets of the early Tang stage were the "Four Distinguished Poets of Early Tang dynasty", including Wang Bo (650–676), Yang Jiong (650–?), Lu Zhaolin (approx. 630–680), and Luo Binwang (approx. 638–?), as well as the "Poetry Bone", Chen Zi'ang (659–700). Their works established a good foundation for the further development of the Tang poetry.

随着时光推移，唐朝国力达到鼎盛时期，唐诗发展也达到了顶峰，出现了百花齐放的繁荣景象，此为盛唐。盛唐时期的浪漫主义诗人李白（701—762）和现实主义诗人杜甫（712—770）即是这一时期最杰出的代表。李白和杜甫不仅是唐诗最高成就的代表，也是中国文化在世界上的重要代表。他们是世界级的中国古代历史文化名人，代表名篇数不胜数。此外田园山水诗派的王维（701—761）、孟浩然（689—740）和边塞诗派的高适（约 700—765）、王昌龄（？—约 756）等人的诗歌也各具特色，各有千秋。

As time went by, the country reached its most prosperous period when the Tang poetry also got to the top. There appeared the diversified flourishing situation. This is the blooming Tang. The blooming Tang period had two most outstanding representatives: the romantic poet, Li Bai (701–762) and the realistic poet, Du Fu (712–770). They not only stood for the highest achievement of the Tang poetry but also the fascinating Chinese culture in the world. They were the world-class cultural celebrities of ancient Chinese history who had left countless masterpieces to the descendants. And the poems of the landscape and pastoral poets like Wang Wei (701–761), Meng Haoran (689–740) and the ones of the frontier fortress poets like Gao Shi (approx. 700–765), Wang Changling (?–756) are also with respective features and have their own merits.

安史之乱对国家经济政治文化破坏严重，唐王朝的国力逐渐下滑，进入缓慢衰落的阶段，唐诗也逐步走向成熟，进而开始出现衰落的态势，此为中唐。中唐时期成绩最卓著的诗人要数“诗魔”白居易（772—846）。他的诗通俗易懂，深受民众喜爱，代表作有《长恨歌》《琵琶行》。但中唐时期唐诗已现颓势，受朝廷腐败、国力衰退等客观条件影响，中唐诗歌难再有雄壮之美，逐渐出现颓靡消极之音。

An Shi Rebellion caused a severe catastrophe to the nation's economy, politics and culture. The national power gradually went down and slowly entered into the deteriorating stage. And the tang poetry also matured and started to show the declining tendency. This is the middle Tang. The most prestigious poet in the middle Tang period was the Poetry Wizard, Bai Juyi (772–846), whose poems were easy to understand and well accepted by common people, including *Song of Eternal Sorrow* (*Chang Hen Ge*) and *Song of the Lute Player* (*Pi Pa Xing*). However, the Tang poetry had started to appear its declining tendency. Affected by the corruption of the courtyard deterioration of the national power and other objective conditions, the poetry of middle Tang period started to play the dejected and passive sound instead of regaining its past grandeur.

到了唐朝末期，唐诗出现了彻底衰落之前的回光返照的现象，并随着唐朝的逐步灭亡拉下帷幕，此为晚唐。晚唐时期著名的诗人主要有李商隐（约 813—858）、杜牧（803—853）、温庭筠（？—866）。杜牧的怀古诗更是一绝，其《赤壁怀古》是怀古诗中的上乘之作。温庭筠则诗词俱佳，以词取胜，为词这种文体到宋代达到鼎盛开启了先河。唐诗在晚唐时期出现了回光返照，在李商隐、杜牧之后彻底进入低谷期，而词则开始崭露头角。

In the late Tang dynasty, there appeared the last radiance of the setting sun of the Tang poetry, which came to an end along with the perish of the Tang dynasty. This is the late Tang. The famous poets in the late Tang period included Li Shangyin (approx. 813–858), Du Mu (803–853), Wen Tingyun (?–866), etc., who brought the final spectacularity of the declining Tang poetry. And the past-cherishing poems of Du Mu were extraordinary, like his great works titled *Red Cliff Reminiscence* (*Chi Bi Huai Gu*). Wen Tingyun were skilled in both poem and Ci (a lyric classical Chinese poetry using a set of poetic meters derived from base of certain patterns of fixed-rhythm, fixed-tone, variable line-length formal types, or model examples, which were originally based on musical song tunes). He got better reputation on his Ci and initiated the development of this literary form to its prosperous time in the Song dynasty. Tang poetry emitted the last radiance of the setting sun and entered the complete low ebb after Li Shangyin and Du Mu, while Ci started to emerge to the surface.

（二）唐诗体裁 Genres of Tang Poetry

唐诗的诗体主要为古体和近体。唐朝诗人在继承古体创作的同时开拓创新，积极推广使用近体写诗，成就了近体诗的艺术升华。

Tang poetry is mainly divided into ancient and new genres. The poets in the Tang dynasty inherited the writing of ancient poetry and also developed the new poetry which was actively promoted and finally achieved the artistic sublimation of the new genre.

1. 古体诗 Ancient Genre Poetry

顾名思义，古体诗就是按照唐朝以前古代的写诗方法写的诗，诗歌形式比较自由，没有字数、音律、格式等的限制。一首诗里，诗句的字数可以是四个字、五个字、七个字，一般称为“四言体”“五言体”“七言体”，还有的诗里各句字数长短相杂，参差不齐，称为“杂言体”。每首诗的诗句数量也没有特别的限制。四言体古诗，远在《诗经》时代就已被人们采用了，到唐代已经逐渐衰微，很少有人再写，唐代的古体诗以五言、七言和杂言为主。

As its name implies, ancient genre poetry is the poems written according to the methods of the successive dynasties before the Tang dynasty, with relatively free style and without the limitation in the number of characters, rhyme and pattern. In one poem, the number of characters in all these lines could be varied from four, five or seven, which were relatively called “four-character style” “five-character style” and “seven-character style”. And for those with various numbers of characters in each line within one poem, it was called “blend character style”. The number of lines of one poem was also without any specific limitation. The four-character poetry was adopted as far as the era of *The Book of Poetry*, and was on the wane by the Tang dynasty. Few people had ever written it. The ancient poetry of the Tang dynasty was mainly the five-character, seven-character and blend character.

2. 近体诗 New Genre Poetry

近体诗又叫“今体诗”或“格律诗”，是唐代形成的新诗体。经过唐朝诗人们的不懈努力，不断创新，以及主动用近体诗来创作的自觉，近体诗在唐朝成为一种非常重要的诗体，丰富了唐诗创作的形式。与古体诗的自由完全不同，近体诗讲究对称和均衡，近体诗中诗句的句数、每个分句的字数、字句的音调、音律都有严格的限制。

The new genre poetry, also called “present poetry” or “Ge Lv poetry”, is a new poetry style formed in the Tang dynasty. Thanks to the poets' continuous efforts, constant innovations and frequently appliance and practices, it became a significant poetry genre in the Tang dynasty, which was used in half of the verses written in that period of time and enriched the creative styles of Tang poetry. Different from the freedom of the ancient genre, the new genre emphasized the symmetry and balance of the poems in which the number of lines, the number of the characters in each line, the tones and rhymes were all strictly determined.

近体诗主要分为律诗和绝句，按照每句五个字和每句七个字的分类，律诗又主要分为五言律诗和七言律诗；绝句又主要分为五言绝句和七言绝句，简称“五绝”和“七绝”。律诗一般是八句，而绝句一般是四句。从形式上看，绝句短小精悍，只有律诗一半的容量，而写出来的艺术水平却丝毫不亚于律诗。李白、王昌龄都是写绝句的高手，而杜甫则是律诗中的王者，是七言律诗最高艺术成就的代表。

The new genre poetry mainly includes Lvshi (a poem of eight lines) and Jueju (a poem of four lines). According to the number of the characters in each line, it can also be divided into five-character and seven-character. So Lvshi has five-character Lvshi and seven-character Lvshi; and Jueju has five-character Jueju and seven-character Jueju, or the shortened form “five-Jue” and “seven-Jue”. Lvshi usually has eight lines and Jueju is with four lines. In terms of the form, Jueju is short and concise, which only has half information of Lvshi; however, they possess equal artistry in all the aspects. Li Bai and Wang Changling were skillful poets of Jueju, while Du Fu was the king of Lvshi, who represented the highest artistic achievement of Lvshi.

（三）唐诗题材 Themes of Tang Poetry

唐诗的内容丰富多彩、包罗万象，人们所能想到的各个方面、各个层次的内容都有涉猎，其中也包含了人们复杂多变的内心情感。不管写景、叙事、咏史、咏物，还是山水、边塞，都是引发诗人情绪发生、做出反应的诱因。归根结底，诗人都是想要表达自我精神世界的思想、感情和想法，抒发个人的情怀。

The content of Tang poetry is full of variety, including all the aspects people could ever imagine, as well as man's complicated emotions deep inside. The descendants can study the social lives of that period of time through Tang poetry, even analyzing ancient people's thoughts and feelings thousands of years ago. So even if the poetries were varied from one another and with their own features respectively, people are still used to classifying poems on themes as which, ranging from scene-description, narration, history-recording, object-depicting, landscape-description or frontier-writing, all of which are the incentive triggering poets' mood fluctuations. After all, the writers just wanted to deliver their own thoughts, feelings and ideas, and express their personal emotions.

1. 写景（抒情）诗 Landscape (emotion-expressing) Poetry

唐朝版图辽阔，风景秀丽，唐人酷爱游山玩水，漫游是唐朝诗人生活的一个非常重要的组成部分。不管是江南的青山秀水，还是北方的大漠孤烟，不管是巴蜀的崇山峻岭，还是长江的烟雨楼台，全都被诗人写入诗中。而诗人们在看见壮丽山河之后内心不禁产生了无限的感情，或喜，或悲，或愁，或闷，这些情绪都融入了他们写景的诗句当中，产生了情景交融的绝妙效果，于是写景（抒情）诗就出现了。崔颢（约 704—754）的《黄鹤楼》就是一首典型的写景（抒情）诗，描写的是中国四大名楼之一黄鹤楼的风景，诗人即景生情，诗兴大发，脱口而出，一气呵成。

Tang Empire owned a broad territory with beautiful landscape. People were fond of traveling among the mountains and rivers, which was an important part of their lives. Both the graceful scenery of the south of Yangtze River, and the expansive desert of the north areas, both the steep cliffs of Bashu (two ancient cities in Sichuan), and the pavilions and terraces in the valley of Yangtze river, were all recorded in the poems. And the affections generated after the poets seeing all these magnificent landscapes, being happy, sad, worried or depressed, were all blended in those lines which produced an excellent fusion of emotions and scenes. So the landscape poem *Yellow Crane Tower*, by Cui Hao (approx. 704–754) is a typical landscape (emotion-expressing) poetry, describing the scenery of Yellow Crane Tower, one of the Four great Towers of China. The poet was inspired by the splendid landscape and plumped out the verse at one stretch.

2. 叙事（咏怀）诗 Narrative (feeling-expressing) Poetry

唐人写诗经常信手拈来，生活中的奇闻趣事，哪怕是微不足道的小事都可以入诗。然而这并不是单纯的记录，而是通过写诗来表达自身的思想感情：对于社会现实的感悟，对于人生价值的思考，对于济世理想的追求。借讲述事情来表明志向、抒发感情、慨叹命运是唐朝诗人普遍使用的表达方式。杜甫的《石壕吏》就是最典型的代表。

People in the Tang dynasty wrote poems freely without too much hesitation. They were ready to include in poems any news and anecdotes in life, and even the most trivial incidents. However. it was not a mere recording; rather, the poet did so to display his thoughts and feelings: how he brooded over social realities, how he pondered on the values of life, and how he pursued his ideal to serve the world. It was common practice for poets in the Tang dynasty to demonstrate aspirations, express emotions and grieve over destinies through telling narrative stories. Du Fu's *The Pressgang at Stone Moat Village* is a typical example.

3. 咏史（怀古）诗 Historical (past-cherishing) Poetry

中国古代非常注重对历史的记录和考察，唐朝也不例外。诗人可以通过各种途径了解古代的历史。那些具有传奇色彩、举世闻名的历史名人、名胜古迹更加受到追捧和爱戴。咏史怀古诗就是以历史事件、历史人物、历史遗迹为题材的诗歌。诗人通过追忆历史，祭奠古迹来寄托哀思，通过历史的教训来影射讽刺当代的社会现实。

Ancient Chinese stressed the importance of recording and studying history, so did people in the Tang dynasty. Poets acquainted themselves with history in many ways, especially through visiting and adoring the legendary and well-known sites of historical figures and events. Historical (past-cherishing) poetry is the poems that address the themes of historical events, figures and relics. Poets either mourned the ancients through recalling historical events and visiting historical sites； or, alluded to or satirized contemporary social realities through drawing lessons from history.

4. 咏物（言志）诗 Object-chanting (ambition expressing) Poetry

咏物言志诗就是通过对事物的描绘咏叹体现对实现个人理想和价值的向往。咏物诗中所咏之物往往是诗人的化身，因为具备某些自然属性符合诗人对品格的要求，所以被拿来作为主题写诗，达到诗人塑造自我的目的。诗中所咏之物与诗人自身的形象完全融合在一起，成为诗人思想感情的寄托。贺知章的《咏柳》吟咏的就是春天的柳树，将心情寄托于有着美好姿态的杨柳之上，洋溢着诗人的愉悦心情。

Object-chanting poetry (or ambition expressing poetry) describes and chants objects

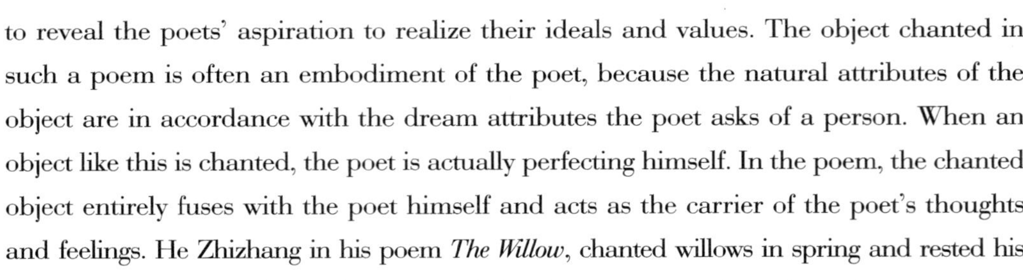

to reveal the poets' aspiration to realize their ideals and values. The object chanted in such a poem is often an embodiment of the poet, because the natural attributes of the object are in accordance with the dream attributes the poet asks of a person. When an object like this is chanted, the poet is actually perfecting himself. In the poem, the chanted object entirely fuses with the poet himself and acts as the carrier of the poet's thoughts and feelings. He Zhizhang in his poem *The Willow*, chanted willows in spring and rested his feelings on the elegant plants. The poet's delightful emotion flows throughout the poem.

5. 山水田园诗 Landscape and Pastoral Poetry

很多唐朝诗人都有山水田园诗的佳作，这并非山水田园诗派诗人们的专利。但王维、孟浩然等山水田园诗派诗人创作的作品堪称典范，并且创作的数量和质量都占优。这类诗主要描写自然风光、农村景物，以及安逸恬淡的隐居生活。诗作意境优美，风格淡雅，语言清丽。

Many poets in the Tang dynasty had masterpieces of landscape and pastoral poems, which were not exclusive to poets of the landscape and pastoral poetic school. Nevertheless, poets of this school like Wang Wei and Meng Haoran created the finest landscape poems and boasted more and better pieces than other poets both on quantity and quality. They mainly described natural landscape, rural scenery and serene and reclusive life in the countryside, all artistic in conception, simple yet elegant in style, and fresh in language.

6. 边塞征战诗 Frontier Fortress Poetry

边塞征战诗以边塞军旅生活为主要题材，或描写奇异的塞外风光，或反映驻守边境的艰辛，是唐朝诗歌的重要组成部分。边塞征战诗的特点非常鲜明，深刻地反映出唐朝边境战事的残酷和驻守边关将士们的艰辛苦楚。诗人通过描写恶劣的自然环境，烘托出将士们坚毅勇敢的英雄气质，也对常年生活在这里的百姓抱有深刻的同情。

Frontier fortress poetry took military life at the frontier fortress as its theme depicting the exotic scenes beyond the borders or reflecting the soldiers' hardship in the frontier areas which was an important part of Tang poetry. It had distinct characteristics, reflecting profoundly the cruel warfare near the borders and the miserable life of frontier soldiers. Through the description of the harsh natural environment, the poets tried to highlight the heroic mettle of the valiant soldiers and also showed their deep sympathy toward the local people.

三、文化关键词

诗仙　Poet Immortal

诗史　poetic history

诗王　King of Poet

古体诗　Ancient Genre Poetry

近体诗　New Genre Poetry

七绝圣手　Best in Seven-Jue Poetry

写景（抒情）诗　Landscape (emotion-expressing) Poetry

咏物（言志）诗　Object-chanting (ambition expressing) Poetry

山水田园诗　Landscape and Pastoral Poetry

边塞征战诗　Frontier Fortress Poetry

第一节　李白

Li Bai

一、诗人简介

李白（701—762），字太白，号青莲居士，祖籍陇西成纪（今甘肃天水附近），生于中亚碎叶城。5 岁时随父迁居绵州彰明（今四川江油）青莲乡，因此自号青莲居士。李白一生除做过三年供奉翰林和短期永王幕僚外，主要是在漫游流浪中度过的，其思想兼有儒、道、侠三家的特点。儒家“兼济天下”的思想支配他积极用世、建立功业。济苍生、安社稷的政治理想是其诗歌的中心主题之一。当他在政治上遭受打击，抑郁不得志时，道家愤世嫉俗、返于自然的思想就在他身上占了主导地位，其作品就表现出放浪形骸的反叛精神，蔑视人间的一切，浮云富贵，粪土王侯。他又深深倾慕古代侠士慷慨悲歌、豪迈不羁的生活态度和他们所奉行的“以武犯禁”“不爱其躯”“羞伐其德”的游侠精神，因此敢于蔑视封建秩序和礼教，冲击传统偶像。李白一生身体力行的政治准则“功成身退”，正是儒、道、侠三者统一的产物。这种强烈要求摆脱羁绊，追求个性解放和精神自由的风格飘逸豪放，是李白诗歌的最大特色。李白的诗歌，形象高度个性化，具有浓厚的主观感情色彩；善于运用大胆的夸张、新颖的比喻和奇特的想象，兴寄无端，瞬息万变；善于运用历史传说和神话故事；语言清新自然而华美豪放。李白著有《李太白集》，被称为“诗仙”，诗歌现存 900 多首，是继屈原之后，我国古代浪漫主义的新高峰。

Li Bai (701–762), also known as Li Po, was renowned as the greatest romantic poet in ancient China. His courtesy name was Taibai and was born in Suiye in Central Asia. His ancestral home was located at Chengji, Longxi (present-day Tianshui, Gansu Province), but when he was five, he moved with his father to Qinglian town, in Changming, Mianzhou (now Jiangyou, Sichuan Province). Except for the three years he served for the Hanlin Academy and Prince Yong, he spent most of his life traveling extensively. His philosophy incorporated the features of Confucianism, Taoism as well as the virtues of chivalry. The Confucian notion of "making the whole world virtuous" was the foundation of his ambitions and optimism. One of the themes of his poetry is his political ambition of providing aid to the common people and bringing peace and stability to the country. When he was frustrated by the unfulfilment of his political ambitions, the Taoist loftiness and retreat in him prevailed and his poems reflected a wild and free persona. On the other hand, he adored the bold and unconstrained mien of ancient errant knights, who would sacrifice their lives for righteousness and never brag about their exploits. Furthermore, he was an iconoclast against feudal principles and etiquettes. Seeking retirement from fame and fortune, the political standard he lived up to in his life, is nothing more than the embodiment of the spirits of Confucianism, Taoism and chivalry. Li Bai's poetry, in general, is characterized by its unconventional spirit and highly personalized imagery. His employment of hyperboles, imageries and allusions is bold, creating exquisite pieces that fully utilize the elements of language. More than 900 poems of Li Bai survived and were compiled in *The Anthology of Li Taibai*. Thanks to the efforts of Li Bai, the "Poet Immortal", the Chinese tradition of Romanticism reached another zenith after Qu Yuan.

李白具有极高的诗歌创作天赋。他的诗歌，激情饱满，境界开阔，想象奇异，语言清新流畅，形象丰富生动，不仅记录了他丰富多彩的生活经历和微妙复杂的内心世界，而且也体现出当时的“盛唐气象”和他所遭遇的社会变化。李白一生中大部分时间都在游历各地，接触到各种宗教文化、民族风情、地方习俗，包括大量传说神话、民歌民谣、音乐舞蹈，他的诗歌创作体现出对这些多元文化异质元素的有机融合。李白胸襟开阔，性格豪放，想象丰富，富有文学天赋，他的大部分诗歌都写作于这个时代，是“盛唐气象”最直接、最生动的写照。李白与唐代另一位伟大诗人杜甫齐名，世称“李杜”。这两位大诗人，被人们称为灿烂的唐诗星空中一对耀眼的双子星。

Li Bai was an extraordinarily talented poet. His poems are full of emotion and fantastic imagination, using clear and fluent language to cover a broad range of topics. His descriptions are rich and dynamic, not merely recording his rich life and fascinating internal realm, but also expressing the spirit of the “High Tang”, and the social and political changes he met. He spent most of his life journeying to all parts of China, encountering different religions, cultures, customs, and practices, including tales and myths, folk songs, music, and dance. His poetic compositions express his amalgamation of this multivariate culture. Li Bai had an open heart and mind, bold and uninhibited character, rich imagination, and literary talent. Most of his poetry, composed during this period, is the most direct and dynamic expression of the “great Tang dynasty”. Li Bai is often associated with another great poet of the Tang dynasty, Du Fu; they are known as “Li Du”. These two poetic geniuses are often referred to as the two brightest stars in the brilliant heaven of Tang poetry.

二、古诗英译赏析

月下独酌

花间一壶酒，独酌无相亲。
举杯邀明月，对影成三人。
月既不解饮，影徒随我身。
暂伴月将影，行乐须及春。
我歌月徘徊，我舞影零乱。
醒时同交欢，醉后各分散。
永结无情游，相期邈云汉。

【许渊冲英译】

Drinking Alone under the Moon

Amid the flowers, from a pot of wine
I drink alone beneath the bright moonshine,
I raise my cup to invite the Moon who blends
Her light with my Shadow and we’re three friends.

The Moon does not know how to drink her share;
In vain my Shadow follows me here and there.
Together with them for the time I stay
And make merry before spring's spent away.
I sing and the Moon lingers to hear my song;
My Shadow's a mess while I dance along.
Sober, we three remain cheerful and gay;
Drunken, we part and each may go his way.
Our friendship will outshine all earthly love,
Next time we'll meet beyond the stars above.

【宇文所安英译】

Drinking Alone by Moonlight

Here among flowers one flask of wine,
with no close friends, I pour it alone.
I lift cup to bright moon, beg its company,
then facing my shadow, we become three.
The moon has never known how to drink;
my shadow does nothing but follow me.
But with moon and shadow as companions a while,
this joy I find must catch spring while it's here.
I sing, and the moon just lingers on;
I dance, and my shadow flails wildly.
When still sober we share friendship and pleasure,
then, utterly drunk, each goes his own way.
Let us join to roam beyond human cares
and plan to meet far in the river of stars.

【赏析重点】

（1）对比分析"举杯邀明月"中"邀"字的翻译方法。

（2）对比分析"我歌月徘徊，我舞影零乱"对仗句式的处理方式。

送友人

青山横北郭，白水绕东城。
此地一为别，孤蓬万里征。

浮云游子意，落日故人情。

挥手自兹去，萧萧班马鸣。

【许渊冲英译】

Farewell to a Friend

Green mountains bar the northern sky;
White water girds the eastern town.
Here is the place to say good-bye,
You'll drift out, lonely thistle down.
Like floating cloud you'll float away;
With parting day I'll part from you.
We wave and you start on your way,
Your horse still neighs: "adieu! adieu!"

【翟里斯（Giles）英译】

A FAREWELL

Where blue hills cross the northern sky,
Beyond the moat which girds the town,
It was there we stopped to say goodbye!
And one white sail alone dropped down
Your heart was full of wandering thought;
For me, my sun had set indeed;
To wave a last adieu we sought,
Voiced for us by each whinnying steed!

【赏析重点】

（1）对比分析“青山横北郭，白水绕东城”中“横”“绕”字的翻译方法。

（2）对比分析文化关键词“青山”“白水”“游子”“故人”“萧萧”的翻译方法。

第二节　杜甫

Du Fu

一、诗人简介

杜甫，字子美，自称少陵野老。生于公元 712 年（唐太极元年），卒于公元 770 年（唐大历五年）。河南巩县（今河南巩义市）人。青年时期南游吴越，北游齐赵。其间曾入洛阳应进士，不第。天宝五年，35 岁的杜甫来到中国当时的政治中心长安，孰料竟在此困居十年，仅被授以右卫率府胄曹参军的小官职。安史之乱爆发，杜甫为叛军所俘，后脱身逃至甘肃凤翔，唐肃宗授以左拾遗。不久因直言进谏被贬为华州司功参军。旋弃官居秦州、同谷，复移家成都，卜居浣花溪畔。经四川节度使严武举荐，任节度参谋、检校工部员外郎。晚年移家出蜀，经湖北漂泊至湖南，后病卒于长沙至岳阳的舟中。

Du Fu (712–770), alias Zimei, self-styled Shaoling Yelao, was born in Gongxian County of Henan (the present Gongyi Gity of Henan Province). In his youth, he traveled to Wu and Yue in the south and Qi and Zhao in the north, and failed in the imperial examinations. In 747 when he was 35 years old, he went to Chang'an, China's political centre at the time, and stayed there for ten years, holding a minor official position. He was taken prisoner during the rebellion of An Lushan and Shi Siming and when he escaped to Fengxiang in Gansu, he was nominated as the imperial advisor. As he was outspoken in his opinions, he was demoted to Huazhou as a secretary. He soon gave up his position and lived in Qinzhou, Tonggu and Chengdu successively. Afterwards recommended by Military Commander Yan Wu in Sichuan, he served under Yan Wu as an advisor and a secretary. In his late years, he left Sichuan and travelled from Hubei to Hunan, finally dying of illness in the boat from Changsha to Yueyang.

杜甫的诗作，被保存下来的有 1400 多首。其深刻的思想内容和丰富多彩的艺术表现手法，无可争辩地证明，杜诗是中国古典文学中一座特别挺拔的高峰。杜诗在内容上最显著的特色就是“以时事入诗”，即客观真实地描写社会、反映时代，因而被称为“诗史”。杜甫生活的时代，正是大唐帝国由盛入衰的时期。这一时期的“安史之乱”、上层腐朽、国事艰难、民间疾苦等，都记录在他那些著名的诗篇之中。

Over 1,400 extant poems by Du Fu have indisputably evidenced themselves as a peak in traditional Chinese literature through their profound content and rich artistic merits. One of the distinguished features, i.e., involving the current affairs into the poems, has earned for Du Fu's poems the renown of "poetic history", for they truthfully depict and reflect the social reality of the time. The age in which Du Fu lived is an age when the Tang Empire went from prosperity to decline. The rebellion of An Lushan and Shi Siming, the corruption of the upper classes, the hardship of the country and the sufferings of the people are all reflected in his famous poems.

作为一位创作天才，杜甫的笔墨也深入社会人生的各个方面。除了浓墨重彩地关注现实之外，其他如歌咏自然风光、凭吊古人遗迹、抒写亲朋情谊、感叹个人身世、刻画飞禽走兽等，都有传颂千古的名篇。杜甫在艺术创作上形成了一种独特的风格，概括起来说就是“沉郁”，即深沉悲愤。杜甫在艺术创作上的成就和特色远不止上述这些方面。其他如语言的精警，格律的工整，笔法的跌宕起伏，声韵的抑扬顿挫，意境浑成而略无经营，结构严谨而不烦绳削等，都达到了难以企及的境界。

As a genius, Du Fu touches upon all the aspects of human life, with his poems covering social realities, natural sceneries, ancient relics, friendly relations, personal experiences, and birds and animals. A touch of gloom marks Du Fu's poems, a profound gloom indeed. What is more, Du Fu reaches the acme of Chinese poetry, for his pithy language, strict scansion, skillful words, resounding rhymes, natural images, and well-formed structures.

二、古诗英译赏析

春夜喜雨

好雨知时节，当春乃发生。
随风潜入夜，润物细无声。
野径云俱黑，江船火独明。
晓看红湿处，花重锦官城。

【许渊冲英译】

Happy Rain on a Spring Night

Good rain knows its time right,
It will fall when comes spring.

With wind it steals in night;
Mute, it wets everything.
Over wild lanes dark cloud spreads;
In boat a lantern looms.
Dawn sees saturated reds;
The town's heavy with blooms.

【宇文所安英译】

Delighting in Rain on a Spring Night

A good rain knows its appointed time,
right in spring it brings things to life.
It enters the night unseen with the wind
and moistens things finely, without a sound.
Over wilderness paths, the clouds are all black,
a boat on the river, its fire alone bright.
At daybreak look where it's wet and red,
the flowers will be heavy in Brocade City.

【赏析重点】

（1）对比分析"随风潜入夜，润物细无声"中"潜""细"字的翻译方法。

（2）分析文化关键词"红湿处""锦官城"的含义和翻译方法。

月夜

今夜鄜州月，闺中只独看。
遥怜小儿女，未解忆长安。
香雾云鬟湿，清辉玉臂寒。
何时倚虚幌，双照泪痕干。

【许渊冲英译】

A Moonlit Night

On the moon over Fuzhou which shines bright,
Alone you would gaze in your room tonight.
I'm grieved to think our little children dear,
Too young to yearn for their old father here.
Your cloudlike hair is moist with dew, it seems;
Your jade-white arms would feel the cold moonbeams.

O when can we stand by the window side,
Watching the moon with our tear traces dried?

【宇文所安英译】

Moonlit Night

The moon tonight in Fu-chou
She watches alone from her chamber,
While faraway I think lovingly on daughters and sons,
Who do not yet know how to remember Chang'an.
In scented fog, her cloud like hairdo moist,
In its clear beams, her jade-white arms are cold.
When shall we lean in the empty window,
Moonlit together, its light drying traces of tears.

【赏析重点】

（1）分析文化关键词“云鬟”“玉臂”的含义和翻译方法。

（2）解读“双照泪痕干”的写作特点和翻译思路。

江南逢李龟年

岐王宅里寻常见，
崔九堂前几度闻。
正是江南好风景，
落花时节又逢君。

【许渊冲英译】

Coming across a Disfavored Court Musician on the Southern Shore of the Yangzi River

How oft in princely mansions did we meet!
As oft in lordly halls I heard you sing.
Now the southern scenery is most sweet,
But I meet you again in parting spring.

【霍克斯（Hawks）英译】

On Meeting Li Kuei-nien in the South

Ch'i-prince's homein often see.
Ts'ui Ninth's hallbefore several-times hear.
Truly Chiang-nan good scenery,
falling flower season again meet you.

【赏析重点】

（1）解读“见”“闻”的逻辑含义和翻译方法。

（2）对比分析“落花时节”的翻译方法。

第三节　王维

Wang Wei

一、诗人简介

王维生于公元701年，字摩诘，汉族，祖籍山西祁县，唐朝诗人，外号“诗佛”。开元九年（721）中进士，任太乐丞相。今存诗400余首。王维精通佛学，佛教有一部《维摩诘经》，是维摩诘向弟子们讲学的书，这是王维名和字的由来。“维摩诘”的汉语意思是“因洁净、不受染污而著称的人”，王维以此为名字，正是借此表达自己内心对纯净、高洁的向往，所以他成就较高的诗歌作品都富有自然清净、远离世俗的超脱气息。

Wang Wei was born in 701, a great poet in the Tang dynasty, also known for his courtesy name Mojie and alias Poetic Buddha, was of the Han nationality with his ancestry origin in Qi county, Shanxi province. In the year 721, he passed the Dianshi (final imperial examination) to earn himself the academic title Jinshi, and took the post of Chengxiang (Prime Minister in ancient China). Of many poems he wrote, 400 have been preserved over the ages. He was a master of Buddhism, and his given name Wei and courtesy name Mojie were borrowed from *The Holy Teaching of Vimalakirti* (Weimojie as the transliteration of Vimalakirti mianing “clean and free from pollution”) which was a Buddhist sutra used by Vimalakirti to teach his students. By the names, Wang Wei expressed his pursuit for pure and virtuous heart, so his famous poems were natural and pure and detached from worldly atmosphere.

除了擅长写诗之外，王维的书法和绘画也非常有名，对音乐也很精通。在唐朝诗人之中，他称得上是多才多艺的全能文人。他将音乐、书法、绘画与诗歌融为一体，互相配合，相得益彰。王维的诗句往往营造出山水画一般的色彩和意境，让人读过之后仿佛置身鸟语花香、悠然恬静的自然世界。而他的山水画中又能体现出诗句的意境，所谓“诗中有画，画中有诗”，就是对王维诗画的最高评价。

In addition to writing poems, Wang's calligraphy and paintings were also very famous and he was proficient in music. Among poets in the Tang dynasty, he was a versatile and all-round scholar. He combined music, calligraphy, painting and poems, which complemented one another. His poems tended to portray an atmosphere with colors like Chinese paintings, which would set people in the leisurely quiet natural world with birds twittering and flowers fragrance after reading them. Also his landscape paintings reflected the poems' atmosphere. So the judgment "poetic paintings, paintings in poems" was the highest praise of his poems and paintings.

二、古诗英译赏析

九月九日忆山东兄弟

独在异乡为异客，
每逢佳节倍思亲。
遥知兄弟登高处，
遍插茱萸少一人。

【许渊冲英译】

Thinking of my Brothers on Mountain Climbing Day

Alone, a lonely stranger in a foreign land,
I doubly pine for kinsfolk on a holiday.
I know my brothers would, with dogwood spray in hand,
Climb up mountain and miss me so far away.

【宇文所安英译】

On the Double Ninth: Remembering My Brothers East of the mountains

Alone in a strange land,
and I here, a stranger
Each time this holiday comes
I long doubly for my kin,
And know that brothers far away
are climbing someplace high,
Decking themselves with dogwood twigs, short one person.

【赏析重点】

（1）分析“九月九日”的文化内涵和翻译方法。

（2）分析“遍插茱萸少一人”的逻辑关系和翻译思路。

鹿柴

空山不见人，
但闻人语响。
返景入深林，
复照青苔上。

【许渊冲英译】

The Deer Enclosure

In pathless hills no man's in sight,
But I still hear echoing sound.
In gloomy forest peeps no light,
But sunbeams slant on mossy ground.

【保罗·卢泽（Paul Rouzer）英译】

Deer Fence

No one is seen in deserted hills,
only the echoes of speech are heard.
Sunlight cast back comes deep in the woods
and shines once again upon the green moss.

【赏析重点】

分析文化关键词“空山”“人语”的内涵和翻译方法。

相思

红豆生南国，春来发几枝。
愿君多采撷，此物最相思。

【许渊冲英译】

Love Seed

The red beans grow in Southern land.
How many load in spring the trees?
Gather them till full is your hand;

They would revive fond memories.

【保罗·卢泽（Paul Rouzer）英译】

The Acacia Tree

Its red beanlike seeds grow in the southern lands;

When autumn comes it puts out many branches.

Id like you to pick and gather them,

For these things most show my longing for you.

【赏析重点】

对比分析题目“相思”的不同翻译思路。

送元二使安西

渭城朝雨浥轻尘，客舍青青柳色新。

劝君更尽一杯酒，西出阳关无故人。

【许渊冲英译】

A Farewell Song

No dust is raised on the road wet with morning rain,

The willows by the hotel look so fresh and green.

I invite you to drink a cup of wine again,

West of the Sunny Pass no friends will be seen.

【保罗·卢泽（Paul Rouzer）英译】

Seeing off Yuan Two on his mission to Anxi

Morning rain at Wei City dampens the light dust;

The hostel is all green—the willow hue is new.

I urge you to drain yet another cup of ale;

Once you head west out of Yang Pass there will be no old friend.

*The Yang Pass was in Gansu and led to points west.

【赏析重点】

（1）对比分析“渭城朝雨浥轻尘”的翻译思路。

（2）分析“西出阳关无故人”句式特点和翻译方法。

第四节　白居易

Bai Juyi

一、诗人简介

白居易（772—846），汉族，字乐天，晚年又号香山居士，河南新郑（今郑州新郑）人，我国唐代伟大的现实主义诗人，中国文学史上负有盛名且影响深远的诗人和文学家，他的诗歌题材广泛，形式多样，语言平易通俗，有“诗魔”和“诗王”之称。官至翰林学士、左赞善大夫。有《白氏长庆集》传世，代表诗作有《长恨歌》《卖炭翁》《琵琶行》等。

Bai Juyi (772–846), of the Han nationality, with the courtesy name Letian and pseudonym of Xiangshan Jushi, was from Xinzheng of Henan province. He was a great realistic poet in the Tang dynasty, and was one of the most influential poets and literators in the history of Chinese literature. His poems were wide-ranging in subject matters, multiple in form and simple in language, and he was well-known as the King of Poet and the Magic Poet. His political life was also very active, once being a member of the Hanlin Academy and Reminder of the Left. His popular works include *Bai's Changqing Collection*, *The Song of Everlasting Sorrow*, *The Elderly Charcoal Seller*, *The Song of the Pipa Player*, etc.

二、古诗英译赏析

赋得古原草送别

离离原上草，一岁一枯荣。
野火烧不尽，春风吹又生。
远芳侵古道，晴翠接荒城。
又送王孙去，萋萋满别情。

【许渊冲英译】

Grass on the Ancient Plain

—Farewell to a Friend

Wild grasses spread o'er ancient plain;
With spring and fall they come and go.

Fire tries to burn them up in vain;
They rise again when spring winds blow.
Their fragrance overruns the way;
Their green invades the ruined town.
To see my friend going away;
My sorrow grows like grass o'er grown.

【阿瑟韦利（Arthur Waley）英译】

Grass

Part part plain on grass
One year one wither flourish
Prairie fire burn not destroy
Spring wind blow again life
Distant fragrance invade old path
Clear emerald meet ruined town
Again see off noble friend go
Crowded full parting feeling
The grass is spreading out across the plain,
Each year, it dies, then flourishes again.
It's burnt but not destroyed by prairie fires,
When spring winds blow they bring it back to life.
Afar, its scent invades the ancient road,
Its emerald green overruns the ruined town.
Again I see my noble friend depart,
I find I'm crowded full of parting's feelings.

【赏析重点】

分析本诗中的不可译要素。

夜雪

已讶衾枕冷，复见窗户明。
夜深知雪重，时闻折竹声。

【许渊冲英译】

Snowing at Night

Surprised to feel my quilt and pillow cold,
I wake up but to see the window bright.

Heavy with snow, I know night has grown old,
At times I hear bamboos snapped by snow white.

【阿瑟韦利（Arthur Waley）英译】

Night Snow

Startled at the cold stiffness of my pillow,
I see that the window is a sheet of pure white.
Deep in the night, the weight of snow increases
Until I hear bamboo snapping in the darkness.

【赏析重点】

对比分析“夜深知雪重”的逻辑关系和翻译思路。

拓展训练 | Extension Training

1. 课后思考

（1）请用英文简要介绍唐诗的特点。

（2）分析总结唐诗常用修辞手法的翻译策略。

2. 文化外宣汉英翻译

（1）唐诗指的是中国唐朝（618—907）期间或前后写的诗，常常被视为中国诗歌的黄金时代。据编撰，全唐诗包括 2200 多位作者所写的约 50000 首唐诗。在唐代，诗歌是社会各阶层社会生活的重要组成部分。文人要求掌握这些诗歌以参加文职选拔考试，但理论上人人都能接触这门艺术。因此出现了大量的诗作和诗人，其中部分诗作保留至今。这一时期两个最著名的诗人是杜甫和李白。

（2）近体诗或称律诗，形成于 5 世纪之前。到唐朝时，发展为固定的平仄形式，以确保每一联句中的中古汉语四个声调之间的平衡，即平声、上声、去声、入声。唐朝近体诗达到最高峰，王维和崔颢是近体诗最著名的代表，而杜甫是最精通近体诗的典范。近体诗的基本形式是律诗，有八行。除了声调的限制外，第二联和第三联的诗行要形式对仗。诗行要内容对称，其中每个词的词性要相同。近体诗的另一种形式是绝句或称四行诗，有律诗前四行的声调，形式无须对应。

（3）“盛唐之音”指唐玄宗开元（713—741）、天宝（742—756）年间的诗歌创作与艺术成就。与初唐、中唐、晚唐时期的诗歌相对应。这一时期是“安史之乱”前唐帝国的黄金时代，当时，社会稳定，政治清明，经济繁荣，南北文化融合，中外交通发达，这一切为“盛唐之音”营造了很好的社会氛围和文化基础。在唐诗初、盛、中、晚四个阶段中，盛唐最短，但艺术成就最为辉煌，被后人誉为“盛唐气象”。这一时期，不但出现了诗仙李白、诗圣杜甫，还出现了张九龄、孟浩然、王维、王昌龄、王之涣等一大批卓有成就的诗人。他们赞美山川，向往功业，抒发个人情志，记述社会现实，诗风豪迈浑厚，意境宏阔高远，语言清新天然，富有生命活力与进取精神，创造了中国古典诗歌的最高成就。就诗派而论，这一时期有山水田园诗派、边塞诗派等。

第八章　宋词英译

Translation of the Song Ci-Poetry

一、学习目标

（1）用英文介绍宋词分类和特点。

（2）掌握宋词文化关键词英译。

（3）对比鉴赏代表性宋词中外译者翻译方法。

二、文化背景

词，是古典诗歌的一种。词的名称很多，因为它可以配乐歌唱，所以也叫曲子词；因为它的句子长短不齐，也被称为长短句。词有很多种调名，叫作词牌，如西江月、满江红、如梦令等。词作为一种新体诗歌，宋代时发展到了鼎盛时期。“宋词”与“唐诗”一样，在中国文学史上占有相当重要的地位。

Ci is one of the ancient poetry forms and can be sung to music, so it's also known as musical ci poetry. As the length of the lines in a ci poem can differ, it is also called “long and short-line verses”. There are various tunes used for ci poems, so they can be sung in different ways. Ci-poetry reached its zenith during the Song dynasty (960–1279). Like Tang poetry, the Song ci-poetry holds a very important position in the history of Chinese literature.

（一）宋词分类 Categorization of ci-poems of the Song dynasty

宋词的分类，一般习惯以豪放派和婉约派这两大创作风格来统分词人和词作。婉约，即婉转含蓄。婉约词派的特点主要是内容侧重儿女风情，结构深细缜密，音律婉转和谐，语言圆润清丽，有一种柔婉之美。豪放，即豪迈放达。豪放派特点大体是创作视野较为广阔，气象恢宏豪放，喜用诗文的手法、句法写词，语词宏博，写事较多。婉约派恪守音律，注意词与曲的搭配，题材多在婉约的范畴。豪放派则打破音乐的束缚，自由发挥，将词的内容扩展到政治、思想等广阔的领域，以豪迈为主。

The poets and ci-poems of the Song dynasty are generally divided into two writing styles, heroic school and graceful school. Graceful school, mild and implicit, with a major feature of emphasizing the content on romance affairs, has an exquisite and deliberate structure, harmonious rhythm and mellow and graceful wording, possessing a delicate beauty. While heroic school, bold and indulgent, with a major feature of a wide range of subjects and grand disposition, mostly involves some poetic expression and sentence structure, with some formal words and phrases, mostly concentrating on narration. The graceful school strictly follows the rhythm regulation, stresses the collocation of ci-poem and music, and has a relatively fixed range of themes. However, the heroic school tends to break the fetter of music, improvises freely and expands the content to a broader realm including politics and philosophy. As each poet has personal characteristic and mostly once wrote ci-poems of both features; therefore, though poets might be categorized by the two schools, it is not very rigorous.

宋词的结构比唐诗复杂得多，因为其本身是音乐文学，所以根据所搭配的乐曲种类的不同可以分为九种：令、引、慢、三台、序子、法曲、大曲、缠令、诸宫调。

The structure of ci-poem is much more complicated than that of Tang Poetry. As it is a kind of musical literature, so according to the accompanying music, it can be divided into: ling, yin, man, santai, xuzi, faqu, daqu, chanling, and zhugongdiao.

宋词还可以根据每首词的字数大致可分小令（58 字以内）、中调（59~90 字以内）和长调（91 字以上，最长的词有 240 字）。每首词，有的只有一整段文字，称为单调；有的分成对称的上下两阕，称为双调；有的分成三段或四段，称为三叠或四叠。

According to the number of the characters in each ci-poem, it can also be divided into xiaoling (within 58 characters), zhongdiao (middle Diao, within 59–90 characters) and changdiao (long Diao, above 91 characters, the longest with 240 characters). The ci-poem only has one paragraph, called dandiao (single Diao); the ci-poem has two parts (Que), called shuangdiao (double Diao); some have three or four paragraphs, called sandie (three Die) or sidie (four Die).

宋词的词牌名也有很大的学问。唐诗只有几种格律的规则，而宋词的词牌却有一千多种，而且每种词牌要求的押韵、形式及字数等都不同。这些丰富多样的词牌名有些来自乐曲的名称，比如《菩萨蛮》，据说是由于唐代大中初年（847—860），女蛮国进贡，她们梳着高髻，戴着金冠，满身配饰看起来像菩萨，当时教坊因此谱成《菩萨蛮曲》。

The title (Cipai) of ci-poem also has many regulations. Tang Poetry only has several metrical rules. However, the title of ci-poem includes more than1,000 variations, which have specific rhymes, forms and number of characters. Those colorful title names are originated from some music names. Like the *Exotic Bodhisattva* (*Pu Sa Man*), which is originated from a legend that in the early Period Dazhong (847–860) of the Tang dynasty, a exotic group of envoys paid tribute to the authority, who were with high buns and wore gold crowns and with their bodies decorated by ornaments and jewels like Bodhisattva. The imperial musician then created the music called *Exotic Bodhisattva*.

（二）宋词主题 Themes of Ci-poems of the Song dynasty

在最初，宋词的题材比唐诗的题材相对集中，婉约派的词作内容大多局限于儿女情长、离愁别绪、羁旅俚俗、酒宴娱乐等方面；豪放派较之扩大了范围，多为爱国、怀古、咏史等政治性题材。南宋时，词人们创作的题材越来越广泛，将生活中的许多题材都写入了词中。然而宋词最出彩的题材依然是写情，尤其是爱情；爱国题材和思考人生哲理的题材也颇有深度。除此之外，咏物、赠答等题材的创作也丝毫不输给诗歌。

The themes of ci-poems were relatively more concentrated than the ones of Tang Poetry at early period. The poet of graceful school mostly depicted the love romance, sorrow of separation travels and folk customs, feasts and entertainment, etc., while the poets of heroic school expanded the range to some political subjects including patriotism, nostalgia and history-retrospect, etc. In the Southern Song dynasty, although writers added more and more themes referring to daily life into their ci-poems, the most distinguished subject was still the emotion-expression, especially the love romance. Besides, the patriotic and philosophical themes were also depicted profoundly. Additionally, ci-poems of object-description and acknowledgement could also rival the poetry.

爱情词，顾名思义，是关于爱情的词。爱情词是宋词词作中最常见的题材之一，不管是婉约派词人还是豪放派词人都不乏名作，且风格各不相同。南宋著名词人陆游与他的前妻唐婉之间互相表白创作的沈园题词《钗头凤》，在宋词的爱情词中颇具浪漫的悲剧色彩，他们的爱情故事在民间也流传甚广。

Romance ci-poem, just as its name implies, depicts love, which was one of the most common themes in ci-poems of the Song dynasty. Many poets of graceful school or heroic school wrote some masterpieces of romance ci-poems, which varied from one another on styles, points of view, and writing patterns. The prestigious poet, Lu You of the Southern Song dynasty (1127–1279) and his ex-wife Tang Wan once wrote inscriptions, *Chai Tou Feng* on the walls of Garden Shen to express their emotion for each other, which enjoyed a reputation of romance and tragedy in the Song ci-poems. Their love story also prevailed among the folks.

爱国或怀古咏史的题材是豪放派词作中最常见的题材。宋朝的国情注定词人们因为国难家仇而满腔热忱，因此爱国词的创作在南宋非常普遍，而婉约派词人也不乏此类题材的创作。艺术水平最高的代表是豪放派词人辛弃疾，他的词作兼有对历史和现实的思考，并且将个人的命运和以史为鉴的现实结合在一起，充满豪气激情，义薄云天。

Patriotic ci-poem (history-chanting ci-poem) is one of the most common subjects in ci-poems of heroic school. Due to the tough political situation, poets of the Song dynasty were bound to have passion and enthusiasm for saving their country from national calamity. So the patriotic ci-poems were widely written across the county in the Southern Song dynasty. And poets of the graceful school also created many related ci-poems. The representative writer with the highest artistic level is Xin Qiji from heroic school. His works contain the deliberation on history and reality, as well as combining his personal destiny and history lessons together. His ci-poems are full of heroic spirit and infuriation.

三、文化关键词

宋词　Ci-poems of the Song dynasty

豪放派　heroic school

婉约派　graceful school

音乐文学　musical literature

小令　Xiaoling

中调　Zhongdiao (middle Diao)

长调　Changdiao (long Diao)

词牌　cipai (title name)

第一节　苏轼

Su Shi

一、诗人简介

苏轼（1037—1101），北宋文学家、书画家。字子瞻，又字和仲，号东坡居士。汉族，眉州眉山（今属四川）人。与父苏洵，弟苏辙合称三苏。他在文学艺术方面堪称全才。与欧阳修并称欧苏，为唐宋八大家之一；诗清新豪健，善用夸张比喻，在艺术表现方面独具风格，与黄庭坚并称苏黄；词开豪放一派，对后代很有影响，与辛弃疾并称苏辛；书法擅长行书、楷书，能自创新意，用笔丰腴跌宕，有天真烂漫之趣，与黄庭坚、米芾、蔡襄并称宋四家；画学文同，喜作枯木怪石，论画主张神似。诗文有《东坡七集》等，词有《东坡乐府》。

Su Shi (1037–1101), was courtesy named Zizhan or Hezhong, with the pseudonym of Dongpo Jushi. He was of the Han nationality, from Meishan of Mei prefecture (now part of Sichuan province), and was a writer, calligrapher, and painter in the Northern Song dynasty. With his father Su Xun and his younger brother Su Zhe, he was known as one of the Three Su's. He was versatile in literature, and is jointly known as Ou-Su with Ouyang Xiu, and was one of the Eight Great Prose Masters of the Tang and Song Dynasties. His poems were powerful in rhythm and fresh in images, frequently using exaggerations and metaphors, forming his own unique style. He was also jointly known as Su-Huang with Huang Tingjian for his calligraphy. His ci-poetry was typical of the powerful and free school, greatly influencing later generations, and he was also jointly known as Su-Xin with Xin Qiji in this regard. His calligraphy strength tended to be in running script and regular script, innovative and rich, unstrained and brilliant in writing, and he was one of the Four Masters of Song Calligraphy with Huang Tingjian, Mi Fu, and Cai Xiang. Drawn from Wen Tong's, his paintings featured dead wood and grotesque rocks, advocating alikeness in spirit. His poems and proses are included in *Dongpo Qiji* (*Seven Collections of Dongpo*), and his ci-poems are included in *Dongpo Yuefu*.

二、诗词英译赏析

水调歌头

明月几时有，把酒问青天。不知天上宫阙，今夕是何年。我欲乘风归去，又恐琼楼玉宇，高处不胜寒。起舞弄清影，何似在人间。

转朱阁，低绮户，照无眠。不应有恨，何事长向别时圆？人有悲欢离合，月有阴晴圆缺，此事古难全。但愿人长久，千里共婵娟。

【林语堂英译】

Mid-Autumn Festival, to the tune of Shuitiaoketou

How rare the moon so round and clear!
With cup in hand I ask of the blue sky,
I do not know in the celestial sphere
What name this festive night goes by?
I want to fly home, riding the air,
But fear the ethereal cold up there,
The jade and crystal mansions are so high!
Dancing to my shadow,
I feel no longer the mortal tie.
She rounds the vermilion tower,
Stoops to silk-pad doors,
Shines on those who sleepless lie.
Why does she, bearing us no grudge,
Shine upon our parting reunion deny?
But rare is perfect happiness,
The moon does wax, the moon does wane,
And so men meet and say goodbye.
I only pray our life be long,
And our souls together heavenward fly!

【许渊冲英译】

Prelude to Water melody Sent to Ziyou on Mid-autumn Festival

On the mid-autumn festival, I drank happily till dawn and wrote this in my cups while thinking of Ziyou.

When did the bright moon first appear?
Wine-cup in hand I ask the blue sky.
I do not know what time of year
It would be tonight in the palace on high
Riding the wind, there I would fly,
But I'm afraid the crystalline palace would be
Too high and too cold for me
I rise and dance, with my shadow I play
On high as on earth, would it be as gay?
The moon goes round the mansions red
with gauze windows to shed
Her light upon the sleepless bed
against man she should not have any spite.
Why then when people part is she oft full and bright?
Men have sorrow and joy, they part and meet again;
The moon may be bright or dim, she may wax or wane.
There has been nothing perfect since olden days.
So let us wish that man live as long as he can!
Though miles apart, we'll share the beauty she displays.

【赏析重点】

（1）对比分析“悲欢离合”“阴晴圆缺”的不同翻译方法。

（2）对比赏析原文和译文的韵律特点。

（3）诵读原文、译文，感受中文、英文节奏特点。

江城子·乙卯正月二十日夜记梦

十年生死两茫茫，不思量，自难忘。
千里孤坟，无处话凄凉。
纵使相逢应不识，尘满面，鬓如霜。
夜来幽梦忽还乡，小轩窗，正梳妆。
相顾无言，惟有泪千行。
料得年年肠断处，
明月夜，短松冈。

【林语堂英译】

A Dream, to the Tune of Chiangch'engtse

Ten years have we been parted:
The living and the dead—
hearing no news,
Not thinking
And yet forgetting nothing!
I cannot come to your grave a thousand miles away
To converse with you and whisper my longing;
And even if we did meet
How would you greet
My weathered face, my hair a frosty white?
Last night
I dreamed I had suddenly returned to our old home
And saw you sitting there before the familiar dressing table,
We looked at each other in silence,
With misty eyes beneath the candle light.
May we year after year
In heartbreak meet,
On the pine-crest,
In the moonlight!

【许渊冲英译】

Riverside town

Dreaming of My Deceased wife on the night of the 20th Day of the 1st Month

For ten long years the living of the dead knows nought.
Should the dead be forgot
And to mind never brought?
Her lonely grave is a thousand miles away
To whom can I my grief convey'
Revived e'en if she be, could she still know me
My face is worn with care
And frosted is my hair.
Last night I dreamed of coming to my native place
She's making up her face

At the window with grace
We gazed at each other hushed
But tears from our eyes gushed
When I am woken, I fancy her heart-broken
On the mound clad with pines,
Where only the moon shines

【赏析重点】

（1）对比分析“尘满面，鬓如霜”“小轩窗，正梳妆”句式结构转换。

（2）诵读原文、译文，感受中文、英文节奏特点。

第二节　李清照
Li Qingzhao

一、诗人简介

李清照（1084—1155），济南章丘（今属山东）人，号易安居士。宋代女词人，婉约词派代表。所作词，前期多写其悠闲生活，后期多悲叹身世，情调感伤，也流露出对中原的怀念。形式上善用白描手法，自辟途径，语言清丽。论词强调协律，崇尚典雅，提出词“别是一家”之说，反对以作诗文之法作词。能诗，留存不多，部分篇章感时咏史，情辞慷慨，与其词风不同。有《易安居士文集》《易安词》，已散佚。后人有《漱玉词》辑本。今人有《李清照集校注》。

Li Qingzhao (1084–1155), born in Zhangqiu, Jinan city (now part of Shandong province), also known as Yi'an Jushi, was a female lyric poet of the Song dynasty. She was the representative of the graceful and restrained school. Her early works most portrayed her carefree days, but her later works turned to the pessimistic writing of her birth as well the memories of the central plains. As for the form, she tended to use the technique of Baimiao (outlining). She tried to form her own style, elegant in language and rhythm, and opposed to the method of writing prose as that of poets. She also wrote poems, but a few poems are still extant. Different from her ci-poetry, her poems were praising the times in which she lived and expressing her ambitions. She created the works of *Yi'an Jushi's*

Collected Works and *Yi'an's Ci-poetry*, which were lost to time. Later generations compiled the *Shuyu Ci*. Contemporary people compiled the *Li Qingzhao Ji Jiao Zhu* (*Notes on Li Qingzhao's Collected Works*).

二、诗词英译赏析

如梦令·昨夜雨疏风骤

昨夜雨疏风骤，浓睡不消残酒。
试问卷帘人，却道海棠依旧。
知否，知否？
应是绿肥红瘦。

【许渊冲英译】

Tune："Like a Dream"

Last night the wind blew hard and rain was fine;
Sound sleep did not dispel the aftertaste of wine
I ask the maid rolling up the screen.
The same crab-apple tree, she says, is seen
But don't you know,
"O don't you know
The red should languish and the green must grow?"

【王红公（Rexroth, Kenneth）、钟玲合译】

Spring Ends to the Tune a Dream Song

Last night fine rain, gusts of wind,
Deep sleep could not dissolve the leftover wine.
I asked my maid as she rolled up the curtains,
"Are the begonias still the same?
Don't you know it is time
For the green to grow fat and the red to grow thin?"

【赏析重点】

（1）对比分析词牌名翻译方法。

（2）对比分析"雨疏风骤""绿肥红瘦"翻译方法。

声声慢·寻寻觅觅

寻寻觅觅，
冷冷清清，
凄凄惨惨戚戚。
乍暖还寒时候，
最难将息。
三杯两盏淡酒，
怎敌他晚来风急？
雁过也，正伤心，
却是旧时相识。
满地黄花堆积，
憔悴损，
如今有谁堪摘？
守着窗儿，
独自怎生得黑？
梧桐更兼细雨，
到黄昏、点点滴滴。
这次第，
怎一个愁字了得！

【许渊冲英译】

Grief Beyond Belief

Tune: "Slow, Slow Song"

I look for what I miss;
I know what it is.
I feel so sad, so drear,
So lonely, without cheer.
How hard is it
To keep me fit
In this lingering cold!
Hardly warmed up
By cup on cup
Of wine so dry,

Oh, how could I
Endure at dusk the drift
Of wind so swift?
It breaks my heart, alas,
To see the wild geese pass,
For they are my acquaintances of old.
The ground is covered with yellow flowers,
Faded and fallen in showers.
Who will pick them up now?
Sitting alone at the window, how
Could I but quicken
To pace of darkness that won't thicken?
On plane's broad leaves a fine rain drizzles
As twilight grizzles.
Oh, what can I do with a grief
Beyong belief!

【王红公（Rexroth, Kenneth）、钟玲合译】

Autumn Love "A Weary Song to a Slow Sad Tune"

Search. Search. Seek. Seek.
Cold. Cold. Clear. Clear.
Sorrow. Sorrow. Pain. Pain.
Hot lashes. Sudden chills.
Stabbing pains. Slow agonies.
I can find no peace.
I drink two cups, then three bowls
Of clear wine until I can't
Stand up against a gust of wind.
The ground, pile up, faded, dead.
Wild geese fly overhead.
They wrench my heart.
They were our friends in the old days.
Gold chrysanthemums litter
The ground, piled up, faded, faded.
This season I could not bear

To pick them. All alone.
Motionless at my window,
I watch the gathering shadows
Fine rain sifts through the wur-t'ung trees
And drips, drop by drop, through the dusk
What can I ever do now?
How can I drive off this word-
Hopelessness?

【赏析重点】

（1）对比分析“寻寻觅觅，冷冷清清，凄凄惨惨戚戚”的翻译方法。

（2）对比分析“这次第，怎一个愁字了得”翻译思路差异。

第三节 辛弃疾

Xin Qiji

一、诗人简介

辛弃疾（1140—1207），南宋词人。原字坦夫，改字幼安，别号稼轩，历城（今山东济南）人。出生时，中原已为金兵所占。一生力主抗金。曾上《美芹十论》与《九议》，条陈战守之策，显示其卓越的军事才能与爱国热忱。其词抒写力图恢复国家统一的爱国热情，倾诉壮志难酬的悲愤，对当时执政者的屈辱求和颇多谴责；也有不少吟咏祖国河山的作品。题材广阔又善化用前人典故入词，风格沉雄豪迈又不乏细腻柔媚之处。作品集有《稼轩长短句》，今人辑有《辛稼轩诗文钞存》。

Xin Qiji (1140–1207), had the courtesy name of Tanfu that was later changed to You'an, along with the pseudonym Jiaxuan, and was from Licheng (now Jinan of Shandong province). He was a poet of the Southern Song dynasty. At the time when he was born, the Zhongyuan Area (central plains, comprising the middle and lower reaches of the Huanghe River) was occupied by the Jin (Jurchen). So he advocated anti-Jin battles throughout his life. He wrote the *Mei Qin Shi Lun* (*Ten Humble Arguments*) and *Jiu Yi* (*Nine Arguments*), stating strategies for defense and offense, which demonstrated his outstanding military ability and patriotic feelings. His works were full of the enthusiasm for reunifying the country, the anger for all the difficulty in fulfilling great aspirations, and criticizing the imperial officials for their humbleness. There were also works praising the rivers and mountains of the country. Subject matters were extensive in his works, which frequently cited the anecdotes of the ancestors, with their style steady and powerful but at the same time delicate and gentle. His collected works include *Jiaxuan Chang Duan Ju* (*Lyrics of Jiaxuan*) and *Xin Jiaxuan Shi Wen Chao Cun* (*Treasure Writings of Xin Jiaxuan*) compiled by contemporary editors.

二、诗词英译赏析

丑奴儿（书博山道中壁）

少年不识愁滋味，爱上层楼。
爱上层楼，为赋新词强说愁。
而今识尽愁滋味，欲说还休。
欲说还休，却道天凉好个秋。

【许渊冲英译】

Tune: "Song of Ugly Slave - Written on the Wall on My Way to Boshan"

While young, I knew no grief I could not bear;
I'd like to go upstairs.
I'd like to go upstairs
To write new verses with a false despair.
I know what grief is now that I am old;
I would not have it told.
I would not have it told,
But only say I'm glad that autumn's cold.

【杨宪益英译】

Written on the Wall on My Way to Boshan

-to the Melody Chou Nu Er

As a lad I never knew the taste of sorrow,
But loved to climb towers,
Loved to climb towers,
And drag sorrow into each new song I sung.

Now I know well the taste of sorrow,
It is on the tip of my tongue,
On the tip of my tongue,
But instead I say, "What a fine, cool autumn day! "

【赏析重点】

（1）对比分析"爱上层楼"的翻译差异。

（2）对比分析"欲说还休"的结构转换。

西江月·夜行黄沙道中

明月别枝惊鹊，清风半夜鸣蝉。稻花香里说丰年，听取蛙声一片。

七八个星天外，两三点雨山前。旧时茅店社林边，路转溪桥忽见。

【许渊冲英译】

The Moon over the West River

Startled by magpies leaving the branch in moon,
I hear cicadas shrill in the breeze at midnight.
The ricefields sweet smell promises a bumper year;
Listen, how frogs' croaks please the ear!
Beyond the clouds seven or eight stars twinkle;
Before the hills two or three raindrops sprinkle.
There is an inn beside the village temple. Look!
The winding path leads to the hut beside the brook.

【赏析重点】

（1）赏析"听取蛙声一片"意象特点和翻译方法。

（2）赏析"七八个星天外，两三点雨山前"增译翻译效果。

拓展训练 | Extension Training

1. 课后思考

（1）请用英文简要介绍宋词。

（2）总结归纳宋词用词特点和翻译策略。

2. 文化外宣汉英翻译

（1）宋词的题材比唐诗的题材相对集中，婉约派的词作内容大多局限于儿女情长、离愁别绪、羁旅俚俗、酒宴娱乐等方面；豪放派较之扩大了范围，多为爱国、怀古、咏史等政治性题材。南宋时，词人们创作的题材越来越广泛，将生活中的许多题材都写入了词中。然而宋词最出彩的题材依然是写情，尤其是爱情；爱国题材和思考人生哲理的题材也颇有深度。除此之外，咏物、赠答等题材的创作也丝毫不输给诗歌。

（2）宋词的分类，一般习惯以豪放派和婉约派这两大创作风格来统分词人和词作。婉约，即婉转含蓄。婉约词派的特点主要是内容侧重儿女风情，结构深细缜密，音律婉转和谐，语言圆润清丽，有一种柔婉之美。豪放，即豪迈放达。豪放派特点大体是创作视野较为广阔，气象恢弘豪放，喜用诗文的手法、句法写词，语词宏博，写事较多。豪放派常打破音乐的束缚，自由发挥，将词的内容扩展到政治、思想等广阔的领域，以豪迈为主。婉约派则恪守音律，注意词与曲的搭配，题材多在婉约的范畴。

（3）意象是指文学作品中表达作者主观情感和独特意境的典型物象。“意”指作者的思想情感；“象”是外在的具体物象，是寄寓了作者思想情感的艺术形象。在文学创作中，“意象”多指取自大自然中能够寄托情思的物象。“意象”强调文学作品的思想内容与形象之美的和谐，是一种成熟的文艺形态。

第九章　元曲英译

Translation of the Qu Poetry

一、学习目标

（1）用英文介绍元曲特点。

（2）掌握元曲文化关键词英译。

（3）对比鉴赏代表性元曲中外译者翻译方法。

二、文化背景

元朝文学的主要成就是元曲。元曲按地区分为南曲和北曲：南曲兴于南宋，流行于江浙一带；北曲兴于金元，随着元代蒙古族征服全国，逐渐由北而南风靡各地。元曲按种类分为散曲和剧曲（杂剧）：散曲曲词是独立成章的，而剧曲则是戏剧中的唱段。散曲属于诗歌的范畴，而剧曲属于戏剧的范畴。散曲又分为小令、套曲和带过曲：小令是一段单一的曲词，套曲是由多个曲牌连缀成套的曲词，带过曲是在几段曲词之间起连接作用的曲词。

The main literary achievement in the Yuan dynasty was Yuan Drama. Regionally there are two types of qu, South and North, the former originating in the Southern Song dynasty to become prevalent in Jiangsu and Zhejiang, the latter in the Jin and Yuan dynasties to grow increasingly popular from North to South alongside the Mongolian conquest. It again divides itself into Sanqu (i.e., verse for songs, each of which is independent) and Zaju (i.e., verse for songs to comprise an opera). Sanqu is a type of poetry but Zaju an element of the opera. Sanqu is subdivided into xiaoling, taoqu and daiguoqu, meaning respectively, verse 1) to a single tune, 2) to one of a series of tunes as a tune suite, and 3) to a transitional tune within a number of tunes.

元曲与宋词有许多相同之处，同是发源于民间的文学，同是和乐填词、亦诗亦歌的形式。但是，元曲又与传统诗词大异其趣，其主要不同之处在于，元曲来自民间最底层，更贴近人民生活，因而语言犀利、明快、戏谑、生动，多用今译俗语，一反传统文人辞章的儒雅风格，更加自由开放，充满市井气息，是当时都市底层人民喜闻乐见的文学形式。

Yuan qu and Song ci have a lot in common: they both originate in folk literature and are both the verse components of music, both to be read as poetry and played as song. The difference is that, belonging to the rank-and-file, Yuan qu is sharp, lucid or cynical-toned, composed in oral speech of the day, full of folk sayings, smells a marketplace odor, and indicates a broadened individualism; it contrasts so sharply to the old-time works that it seems to have soon found itself in popular favor.

由于元曲都是随乐而歌的，所以每一首元曲通常都要标明它的乐调名称和曲牌。中国古代以宫、商、角（jué）、变徵（一说清角）、徵、羽、变宫为七声。乐调中以任何一个音声为主，即可构成一种调式。以宫声为主的调式称为“宫”，以其他六个音声中任何一声为主的调式都统称为“调”，合称为“宫调”。不同的宫调表达着不同的情感，或激昂雄壮，或缠绵忧伤，各有特色。

As verse for the song, qu was given two identifying tags: name of the melody to which musical sounds were arranged and name of the tune to which the verse was composed. In ancient China, gong, shang, jue, bianzhi (or qingyue), zhi, yu, and biangong were names of the seven musical sounds. When gong was to be the principal sound in the arrangement, the melody fell into the category gong, whereas any of the other six sounds was to be principal. The melody would alike be tagged diao. Since gong-diao thus represented varied forms and capacities of the melody, it gave expression to moods running all the way from foaming indignation to militant grandeur, from sentimental affection to dark melancholy.

元曲也有曲牌，这和词有词牌一样。曲牌规定了每首曲的长短和句式。但是，曲和词不同的是，词常常有上下片，甚至多到三片或四片，就像我们现在一首歌曲常常有两段甚至三段或四段歌词一样，唱起来有回环往复的感觉。而曲却不分片，只有一段，称为单调。这是因为曲常常以叙事文学的形式出现，所以不方便重复歌唱。而且，词的用韵比较稀疏，可以隔行押韵，而曲的用韵密集，几乎句句用韵；词牌对词的句式、字数都有严格规定，不能随意更改，而曲牌则比较随意，允许作者根据需要适当改变句式，增加衬字。

As is the case of Song ci, the tune dictates number of words in the verse and form of the line. They are different in that ci is often composed of 3 or even 4 stanzas, like the modern song that comprises several stanzas to be sung repeatedly, whereas a piece of qu is a single (mono) verse. This feature of qu suits its narrative form, but is unfit for the words to be voiced repeatedly. Also, while ci is rhymed every two or several lines, qu has to be rhymed at the end of virtually each line. Again, while the ci tune restricts line form and the number of words, qu is flexible as to be allowed to have its line form and number of words somewhat varied, as deemed necessary by the composer. Such liberty benefits qu creation and makes for easier understanding for the audience, to aid qu's popular influence.

中国诗歌发展到元代，诗、词、曲三种形式已经齐备。后人常说“诗庄、词媚、曲俗”，意思是，诗比较典雅、严肃、庄重，多用来言志抒怀；词比较通俗、轻松、细腻，多用来表达情感；曲则更加诙谐戏谑、激昂慷慨，多用来鞭挞讽刺社会和世人心态。在元曲出现以后，中国古代诗歌的形式就没有更多新的变化了，只是在诗、词、曲三种形式中转换摇摆，所以有人说元曲是中国古代诗歌形式中最后的辉煌。

Joining poetry and ci, qu combines with them to constitute a homogeneous system of Chinese poetry. Critics in the ensuing ages have branded them in that order, as majestic, courtly, and vulgar, meaning that shi, elegant, solemn, and elevated in style, suits expression of aspirations, ideals, and profound feelings; ci, with its comparatively easy text and a style that is brisk and entertaining, gives expression to sentimental emotions; whereas qu, popularly favored and playfully, ironically, or indignantly worded, is a ready means for social satire and depiction of mentality of the rank-and-file. Upon completion of these three forms, Chinese poetry came to a standstill, to shift aimlessly from one to another, now and again. And this happened, say critics, only after qu had exhibited the afterglow.

三、文化关键词

杂剧　Zaju Opera

曲牌　qupai (name of the tune)

乐调　name of the melody

散曲　Sanqu (verse for songs, each of which is independent)

剧曲（杂剧）　Zaju (verse for songs to comprise an opera)

第一节　关汉卿

Guan Hanqing

一、名家简介

关汉卿（约 1220—1300），元代杂剧作家，是中国古代戏曲创作的代表人物，号已斋、已斋叟。汉族，解州人（今山西省运城）。关汉卿创作了 60 多个剧本，现在还留存有十多个优秀的剧目，其代表作是《窦娥冤》。他的杂剧和散曲作品直言讴歌处在社会最底层的人们，写他们的高尚品格、聪明才智、勇敢精神、善良心地和真挚情感。他也敢于大胆揭露现实社会的黑暗，抨击贪官污吏的罪恶。他被誉为中国戏剧的奠基人，并被列为“元曲四大家”（马致远、郑光祖、白朴）之首。

Guan Hanqing (about 1220–1300), pseudonym Yizhai and Yizhaisou, was of the Han nationality and was from Xiezhou (now Yuncheng of Shanxi province). He was a playwright in the Yuan dynasty, with over 60 pieces of theatrical works attributed to him, of which more than 10 are traditionally considered masterpieces with *Dou E Yuan* (literally: Dou E as Victim of Injustice) as the most representative. He composed his plays and works of Zaju in praise of human qualities more often ascribed to people from the lower classes, their ingenuity, gallantry, kindness, and sincerity in love and friendship, in support and justification of popular attempts and movements, and as forthright revelation of official corruption and vices. He has been considered as the pioneer of Chinese drama and the top of the Four Great Yuan Playwrights, the other three being Ma Zhiyuan, Bai Renfu, and Zheng Guangzu.

二、元曲英译赏析

沉醉东风

咫尺的天南地北，霎时间月缺花飞。手执着饯行杯，眼阁着别离泪。刚道得声“保重将息”，痛煞煞教人舍不得。“好去者望前程万里。”

【辜正坤英译】

Untitled to the Tune of Heart-inebriating East Wind

Close to me now the next minute you'll be far away, And in an instant the moon wanes and flowers fade and decay. With the cup in my shaking hand, Tearfully I send you off to a distant land. Waving goodbye I say "Take care," Oh, this leave-taking sorrow I cannot bear. Now gradually you are out of sight, I can only wish you a future so gloriously bright.

【许渊冲英译】

Tune: Intoxicated in East Wind Farewell Song

We stand so near yet we'll be poles apart soon; In a moment flowers will fall and wane the moon. We hold in hand the farewell cup, In our eyes tears well up. I have just said, "Take care to keep fit." How painful is it to tear myself away! I can only say, "Go your way for the bright day."

【赏析重点】

（1）对比分析曲名“沉醉东风”的翻译方法。

（2）分析“咫尺的天南地北”含义和翻译思路。

（3）分析“痛煞煞教人舍不得”的语气特点和翻译方法。

白鹤子

香焚金鸭鼎，闲傍小红楼。

月上柳梢头，人约黄昏后。

【许渊冲英译】

Tune: Song of White Crane

Incense in golden censer burned.
I stand in red bower unconcerned
The moon atop the willow tree,
At dusk my lover trysts with me.

【赏析重点】

分析“月上柳梢头，人约黄昏后”的结构特点和翻译方法。

第二节 马致远

Ma Zhiyuan

一、名家简介

马致远，字千里，号东篱，大都人，中国元代著名大戏剧家、散曲家，与关汉卿、郑光祖、白朴并称“元曲四大家”。所做杂剧今知有 15 种，《汉宫秋》是其代表作；散曲 120 多首，有辑本《东篱乐府》，其中《秋思》最为著名。与关汉卿作品中泼辣的世俗情调相比，马致远的作品更多一些文人气质，用语高雅，情调别致，感情细腻，意象优美。因此，他的散曲颇受元代文人喜爱，他也因此获得“曲状元”的美名。

Ma Zhiyuan (1250–1321), courtesy name Dongli, was a Chinese poet and celebrated playwright, a native of Dadu (大都 , present-day Beijing) during the Yuan dynasty. He is considered to be one of the Four Great Yuan Playwrights, along with Guan Hanqing, Zheng Guangzu, and Bai Renfu. Among his achievements is the development and popularizing of the new sanqu (散曲) lyric form of poetry. The poem "*Autumn Thoughts*" (秋思) is the most widely known of his sanqu poems. In contrast, while Guan Hanqing's works are pungent-, familiar-toned, Ma's exhibit an elegant style, a larger degree of humanity, minutely varied emotions, and graceful images, which explain, probably, his being traditionally hailed as the qu champion.

二、元曲英译赏析

天净沙・秋思

枯藤老树昏鸦，
小桥流水人家，
古道西风瘦马。
夕阳西下，
断肠人在天涯。

【许渊冲英译】

Tune: Sunny Sand Autumn Thoughts

Over old trees wreathed with rotten vines fly crows;

Under a small bridge beside a cot a stream flows;
On ancient road in western breeze a lean horse goes.
Westwards declines the setting sun.
Far, far from home is the heart-broken one.

【辜正坤英译】

Thoughts on Autumn to the Tune of Sky Scouring Sand

A withered vine, an old tree gaunt and a raven croaking on high;
A small bridge, the murmuring water and a thatched cottage nearby;
An ancient path, the west wind and a bony horse is heard to neigh;
Lo! The sun sets today;
At the earth-end a heart-broken traveller plods his weary way.

【赏析重点】

（1）对比分析原文与译文的韵律特点。

（2）分析“枯藤老树昏鸦，小桥流水人家，古道西风瘦马”的句式特点和翻译方法。

寿阳曲・潇湘夜雨

渔灯暗，客梦回。一声声滴人心碎。
孤舟五更家万里，是离人几行清泪。

【辜正坤英译】

The Night Rain on the Xiaoxiang River to the Tune of Life-giving Sun

The lamplight is dim; Broken is the strangers dream; By drops of heart-rending rain.

Like a traveler's passion-ridden tear in vain, At dawn in the lonely fishing boat I roam, Thousands of miles away from my home.

【许渊冲英译】

Tune: Song of Long-lived Sun Night Rain on the River

Dim fishers lanternlight, I wake up from my dream. The rain drips drop by drop to break my heart.

My lonely boat is far from home deep in the night. It rains as tears which stream down from the eyes of those who part.

【赏析重点】

（1）分析“一声声滴人心碎”的语言特征和翻译方法。

（2）对比分析“孤舟五更家万里，是离人几行清泪”英译文的翻译思路。

第三节 赵孟頫

Zhao Mengfu

一、名家简介

赵孟頫（1254—1322），字子昂，号松雪道人，别号鸥波、水精宫道人等。中国吴兴（今浙江湖州）人，宋室后代。元代官僚，书画家。其妻为元朝画家、诗人管道昇。

Zhao Mengfu, courtesy name (zi) Zi'ang, (born in 1254, Huzhou [now Wuxing], Zhejiang province, China, died in 1322), Chinese painter and calligrapher, has been honored as an early master within the tradition of the literati painters (wenrenhua), who sought personal expression rather than the representation of nature. Though he was a descendant of the imperial family of the Song dynasty (960–1279) and had been educated in the imperial university, in 1286, Zhao accepted service in the newly established Mongol court. Zhao's wife, Guan Daosheng, was also a painter of note.

二、元曲英译赏析

后庭花·清溪一叶舟

清溪一叶舟，芙蓉两岸秋。
采菱谁家女，歌声起暮鸥。
乱云愁，满头风雨，戴荷叶归去休。

【许渊冲英译】

Tune: Backyard Flowers

Autumn Thoughts

On the clear stream she rows a leaf-like boat,
Lotus blooms spread autumn hue to the shore.
Who is gathering lotus seed, at dusk afloat?
She startles gulls with her folklore.
From gloomy clouds grief is shed,
Wind and rain overspread,
She goes back with a lotus leaf over her head.

【辜正坤英译】

Untitled

to the Tune of Flower in the Backyard

A leaf-like boat sails along the limpid stream,
On either bank one can see autumn lotuses gleam.
Where from are Lotus-gathering girls singing a song?
At their singing the startled evening water birds throng.
Riotous clouds wrinkle the sky,
In the wind and rain on high,
Lotus left on heads they sail back home in team.

【赏析重点】

（1）对比分析“清溪一叶舟，芙蓉两岸秋”译文的翻译方法。

（2）分析“乱云愁，满头风雨，戴荷叶归去休”的句式特点和翻译思路。

拓展训练 | Extension Training

1. 课后思考

（1）请用英文简要介绍元曲。

（2）总结归纳元曲语言特点和翻译策略。

2. 文化外宣汉英翻译

（1）中国文学中，曲或元曲是由散曲和杂剧构成的。散曲包括诗歌，而杂剧是中国戏剧的一种形式。曲在南宋后期开始流行，元朝达到鼎盛时期。因此常称为元曲。散曲和词都是抒情诗，有特定的调子，但散曲又不同于词，它更口语化，可添加衬字。散曲还可以分为小令和散套，散套由多个调子组成。

（2）晚唐和宋代的古文运动主张清晰和准确，不主张华丽的骈体文或自汉代以来流行的平行散文风格。平行散文结构呆板，过于华丽而忽视内容，因此受到批评。古文风格倡导者的目的是要继承前汉散文的精神，而不是直接模仿。他们使用口语元素，使文字变得更直接。古文运动的发起人是韩愈和柳宗元，他们不仅是大作家也是大理论家，为古文运动奠定了基础。两人都热衷于促进古文运动，热衷于教年轻人，使运动得以发展。

第十章　古典小说英译

Translation of Chinese Classic Novels

一、学习目标

（1）用英文介绍中国四大名著。

（2）掌握中国古典小说书名英译。

（3）对比鉴赏代表性中国古典小说中外译者翻译策略。

二、文化背景

中国古代小说的萌芽和神话传说有密切的关系。我们祖先口头创作的神话和传说经人记录下来，逐渐形成了书面的作品，其中以《山海经》最具代表性，这部作品表面上好像是一部讲地理的著作，实际上带有明显的小说特性，书中讲到的一山一水，常常连带着相关的故事，如“北山经”中记载了精卫填海的故事，反映了我们祖先征服自然的决心和克服困难的战斗精神。战国时期还有无名氏的《穆天子传》，是一本根据周穆王周游天下改编的传说，带有类似历史小说的特点。

The origin of fiction is closely linked with myths and legends which, at first handed down by word of mouth, were gradually recorded as written literature. The most representative one is *Shan Hai Jing*, or *Classic Mountains and Seas*. While intended as a geographical record, it contains less fact than fiction and its accounts of different mountains and streams embody beautiful legends, some with a deep meaning like the story of the bird called Jing-wei. This myth also reflects our forbears' determination to conquer nature and their courage in the face of obstacles. Another work of this period is *The Travels of King Mu* by an unknown writer. A mixture of history and fancy, this is based on the legend that King Mu of the Zhou dynasty travelled all over the world.

汉代，小说有了进一步发展，如韩婴的《韩诗外传》、刘向的《说苑》《新序》等书包含了很多短篇故事，不仅内容具有教育意义，叙述也很动人。魏晋以后，小说的数量和质量都有很大提高，主要有两类：一类以记鬼神为主，另一类以记人事为主。代表作品包括干宝的《搜神记》和刘义庆的《世说新语》。《搜神记》里的故事有些采自史书，有些来自民间，这些故事既有反映劳动人民对自然的斗争，也有反映对压迫者的反抗，如“干将莫邪”的故事。《世说新语》记载的都是历史上人物的言行，通过作者生动而真实的描绘，使人们能够看到这些人物的性格和风度。

The Han Period saw further developments in fiction. *Anecdotes on the Book of Songs* by Han Ying, and *The Garden of Anecdotes* and *New Discourses* by Liu Xiang contain many short tales which point a moral and are good stories into the bargain. During the Wei and Jin dynasties more fiction was written, of a higher standard than heretofore. It fell into two main categories: stories about the supernatural, and anecdotes about famous men. *Sou Shen Ji*, or *Anecdotes about Spirits and Immortals* by Gan Bao is an example of the former, and *New Anecdotes* by Liu Yi-ching of the latter. Some of the tales in *Sou Shen Ji* are based on historical records, and others have a folk origin. A number of them reflect man's struggle against nature or resistance to oppression, such as the story of *Ganjiang and Moye*. *New Anecdotes* deal with the conversation and behaviour of historical figures. By means of graphic and truthful descriptions Liu Yi-ching conjures up these men for us with all their personal idiosyncrasies and sheds light on the customs of the time and the luxurious mode of life of the rulers.

小说在隋唐以后，主要以传奇形式得到更快的发展。唐后期阶段，这类作品不仅数量多，而且质量高。如《长恨传》《莺莺传》《南柯太守传》《霍小玉传》等都产生在这个时期。这些作品大多形象地描绘了当时的社会现实，如《长恨传》写出了统治阶级的腐朽生活和争权夺利的丑恶；《莺莺传》《霍小玉传》写出了妇女在恋爱和婚姻中悲惨的遭遇。这些作品在人物塑造和语言运用上也有较高的成就，能用简练、自然的语言，生动地写出人物的特征。

Fiction made rapid strides in the form of chuan qi during the Sui and Tang dynasties. Towards the end of the dynasty this genre became popular, and the middle of the eighth century to the early part of the ninth is the second period, when many chuan qi of a high quality were produced. To this time belong the famous *Everlasting Remorse*, *The Story of Ying-ying*, *The Governor of the Southern Tributary State* and *Prince Huo's Daughter*. Taken as a whole these Tang stories give us a vivid and accurate picture of society. *Everlasting Remorse* shows the decadent ways and vicious struggle for power of the ruling class. *Prince Huo's Daughter* and *The Story of Ying-ying* describe the unhappy lot of women and their tragic love stories. The characterization and language are magnificent.

Most of the writers have a warm, natural style, and by means of significant details bring out the salient features of their characters.

宋元时期的小说大都记载于《京本通俗小说》等选本中。这些作品虽然不免夹杂迷信等缺点，但大都是以当时的现实社会现象和现实生活为素材而构成的。这个时期出现的“讲史”话本与后来的章回小说有密切的关系，如《宣和遗事》中关于宋江诸人的描述就是《水浒传》中梁山英雄故事的最早蓝本。

Most of the Song and Yuan stories dealing with city life can be found in such collections as *Popular Tales of the Capital*. Although these stories contain elements of superstition or vulgarity, they deal in the main with the actual society and life of the time. The historical stories in this period are the immediate forerunners of the traditional novels. Thus the descriptions of Song Jiang and other peasant leaders given in *the Tales of the Xuan Ho Period* are the earliest sources for the adventures of *Outlaws of the Marsh*.

明前期的小说主要是从宋元话本基础上发展而来的章回小说，代表性作品包括《水浒传》和《三国演义》。《水浒传》中的一百单八条好汉是最具特色的人物塑造，人物个性分明，如淳朴、坦率、公平、仁厚、忠诚的李逵；钢制强硬、勇力过人的武松；武艺过人、性格豪爽、见义勇为的鲁智深等。其次，《水浒传》还生动描绘了很多精彩场面，如智取生辰纲、三打祝家庄、鲁智深大闹五台山、林冲雪夜奔梁山、景阳冈武松打虎等。《三国演义》是以动荡纷扰的历史阶段为背景，揭露了政治集团的明争暗斗，表达了人民对政治人物的憎爱与取舍。

The novels written at the beginning of the Ming dynasty developed from the story-tellers' scripts of the Song and Yuan dynasties. The most important are *Outlaws of the Marsh* and *Three Kingdoms*. *Outlaws of the Marsh* describes the heroic exploits of the peasant army led by Song Jiang during the Northern Song dynasty. A hundred and eight brave men in this epic novel are all robust characters with a strong sense of justice and tremendous courage capable of fighting to the death, and able to distinguish clearly between right and wrong, friend and foe. Depicting all these outlaws, the author made each a sharply defined individual. Li Kui is a true peasant, simple blunt, generous and sincere. Wu Song is a man of iron, of stupendous strength and courage. Lu Zhi-shen is another incomparable fighter, hot-headed, trusty, a champion of the weak. In addition to brilliant characterization *Outlaws of the Marsh* presents us with many unforgettable scenes like "*The Gift Is Taken by Guile*", "*The Three Attacks on Chu Family Village*", "*Lu Zhi-shen Spreads Havoc on Mount Wutai*", "*Lin Chong Ascends the Mountain One Snowy Night*", and "*Wu Song Kills the Tiger on Jingyang Ridge*". *Three Kingdoms* has as its background the stirring and troubled times during the third century when China was divided into three kingdoms. It shows us the open clashes and secret feuds between different political groups, and the popular estimate of the chief figures of the time.

明后期的小说逐渐失去了宋元时期话本的特点，如名著《西游记》主要是吴承恩个人的创作，其中的孙悟空形象是猴性和人性的巧妙融合，他的败敌制胜的机智和勇敢，为崇高目的而排除困难、斗争到底的毅力，无疑是中国古典文学中最辉煌的形象之一。明中叶以后，出现了众多小说总集，如《清平山堂话本》、“三言”（《喻世明言》《警世通言》《警世恒言》）、“二拍”（《初刻拍案惊奇》《二刻拍案惊奇》）等。它们的题材和宋元话本一样不免有可惊可喜的离奇故事，但和明代的社会现实大都有着密切的血肉关系。

Unlike the story-teller's scripts that had developed from the historical tales of the Song and Yuan Dynasties, *Journey to the West* is by and large the work of one man, Wu Cheng-en. Although this story is full of spirits and monsters, the author has made of it an epic of the human spirit and man's stubborn resistance to all the powers of darkness. Monkey Sun Wu-kong's courage and perseverance in the face of enormous odds are even more evident. A wily, fearless fighter but kind and loyal friend, he radiates optimism and humour. He's undoubtedly one of the most popular figures in all Chinese literature. During the later half of the dynasty a number of collections appeared, notably *Tales of Qin Ping Hermitage*, *San Yan* (*Stories to Teach Men*), *Er Pai* (*Stories to Warn Men and Stories to Awaken Men*), which contained many works of a high quality. Some of them, it is true, border on the fantastic like certain of the Song and Yuan stories, but for the most part they deal with everyday life.

清代的小说达到了更高的繁荣程度，最著名的是蒲松龄的《聊斋志异》、吴敬梓的《儒林外史》和曹雪芹的《红楼梦》。《聊斋志异》取材于神仙狐鬼的故事，作者讽刺了残暴贪污的官吏，批判了科举制度，同时又同情人民的苦难，同情妇女，肯定真挚的爱情和反礼教的行为。《儒林外史》的核心思想是反封建，包括吃人的封建礼教和丑恶的科举制度。《红楼梦》描写了典型的封建贵族的生活，作者曹雪芹一方面揭露了腐朽、没落的封建家庭，一方面也创造了两个光辉的正面人物贾宝玉和林黛玉，他们具有富于煽动力的叛逆性格，坚决反对封建传统的一切，他们之间产生了忠诚而纯洁的爱情，但是由于这种和封建制度尖锐对立的性格必然为腐朽势力所不能容忍，两人终无法逃脱悲剧的命运结果。

The Ming dynasty is the great age of the novel. The masterpieces of this period were:

Strange Tales of Liao Zhai by Pu Song-ling, *The Scholars* by Wu Jing-zi, and *A Dream of the Red Mansion* by Cao Xue-qin. *Strange Tales of Liao Zhai* takes its material from stories about ghosts and supernatural beings, as well as the amazing adventures of men. Through these tales Pu Song-ling satirized rapacious officials, denounced the examination system, showed his sympathy for the sufferings of the people and the hard lot of women, and applauded true love and the defiance of convention. With the main thought of anti-feudalism, the author of *The Scholars* directed his biting satire primarily against the inhuman feudal morality, and secondly against the examination system. *A Dream of the Red Mansion* described a rich, aristocratic family. In addition to the realistic descriptions of a landowning family in the eve of the collapse of feudalism, Cao Xue-qin also created two immortal characters—Jia Bao-yu and Lin Dai-yu, young rebels who stubbornly oppose old traditions. And because the two young people both hated feudal oppression and longed for freedom to develop their individuality, a true love sprang up between them. For young rebels like this could not be tolerated by the forces of feudalism, their tragic romance was unavoidable.

三、文化关键词

神话传说　myths and legends

话本　story-teller's scripts

《山海经》 *Classic of Mountains and Seas*

《搜神记》 *Anecdotes about Spirits and Immortals*

《聊斋志异》 *Strange Tales of Liao Zhai*

《水浒传》 *Outlaws of the Marsh*

《三国演义》 *Three Kingdoms*

《西游记》 *Journey to the West*

《红楼梦》 *A Dream of Red Mansion*

第一节 《水浒传》

Outlaws of the Marsh

一、典籍简介

《水浒传》叙述以宋江为首的一百零八位英雄好汉的故事。宋江在历史上确有其人。北宋末年，他领导农民起义军与官府对抗，活动在今天的山东、河北、河南、江苏一带。《水浒传》吸纳了宋、元有关宋江三十六人的民间传说和戏曲故事中的某些成分，但在本质上它是作家个人的创作。《水浒传》的成功之处在于对宋江等人被逼上梁山的曲折过程进行了个性化的真实的描写。这些形象在中国已成为家喻户晓的典型。如鲁智深、林冲、武松、李逵、宋江、石秀、燕青等。作者在刻画人物方面所表现出来的艺术创造能力，在中国今译小说史上是空前的。《水浒传》的影响极其深远。在文学上，它为后世小说创作提供了丰富的艺术经验，同时也为后世文学提供了题材的来源。

Outlaws of the Marsh recounts the doings of the 108 heroes, led by Song Jiang, of Mount Liangshan. This Song Jiang was in fact a historical figure, who led a peasant revolt in the area of what are now the provinces of Shandong, Hebei, Henan and Jiangsu in the closing years of the Northern Song dynasty (960–1127). While *Outlaws of the Marsh* is a collection of stories from folk legends and dramas of the Song and Yuan Dynasties, it also in essence bears the mark of the creativity of the individual author. The success of *Outlaws of the Marsh* as a novel lies in the fact that it describes the tortuous course of the adventures of the Liangshan outlaws in a uniquely true-to-life way. These characters have become household names in China, including Sagacious Lu, Lin Chong, Wu Song, Li Kui, Song Jiang, Shi Xiu and Yan Qing. The artistic creative skill of the author in delineating these characters is unsurpassed in the history of Chinese vernacular fiction. The influence of *Outlaws of the Marsh* has been extremely far reaching. It provided a wealth of artistic experience for the creation of novels by later generations as well as material sources for later literary scholars.

二、作者简介

施耐庵，元末明初的文学家，本名彦端，祖籍泰州海陵县或苏州吴县阊门（今江苏苏州），博古通今，才气横溢，举凡群经诸子，辞章诗歌，天文、地理、医卜、星象等，一切技术无不精通，35岁曾中进士，后弃官归里，闭门著述，与拜他为师的罗贯中一起研究《三国演义》《三遂平妖传》的创作，搜集整理关于梁山泊宋江等英雄人物的故事，最终写成"四大名著"之一的《水浒传》。

Shi Nai'an, also known as Yanduan, was a native of Hailing county of Taizhou or Changmen, Wu County, Suzhou (now Suzhou city, Jiangsu province). He was an author in the Late Yuan dynasty and the early Ming dynasty. He was versatile and talented, familiar with classics and masters both in modern times and ancient times. He also was familiar with poems, prose, astronomy, geography, medicine and aspect astrology, etc. At the age of 35, he passed the imperial examination and was selected as Jinshi, but later he gave up the official title and returned to his hometown. There he created his works and together with his disciple Luo Guanzhong, he studied the writing of *San Guo Yan Yi* (*Three Kingdoms*) and *Sansui Ping Yao Zhuan* (*Taming Devils*). After collecting the stories of the heroes of Liangshan Po such as Song Jiang, he finally completed the writing of *Shuihu Zhuan* (*Outlaws of the Marsh*), one of the "*Four Chinese Classic Novels*".

三、典籍英译赏析

（一）人物描写

【原典 1　花和尚鲁智深】

头裹芝麻罗万字顶头巾，脑后两个太原府纽丝金环，上穿一领鹦哥绿纻丝战袍，腰系一条文武双股鸦青绦，足穿一双鹰爪皮四缝干黄靴。生得面圆耳大，鼻直口方，腮边一部貉胡须。身长八尺，腰阔十围。

【沙博理英译】

His head was bound in a bandanna with figured swastikas, buckled in the back with twisted gold rings from Taiyuan. A raven black plaited sash bound his parrot-green warrior's gown at the waist. On his feet were yellow boots embossed with four welts of brown leather in hawk talon design. He had large ears, a straight nose and a broad mouth. A full beard framed his round face. He was eight feet tall and had a girth of ten spans.

【赛珍珠英译】

On his head he wore a hat of spotted silk, on the back of which were two twisted golden circles from T'ai Yuan Fu. On his upper body he wore a coat of the blue of a parrot's feathers. About his waist was a double girdle the color of the greenish black of a crow's plumage. On his feet were leather boots, and they were like the claws of an old eagle, dry yellow in color, and with four seams. His face was round; his ears were very large; his nose was straight and his mouth was square. He wore a fanshaped beard clean around his jaws. His body was eight feet in height, and his girth was enormous.

【赏析重点】

（1）分析描写语言"芝麻罗万字顶头巾""太原府纽丝金环""鹦哥绿纻丝战袍""文武双股鸦青绦""鹰爪皮四缝干黄靴"的语言特点和翻译方法。

（2）对比分析"鼻直口方""腰阔十围"中文化要素的翻译差异。

【原典 2　豹子头林冲】

头戴一顶青纱抓角儿头巾，脑后两个白玉圈连珠鬓环。身穿一领单绿罗团花战袍，腰系一条双搭尾龟背银带。穿一对磕瓜头朝样皂靴，手中执一把折迭纸西川扇子。那官人生的豹头环眼，燕颔虎须，八尺长短身材，三十四五年纪。

（《水浒传》第七回）

【沙博理英译】

The gentleman wore a black muslin cap with its two corners gathered together, a pair of interlinked circlets of white jade held the knot of hair at the back of his head. He was dressed in a green officer's robe of flowered silk, bound at the waist by a girdle made of double strips of beaver and fastened by a silver clasp shaped like a tortoise back. His feet were shod in square-toed black boots. In his hand he carried a folding Chengdu fan. About thirty-five years old, he had a head like a panther, round eyes, a chin sharp as a swallows beak, whiskers like a tiger and was very tall.

【赛珍珠英译】

On his head was a sky-blue muslin hat with the two corners gathered together. At the back were two clasps of white jade and circles of beaded jewels at the side. On his body was a robe made of a single thickness of thin green striped silk and upon it was woven a pattern of round flowers. Around his waist was a girdle made of double strips of beaver's fur and silver with markings of tortoise shell. On his feet were a pair of square-toed high black boots, and in his hand a folded paper Szechuan fan. His head was shaped like a leopard's, his eyes round, and on his swallow-like throat, his whiskers were like those of a tiger. His body was eight feet tall and he was thirty or forty years old.

【赏析重点】

（1）分析“白玉圈连珠鬓环”“单绿罗团花战袍”“双搭尾龟背银带”“磕瓜头朝样皂靴”的中文特点和翻译方法。

（2）分析“豹头环眼”“燕颔虎须”用词特点和翻译方法。

（二）动作描写

【原典 1　鲁智深拳打镇关西】

扑的只一拳，正打在鼻子上，打得鲜血迸流，鼻子歪在半边，却便似开了个油酱铺，咸的、酸的、辣的，一发都滚出来。郑屠挣不起来，那把尖刀，也丢在一边，口里只叫：“打得好！”鲁达骂道：“直娘贼，还敢应口！”提起拳头来，就眼眶际眉梢只一拳，打得眼棱缝裂，乌珠迸出，也似开了个彩帛铺的，红的、黑的、绛的，都绽将出来。

【沙博理英译】

He landed a punch on Zheng's nose that flattened it to one side and brought the blood flowing like the sauces in a condiments shop—salty, sour and spicy. Zheng struggled vainly to rise. The knife fell from his hand. “A good blow,” he cried.

“Mother-raping thief,” said the major. “How dare you talk back?” He punched the butcher on the eyebrow, splitting the lid so that the eye-ball protruded. Red, black and purple gore flowed like swatches of cloth in a draper's shop.

【赛珍珠英译】

And as he spoke he lifted his fist and with a dull thud he hit Cheng on the bridge of the nose and the fresh blood flowed out. Cheng's nose was broken and bent to the side and of a sudden he smelled as many smells as though he opened a condiment shop—soy bean sauce, salt, sour sweet, hot—all in a second he smelled them all. He tried to get up but he could not. He had cast the pointed knife to one side and he kept yelling, “That's right—you hit me—go on and hit me.” Lu Ta cursed him, saying, “You incestuous beast, do you still dare to answer me?”

And he lifted his great fist and hit Cheng on the eye socket and split open the corner of his eye so that his eyeball burst out. It was now to Cheng as though he had opened a silk shop wherein were silks of many colors, for he saw black and purple and red from the bursting of his eyeball.

【赏析重点】

对比分析“也似开了个彩帛铺的，红的、黑的、绛的，都绽将出来”修辞翻译方法。

【原典2　武松打虎】

那个大虫又饥又渴，把两只爪在地下略按一按，和身望上一扑，从半空里撺将下来。武松被那一惊，酒都做冷汗出了。说时迟，那时快；武松见大虫扑来，只一闪，闪在大虫背后。那大虫背后看人最难，便把前爪搭在地下，把腰胯一掀，掀将起来。武松只一闪，闪在一边。大虫见掀他不着，吼一声，却似半天里起个霹雳，振得那山冈也动，把这铁棒也似虎尾倒竖起来只一剪。武松却又闪在一边。

【沙博理英译】

Both hungry and thirsty, the big animal clawed the ground with its front paws a couple of times, sprang high and came hurtling forward. The wine poured out of Wu Song in a cold sweat. Quicker than it takes to say, he dodged, and the huge beast landed beyond him. Tigers can't see behind them, so as its front paws touched the ground it tried to side-swipe Wu Song with its body. Again he dodged, and the tiger missed. With a thunderous roar that shook the ridge the animal slashed at Wu Song with its iron tail. Once more he swivelled out of the way.

【赛珍珠英译】

Now that great tiger was both hungry and thirsty and it put its front paws down lightly on the ground and leaped and seemed to descend out of space. Wu Sung gave a start of fright and the wine came out on him in cold sweat. To tell it is slow, but it happened too quickly! Wu Sung, seeing the great tiger springing forward, ran and hid behind the beast. Now it was hard for the tiger to see a man behind it, and so it put its front paws down on the earth and lifted up its back and hinder parts and thus struck out. Wu Sung ran and hid again to one side. The tiger seeing it could not catch him by springing or kicking gave a roar and it was as though there was a crack of thunder in the near air. And the very mountain trembled. Then the tiger made its tail that was like a bar of iron to stand erect, and then it beat its tail suddenly down.

【赏析重点】

（1）对比分析动词“按一按”“一扑”“一闪”“一掀”的翻译用词。

（2）对比分析“说时迟，那时快”的译文效果。

【原典3】

原来那大虫拿人只是一扑，一掀，一剪；三般捉不着时，气性先自没了一半。那大虫又剪不着，再吼了一声，一兜兜将回来。武松见那大虫复翻身回来，双手轮起哨棒，尽平生气力，只一棒，从半空劈将下来。只听得一声响，簌簌地，将那树连枝带叶劈脸打将下来。定睛看时，一棒劈不着大虫，原来打急了，正打在枯树上，把那条哨棒折做两截，只拿得一半在手里。

【沙博理英译】

Now this tiger had three methods for getting its victim—spring, swipe and slash. But none of them had worked, and the beast's spirit diminished by half. Again it roared, and whirled around. Wu Song raised his staff high in a two-handed grip and swung with all his might. There was a loud crackling and a large branch of leaves and all, tumbled past his face. In his haste, he had struck an old tree instead of the tiger, snapping the staff in two and leaving him holding only the remaining half.

【赛珍珠英译】

Wu Sung again darted to one side. Before this when the great tiger caught a man it gave one leap and one kick and one beat with its tail and if these three did not avail half its strength of anger went down. Now when the tiger could not catch the man, it roared again and it turned itself about. Wu Sung, seeing that great tiger turn itself about, thus, lifted high his club with both his hands, and with all the strength he had he brought it down and struck it through the air. He heard a thud and a tree fell with a scattering of leaves and branches. When he stared he saw that in his excitement this blow had not hit the tiger, and he had only hit a dead tree and the club was broken in two, and there was but the half of it there in his hand.

【赏析重点】

（1）对比分析“一扑，一掀，一剪”的译文用词。

（2）分析“双手轮起哨棒，尽平生气力，只一棒，从半空劈将下来”译文的结构转换。

第二节　《三国演义》

Three Kingdoms

一、典籍简介

《三国演义》是中国古代第一部长篇章回小说，是历史演义小说的经典之作。

在古往今来的小说中，没有一部作品能够像《三国演义》这样对中国的社会生活产生如此深刻和广泛的影响。小说中的许多故事，直接的或间接的通过戏曲、曲艺和其他通俗文艺形式传播到社会各个阶层和民间各个角落，成为妇孺皆知的话题，从而渗透到中国民间文化意识的深处。

Three Kingdoms was the first full-length novel with clear chapter divisions to appear in ancient China. It is a classic historical romance. No other work of this genre, in past times or present, has had such a deep and wide-ranging impact on Chinese society. The various episodes have been transmitted to every nook and cranny of Chinese society, either directly or indirectly by means of the theater, songs and other channels of popular culture, and are known in every household in the land.

《三国演义》是罗贯中依据陈寿的《三国志》创作而成的。在故事情节的编排和人物形象的描写这些具象的层面上，罗贯中是既“据正史”，又“采小说”。在虚与实、雅与俗这些艺术原则的层面上，罗贯中力求虚实相间、雅俗共赏。《三国演义》描写公元 3 世纪前后近百年的历史风云，始于黄巾起义，止于三家归晋。罗贯中拥刘反曹的政治倾向十分鲜明。不仅把刘备集团安置在情节的中心位置，从刘、关、张桃园结义开始，直到诸葛亮秋风五丈原，构成情节的主干，使刘、关、张和诸葛亮的命运成为读者关注的焦点，而且在全书的人物配置和描写上也始终突出刘备集团的人物。《三国演义》着力描写刘备集团君臣如兄弟的真诚而亲密的关系，同时揭露曹操的损人利己、冷酷残暴的灵魂和曹魏集团内人与人之间的暗算和倾轧，由此形成真善美与假丑恶的鲜明对比，烘托出小说的政治道德主题。

Three Kingdoms was created by Luo Guanzhong, based on the historical work *Sanguo Zhi* (*Annals of the Three Kingdoms*) by Chen Shou. From the arrangement of the plot and the descriptions of the characters, we can indeed see that Luo Guanzhong embellished historical facts with fictional elements. Also his artistic method was to combine invention with authenticity and cater to both refined and popular tastes. The narrative of *Three Kingdoms* covers a period of 100 years, from the rebellion of the Yellow turbans to the replacement of the division of the country into the three kingdoms by the Jin dynasty. Luo Guanzhong's support for Liu Bei and his bias against Cao Cao is abundantly clear in the novels pages. Not only does he place Liu Bei and his company in the center of the plot, he makes the fates of Liu Bei, Guan Yu, Zhang Fei and Zhuge Liang the focus of the reader's attention from the oath taken in the Peach Garden to the death of Zhuge Liang at Wuzhangyuan. The members of this group too are central in the placement and description of the characters in the book. Throughout *Three Kingdoms* there is a sharp contrast between the close fellowship and sincerity which reigns in Liu Bei's camp and the self-seeking scheming and internecine treachery which is the norm among Cao Cao's group. This struggle between good and evil throws into clear relief the novel's propagation of righteous politics.

《三国演义》是中国传统文化的结晶。它既包含着以乐诗书为内核的雅文化，也兼容着以说书、戏曲、占卜等为表现的俗文化；它既有生动而丰富的故事情节和栩栩如生的众多人物形象，又蕴含有历史积累的巨大的智慧。它既通俗又高雅，从而获得上至贵族士大夫、下至平民百姓的喜爱。刘、关、张的结义，曾被后世许多人仿效，关羽崇拜已成为一个至今不衰的文化现象。《三国演义》所提供的军事和政治斗争的策略和经验，世世代代为人们所借鉴。

Three Kingdoms is a crystallization of the heritage of Chinese literature. It includes not only fine writing from the traditional categories of the rites, music, poetry and prose, it also draws from the folk arts, storytelling, drama, divination, etc. As well as a plethora of vigorous plot lines and lifelike characters, the novel contains a wealth of wisdom accumulated through the ages. Its tone is both exalted and down-to-earth, and as a result it is enjoyed by the mighty and the humble alike. The sworn brotherhood between Liu Bei, Guan Yu and Zhang Fei has been held up as a model ever since, and Guan Yu has become an everlasting literary symbol. Furthermore, the political and military intrigues and maneuvers in the novel have served as reference for generations of statesmen and strategists.

二、作者简介

罗贯中（约 1330—约 1400），汉族，山西太原（清徐县）人。名本，字贯中，号湖海散人。他是元末明初著名小说家、戏曲家，是中国章回小说的鼻祖。罗贯中的一生著作颇丰，主要作品有：剧本《赵太祖龙虎风云会》《忠正孝子连环谏》《三平章死哭蜚虎子》，小说《隋唐两朝志传》《残唐五代史演义》《三遂平妖传》《粉妆楼》、代表作《三国演义》等。

Luo Guanzhong (about 1330–1400), Han nationality, was a native of Qingxu County, Taiyuan City, Shanxi Province. Luo's given name was Ben while Guanzhong was his courtesy name and his pseudonym was Huhai Sanren (Leisure Man by Lakes and Seas). Luo was a famous novelist, playwright as well as the originator of traditional

Chinese zhanghui-style (chapter based) novel in the late Yuan and early Ming dynasties. Throughout his life, Luo wrote many works, including plays like *Story of Emperor Taizu of Song dynasty* and *the Heroes*, *Serial admonition of an Upright and Filial Son*, *Sanpingzhang Weeping for Feihuzi* and novels like *The Chronicle of the Sui and Tang Dynasties*, *The End of Tang dynasty and the Period of the Five Dynasties*, *Tale of Sansui Conquering Monsters*, *Fenzhuang Lou* (*Pink Building*) and *Three Kingdoms*, which was Luo's masterpiece.

三、典籍英译赏析

（一）人物描写

【原典 1　刘备】

那人不甚好读书；性宽和，寡言语，喜怒不形于色；素有大志，专好结交天下豪杰；生得身长七尺五寸，两耳垂肩，双手过膝，目能自顾其耳，面如冠玉，唇若涂脂；中山靖王刘胜之后，汉景帝阁下玄孙：姓刘，名备，字玄德。

（第 1 回）

【罗慕士英译】

This man, though no scholar, was gentle and generous by nature, taciturn and reserved. His one ambition was to cultivate the friendship of the boldest spirits of the empire. He stood seven and a half spans tall, with arms that reached below his knees. His ear lobes were elongated, his eyes widely set and able to see his own ears. His face was flawless as jade, his lips like dabs of rouge. This man was a descendant of Liu Sheng, Prince Jing of Zhongshan, a great-great-grandson of the fourth Han emperor, Jing. His name was Liu Bei; his style, Xuande.

【赏析重点】

（1）分析“性宽和，寡言语，喜怒不形于色”的翻译方法。

（2）分析“身长七尺五寸，两耳垂肩，双手过膝，目能自顾其耳，面如冠玉，唇若涂脂”译文的句式结构转换。

【原典 2　张飞】

玄德回视其人：身长八尺，豹头环眼，燕颔虎须，声若巨雷，势如奔马。玄德见他形貌异常，问其姓名。其人曰：“某姓张，名飞，字翼德。世居涿郡，颇有庄田，卖酒屠猪。”

（第 1 回）

【罗慕士英译】

Xuande turned and faced a man eight spans tall, with a blunt head like a panther's, huge round eyes, a swallow's heavy jowls, a tiger's whiskers, a thunderous voice, and a stance like a dashing horse. Half in fear, half in admiration. Xuande asked his name. "The surname," the man replied, "is Zhang; given name, Fei, style, Yide. We've lived in this county for generations, farming our piece of land, selling wine, and slaughtering pigs."

【赏析重点】

分析"豹头环眼，燕颔虎须，声若巨雷，势如奔马"的修辞翻译方法。

【原典3 关羽】

玄德看其人：身长九尺，髯长二尺；面如重枣，唇若涂脂；丹凤眼，卧蚕眉；相貌堂堂，威风凛凛。玄德就邀他同坐，叩其姓名。其人曰：吾姓关，名羽，字长生，后改云长。

（第1回）

【罗慕士英译】

Xuande observed him: a man of enormous height, nine spans tall, with a two-foot-long beard flowing from his rich, ruddy cheeks. He had glistening lips, eyes sweeping sharply back like those of the crimson-faced phoenix, and brows like nestling silkworms. His stature was imposing, his bearing awesome. Xuande invited him to share their table and asked who he was. "My surname is Guan," the man replied, "My given name is Yu; my style, Changsheng, was later changed to Yunchang."

【赏析重点】

分析"面如重枣，唇若涂脂；丹凤眼，卧蚕眉"的修辞翻译方法。

【原典4 曹操】

为首闪出一将：身长七尺，细眼长髯；官拜骑都尉；沛国谯郡人也，姓曹，名操，字孟德。操父曹嵩，本姓夏侯氏；因为中堂侍曹腾之养子，故冒姓曹。曹嵩生操，小字阿瞒，一名吉利。操幼时，好游猎，喜歌舞；有权谋，多机变。

（第1回）

【罗慕士英译】

The leader of this new unit flashed into sight-tall, narrow-eyed with a long beard. This man's rank was cavalry commander. His surname was Cao; his given name, Cao;

his style, Mengde. Cao Cao's father, Cao Song, was originally not a Cao but a Xiahou. However, as the adopted son of the eunuch Cao Teng he assumed the surname Cao. Cao Song was Cao Cao's natural father. In addition Cao Cao had the childhood nickname Ah Man and another given name, Jili. As a youth Cao had loved hunting and delighted in song and dance. He was a boy with ingenious ideas for any situation, a regular storehouse of schemes and machinations.

【赏析重点】

分析"好游猎，喜歌舞；有权谋，多机变"的翻译方法。

【原典 5　吕布】

只见吕布顶束发金冠，披百花战袍，擐唐猊铠甲，系狮蛮宝带，纵马挺戟，随丁建阳出到阵前。

（第 3 回）

【罗慕士英译】

There for all to see was Lv Bu, his topknot bound in a golden crown, wearing a millefleur battle robe, girded with armor and a belt bearing a motif of lions and reptiles. Giving his horse free rein, his halberd poised, Lv Bu followed Ding Yuan to the front of the lines.

【赏析重点】

分析"顶束发金冠，披百花战袍，擐唐猊铠甲，系狮蛮宝带"的语言特点和翻译方法。

【原典 6　诸葛亮】

玄德见孔明身长八尺，面如冠玉，头戴纶巾，身披鹤氅（chǎng），飘飘然有神仙之概。

（第 38 回）

【罗慕士英译】

To Xuande, Kongming appeared singularly tall, with a face like gleaming jade and a plaited silken band around his head. Cloaked in crane down, he had the buoyant air of a spiritual transcendent.

【赏析重点】

分析"面如冠玉，头戴纶巾，身披鹤氅"的语言特点和翻译方法。

（二）武器描写

【原典 1】

云长造青龙偃月刀，又名“冷艳锯”，重八十二斤。

【罗慕士英译】

For Lord Guan, a Green Dragon Crescent-moon Blade, also known as Frozen Glory, weighing eighty-two jin.

【赏析重点】

分析“青龙偃月刀”“冷艳锯”的翻译方法。

【原典 2】

弓箭随身，手持画戟，坐下嘶风赤兔马。

【罗慕士英译】

A quiver of arrows at his side, a figured halberd with two side-blade, Lv Bu sat astride Red Hare as it neighed like the roaring wind.

【赏析重点】

分析“画戟”“嘶风赤兔马”的翻译方法。

【原典 3】

挺丈八蛇矛，飞马大叫：“三姓家奴休走！燕人张飞在此！”

【罗慕士英译】

Holding high his eighteen-span snake-headed spear he flew at Lv Bu, shouting mightily, “Stay! Bastard with three fathers! Know me for Zhang Fei of Yan!”

【赏析重点】

分析“三姓家奴”的文化内涵和翻译方法。

【原典 4】

曹操有宝剑两口，一名“倚天”，一名“青釭”，倚天剑自配之，青釭剑令夏侯恩配之。

【罗慕士英译】

Now, Cao Cao had two swords of exceptional value. One was called Heaven’s Prop, the other Black Pommel, Cao wore the first himself, Xiahou En the second.

【赏析重点】

分析“倚天”“青釭”的翻译方法。

（三）精彩片段描写

【原典 1　桃园三结义】

次日，于桃园中，备下乌牛白马祭礼等项，三人焚香再拜而说誓曰：“念刘备、关羽、张飞，虽然异姓，既结为兄弟，则同心协力，救困扶危；上报国家，下安黎庶；不求同年同月同日生，只愿同年同月同日死。皇天后土，实鉴此心。背义忘恩，天人共戮！”誓毕，拜玄德为兄，关羽次之，张飞为弟。祭罢天地，复宰牛设酒，聚乡中勇士，得三百余人，就桃园中痛饮一醉。

（第 1 回）

【罗慕士英译】

The next day the three men had a black bull, a white horse, and other offerings brought to the peach garden. Amid the smoke of incense they performed their ritual prostration and took their oath: “We three, though of separate ancestry, join in brotherhood here, combining strength and purpose, to relieve the present crisis. We will perform our duty to the Emperor and protect the common folk of the land. We dare not hope to be together always but hereby vow to die the self same day. Let shining Heaven above and the fruitful land below bear witness to our resolve. May Heaven and man scourge whosoever fails this vow.”

So swearing, Xuande became the eldest brother; Lord Guan, the second; and Zhang Fei, the youngest. After the ceremonies they butchered the bull and spread forth a feast in the peach garden for the three hundred local youths they had recruited; and all drank to their heart’s content.

【赏析重点】

（1）分析“同心协力，救困扶危；上报国家，下安黎庶”的语言特点和翻译方法。

（2）分析“不求同年同月同日生，只愿同年同月同日死”的翻译方法。

【原典 2　张翼德大闹长坂桥】

却说文聘引军追赵云至长坂桥，只见张飞倒竖虎须，圆睁环眼，手绰蛇矛，立马桥上；又见桥东树林之后，尘头大起，疑有伏兵，便勒住马，不敢近前。……见飞怒目横矛，立马于桥上，又恐是诸葛孔明之计，都不敢近前。……张飞睁圆环眼，隐隐见后军青罗伞盖、旄钺旌旗来到，料得是曹操心疑，亲自来看。飞乃厉声大喝曰："我乃燕人张翼德也！谁敢与我决一死战？"声如巨雷。曹军闻之，尽皆股栗。曹操急令去其伞盖，回顾左右曰："我向曾闻云长言：翼德于百万军中，取上将之首，如探囊取物。今日相逢，不可轻敌。"言未已，张飞睁目又喝曰："燕人张翼德在此！谁敢来决死战？"曹操见张飞如此气概，颇有退心。飞望见曹操后军阵脚移动，乃挺矛又喝曰："战又不战，退又不退，却是何故！"喊声未绝，曹操身边夏侯杰惊得肝胆碎裂，倒撞于马下。操便回马而走。于是诸军众将一齐望西奔走。

（第 42 回）

【罗慕士英译】

Wen Pin, meanwhile, had tracked Zilong to the bridge. There he found Zhang Fei, tiger-whiskers uncurled, eyes two rings of fury, snake lance in hand. Mounted and poised, Zhang Fei looked out from the bridge. Wen Pin spotted dust rising out of the adjacent copse to the east. Suspecting an ambush, he reined in. ...Cao's commanders contemplated Zhang Fei's menacing glare and leveled lance. And, too, they remembered Kongming's clever traps. ...Zhang Fei's probing eye made out Cao Cao's blue silk umbrella in the distance, his feathered battle-axe and fringed banner. "So he came to see for himself," Zhang Fei thought. He called out: "I am Zhang Fei of Yan. Have you a man who'll fight it out to the death?" The power of Zhang Fei's voice unnerved Cao Cao's men. Cao Cao ordered the command umbrella removed. Turning to his attendants, he said, "Once Lord Guan told me that Zhang Fei had taken the head of a chief general before the eyes of his own legions as easily as removing an object from a sack. Today we have crossed his path and must take care." As Cao Cao spoke Zhang Fei widened his eyes and shouted again: "Here he stands! Zhang Fei of Yan, who'll fight to the death any man that dares!" But Cao Cao daunted by the warrior's indomitable spirit, was content to draw back. Zhang Fei watched the rear lines of Cao Cao's army shuffling about. He lifted his spear and bellowed: "What's it to be? Don't want to fight? Don't want to leave?" The mighty voice still commanded the air when Xiahou Jie, right beside Cao Cao, collapsed and fell from his saddle, panic-stricken. Cao Cao turned and rode back, followed by his commanders.

【赏析重点】

（1）分析"倒竖虎须，圆睁环眼，手绰蛇矛"的中文特点和翻译方法。

（2）分析"如探囊取物""惊得肝胆碎裂"的修辞翻译方法。

（3）分析"战又不战，退又不退，却是何故！"的翻译方法。

第三节 《西游记》

Journey to the West

一、典籍简介

《西游记》的故事是根据一个真实的历史事件衍生出来的。唐代贞观年间僧人玄奘（602—664）只身西行，经中亚细亚去天竺（今印度）取经，历经十七载，一百三十八国往返数万里，写下了佛教文化史和中印文化交流史上辉煌的一页。

The historical background to the novel *Journey to the West* is as follows: In the Zhenguan reign period of the Tang dynasty, a Buddhist monk named Xuanzang (602–664) traveled alone through Central Asia to the land of Tianzhu (present-day India) to seek the original Buddhist scriptures. Journey there and back—covering thousands of miles—took 17 years, and Xuanzang traversed 138 states, writing a brilliant page not only in the history of Buddhist culture but also in the history of Sino-Indian cultural exchanges.

《西游记》用八十七回的主要篇幅描叙唐僧师徒四众披荆斩棘，沿途斩妖降怪的取经历程。在往西天的路上，无论是山野丛林，还是乡村城镇，到处都潜藏着危险。形形色色的妖魔鬼怪，有的明火执仗，有的巧妙伪装，有的控制操纵国君权柄、以合法的官方身份出现，总之是危害地方，阻挠唐僧西行取经，甚至欲擒唐僧杀而食之。孙悟空在与各种妖魔鬼怪的斗争中起着中坚的作用，他不但要与妖魔鬼怪正面作战，而且不时要克服来自内部的师父、师弟的干扰和牵制。以孙悟空为骨干的师徒四众经历千辛万苦，战胜了各种各样的凶恶和狡猾的敌人，终于到达西天，完成了取经的神圣使命。所谓“九九八十一难”的故事虽说都是虚幻的神话，但是唐僧师徒在斗争中所表现得不达目的誓不罢休和藐视强大敌人并与之顽强战斗的精神和品格，却是十分现实的，它正是中华民族的精神和品格的生动写照。《西游记》以神魔为主要描写对象，它创造了一个神奇的充满幻想的世界。但是，这个虚幻的世界却反射着现实社会种种矛盾的光影，那些神魔的性格都是世间凡人性格的概括和升华。

In *Journey to the West* a total of 87 chapters are dedicated to the story of the Tang priest Xuanzang's quest for the Buddhist scriptures. In the course of their journey, they brave a series of dangers and vanquish devils and monsters. The road to the Western Paradise is fraught with danger, whether in mountains and forests or in villages and towns. Demons of all descriptions try to bar their way, even to the extent of endeavoring to kill and eat Xuanzang. Some of these ghostly opponents appear openly hostile, while others are cunningly disguised; some wield power over kingdoms or feign to be officials carrying out their lawful duties. Monkey plays a central role in every battle with the monsters, not only contending with them face to face, but also helping his companions overcome the obstacles and restraints that originate within themselves. After overcoming all kinds of evil and devious enemies, with Monkey as the backbone of the company, the travelers finally reach the Western Paradise and accomplish their sacred mission of taking back the scriptures. In this so-called story of 81 difficulties, although it is filled with myth and fantasy, the staunch spirit and character of the four companions to battle all enemies and overcome all hurdles in order to attain their goal is manifested very clearly, and as such it is a vivid portrayal of the spirit and character of the Chinese nation. With supernatural beings as its protagonists, *Journey to the West* creates a world full of fantasy and illusion but this fantasy world reflects various kinds of contradictions in the society of Wu Cheng'en's time. The characters of the demons are generalizations and sublimations of the characters of ordinary mortals.

二、作者简介

吴承恩（1501—1582），字汝忠，号射阳山人。汉族，淮安府山阳县（今江苏省淮安市楚州区）人。中国明代杰出的小说家，是四大名著之一《西游记》的作者。

Wu Cheng'en (1501–1582), courtesy named Ruzhong, with the pseudonym of Sheyang Hermit, was of Han nationality, and a native of Shanyang County of Huai'an prefecture (now Chuzhou district, Huai'an city, Jiangsu province). He was an outstanding novelist of the Ming dynasty, and also the author of *Journey to the West*, which is one of the Four Classic Chinese novels.

三、典籍英译赏析

（一）人物描写

【原典 1　孙悟空】

猴王听说，教："取我披挂来！"就戴上紫金冠，贯上黄金甲，登上步云鞋，手执如意金箍棒，领众出门，摆开阵势。这巨灵神睁睛观看，真好猴王：

身穿金甲亮堂堂，头戴金冠光映映。手举金箍棒一根，足踏云鞋皆相称。

一双怪眼似明星，两耳过肩查又硬。挺挺身才变化多，声音响亮如钟磬。

尖嘴咨牙弼马温，心高要做齐天圣。

（第 4 回）

【詹纳尔英译】

"Fetch me my armour," said the Monkey King. He then donned his golden helmet, tied on his golden armour, put on his cloud-walking shoes, and took his As-You-Will gold-banded cudgel in his hand. He led his troops out of the cave and drew them up in battle array. The Mighty Miracle God gazed wide-eyed at the excellent Monkey King:

On his body was gleaming golden armour,
On his head a dazzling golden helmet,
In his hand a gold-banded club,
On his feet a pair of cloud-walking shoes to match.
His devil eyes shone like stars,
His ears were long and hard.
His sturdy frame could be transformed at will,
His voice rang clearly as a bell.
The sharp-mouthed Horse Protector with protruding teeth,
Wanted to become a Sage Equaling Heaven.

【赏析重点】

（1）分析"戴上紫金冠，贯上黄金甲，登上步云鞋，手执如意金箍棒"中的动词翻译方法。

（2）分析"身穿金甲亮堂堂，头戴金冠光映映"的语言特点和翻译方法。

【原典 2　猪八戒】

卷上莲蓬吊搭嘴，耳如蒲扇显金睛。獠牙锋利如钢挫，长嘴张开似火盆。金盔紧系腮边带，勒甲丝绦蟒退鳞。手执钉把龙探爪，腰挎弯弓月十轮。纠纠威风欺太岁，昂昂志气压天神。

（第 8 回）

【詹纳尔英译】

His entrails hung from his mouth, rolled up and knotted;
His ears were like rush fans, his eyes shone gold.
His teeth were sharp as steel files,
And when he opened his mouth it was like a brazier.

His golden helmet was tied firmly round his cheeks;
His armour, bound with a silken sash, was a python's sloughed-off skin.
In his hands he held a nailed rake like a dragon's claw,
At his waist hung a curved bow the shape of a half-moon
His martial might overawed the Year Planet;
His overweening spirit threatened the heavenly gods.

【赏析重点】

（1）分析“獠牙锋利如钢挫，长嘴张开似火盆”的修辞特点和翻译方法。

（2）分析“手执钉把龙探爪，腰挎弯弓月十轮”的译文结构转换。

【原典 3 沙僧】

一头红焰发蓬松，两只圆睛亮似灯。不黑不青蓝靛脸，如雷如鼓老龙声。身披一领鹅黄氅，腰束双攒露白藤。项下骷髅悬九个，手持宝杖甚峥嵘。

（第 22 回）

【詹纳尔英译】

A head of matted hair, as red as fire,
A pair of staring eyes, gleaming like lamps.
An indigo face, neither black nor green,
A dragon's voice like drums or thunder.
On his body a cloak of yellow goose-down,
Tied at the waist with white creeper.
Nine skulls hung around his neck,
And in his hands was an enormous staff.

【赏析重点】

分析“身披一领鹅黄氅，腰束双攒露白藤”的译文结构转换。

【原典 4 观音菩萨】

当有观音菩萨，行近莲台，礼佛三匝，道：“弟子不才，愿上东土寻一个取经人来也。”诸众抬头观看，那菩萨：理圆四德，智满金身。缨络垂珠翠，香环结宝明，乌云巧叠盘龙髻，绣带轻飘彩凤翎。碧玉纽，素罗袍，祥光笼罩；锦城裙，金落索，瑞气遮迎。眉如小月，眼似双星。五面天生喜，朱唇一点红。净瓶甘露年年盛，斜插垂杨岁岁青。解八难，度群生，大慈悯：故镇大山，居南海，救苦寻声，万称万应，千圣千灵。兰心欣紫竹，意性爱香藤。他是落伽山上慈悲主，潮音洞里活观音。

（第 8 回）

【詹纳尔英译】

The Bodhisattva Guanyin went up to the lotus throne, and after going round the Buddha three times by way of salutation she said, "Your untalented disciple wishes to go to the East to find a man to come and fetch the scriptures." All present raised their heads to look at the Bodhisattva:

Her understanding filling out the four virtues,
Wisdom filling her golden body.
From her necklace hang pearls and jade,
Her bracelet is made of jewels.
Her hair is black clouds skillfully piled like coiling dragons;
Her embroidered girdle lightly sways, a phoenix wing.
A jade face full of heavenly happiness,
Scarlet lips making a touch of red.
Her pure bottle of sweet dew is ever full,
The willow twigs in it are always green.
She delivers from the eight disasters,
Saves all living beings,
Great is her compassion.
She stays on Mount Tai,
Lives in the Southern Sea,
Seagreen jade buttons,
A gown of white silk gauze,
Bathed with sacred light;
Brocade skirts,
A girdle of gold,
Shielded by propitious vapours.
Eyebrows like crescent moons,
Eyes like a pair of stars.
Rescues the suffering when she bears their cries,
Never failing to answer every call,
Infinitely divine and miraculous.

Her orchid heart admires the purple bamboo;
Her orchid nature loves the fragrant creeper.
She is the merciful ruler of Potaraka Island,
The living Guanyin of the Tide Cave.

【赏析重点】

（1）分析“乌云巧叠盘龙髻，绣带轻飘彩凤翎”的中文特点和翻译方法。

（2）分析“净瓶甘露年年盛，斜插垂杨岁岁青”的翻译方法。

（二）场景描写

【原典1 水帘洞】

你看他瞑目蹲身，将身一纵，径跳入瀑布泉中，忽睁睛抬头观看，那里边却无水无波，明明朗朗的一架桥梁。他住了身，定了神，仔细再看，原来是座铁板桥。桥下之水，冲贯于石窍之间，倒挂流出去，遮闭了桥门。却又欠身上桥头，再走再看，却似有人家住处一般，真个好所在。但见那：

翠藓堆蓝，白云浮玉，光摇片片烟霞。虚窗静室，滑凳板生花。乳窟龙珠倚挂，萦回满地奇葩。锅灶傍崖存火迹，樽罍靠案见肴渣。石座石床真可爱，石盆石碗更堪夸。又见那一竿两竿修竹，三点五点梅花。几树青松常带雨，浑然相个人家。

（第1回）

【詹纳尔英译】

Watch him as he shuts his eyes, crouches, and springs, leaping straight into the waterfall. When he opened his eyes and raised his head to look round, he saw neither water nor waves. A bridge stood in front of him, as large as life. He stopped, calmed himself, took a closer look, and saw that the bridge was made of iron. The water that rushed under it poured out through a fissure in the rocks, screening the gateway to the bridge. He started walking towards the bridge, and as he looked he made out what seemed to be a house. It was a really good place. He saw:

Emerald moss piled up in heaps of blue,
White clouds like drifting jade,
While the light flickered among wisps of coloured mist.
A quiet house with peaceful windows,
Flowers growing on the smooth bench;
Dragon pearls hanging in niches,
Exotic blooms all around.

Traces of fire beside the stove,
Scraps of food in the vessels by the table.
Adorable stone chairs and beds,
Even better stone plates and bowls.
One or two tall bamboos,
Three or four sprigs of plum blossom,
A few pines that always attract rain,
All just like a real home.

【赏析重点】

（1）分析“桥下之水，冲贯于石窍之间，倒挂流出去，遮闭了桥门”的译文结构转换。

（2）分析“虚窗静室，滑凳板生花”的译文结构转换。

（3）分析“一竿两竿修竹，三点五点梅花”的中文特点和翻译方法。

【原典 2　三星洞】

烟霞散彩，日月摇光。千株老柏，万节修篁。千株老柏，带雨半空青冉冉；万节修篁，含烟一壑色苍苍。门外奇花布锦，桥边瑶草喷香。石崖突兀青苔润，悬壁高张翠藓长。时闻仙鹤唳，每见凤凰翔。仙鹤唳时，声振九皋霄汉远；凤凰翔起，翎毛五色彩云光。玄猿白鹿随隐见，金狮玉象任行藏。细观灵福地，真个赛天堂！又见那洞门紧闭，静悄悄杳无人迹。忽回头，见崖头立一石牌，约有三丈余高、八尺余阔，上有一行十个大字，乃是“灵台方寸山，斜月三星洞”。

（第 2 回）

【詹纳尔英译】

Misty clouds scattered colours,
Sun and moon shimmered bright.
A thousand ancient cypresses,
Ten thousand lofty bamboos.
A thousand ancient cypresses,
A soft green drawing the rain from the sky.
Ten thousand lofty bamboos,
And a misty valley is azure blue.
Outside the gate rare flowers spread brocade;
Beside the bridge wafts the scent of jade flowers.

Rocky crags jut, glossy with green moss;
On overhanging cliffs blue lichen grows.
Sometimes the call of the crane is heard
And often you see the phoenix soar.
The call of the crane
Echoes beyond the Ninth Heaven and the Milky Way.
When the phoenix soars,
The brilliance of its wings colours the clouds.
Black apes and white deer can be just made out;
Golden lions and jade elephants prefer to keep hidden.
If you look closely at this happy land,
You will see that it rivals paradise.

He saw that the doors of the cave were shut fast, and that everything was still, with no signs of any people. He turned round and noticed that there was a stone tablet about thirty feet high and eight feet wide at the top of the cliff. On it was carved in enormous letters: SPIRIT-TOWER HEART MOUNTAIN, CAVE OF THE SETTING MOON AND THE THREE STARS.

【赏析重点】

（1）对比“青冉冉”“色苍苍”的颜色翻译方法。

（2）分析“声振九皋霄汉远”“翎毛五色彩云光”中的文化要素翻译方法。

【原典 3　凌霄宝殿】

初登上界，乍入天堂。金光万道滚红霓，瑞气千条喷紫雾。只见那南天门，碧沉沉，琉璃造就；明幌幌，宝玉妆成。两边摆数十员镇天元帅，一员员顶梁靠柱，持铣拥旄；四下列十数个金甲神人，一个个执戟悬鞭，持刀仗剑。外厢犹可，入内惊人：里壁厢有几根大柱，柱上缠绕着金鳞耀日赤须龙；又有几座长桥，桥上盘旋着彩羽凌空丹顶凤。

（第 4 回）

【詹纳尔英译】

First ascent to the upper world,
Sudden entry into paradise.
Ten thousand beams of golden light shone with a reddish glow;
A thousand strands of propitious vapour puffed out purple mist.

See the Southern Gate of Heaven,
Deep green,
Crystalline,
Shimmering bright,
Studded with jewels.
On either side stood scores of heavenly marshals,
Tall as the roofbeams, next to the pillars,
Holding metal-tipped bows and banners.
All around stood gods in golden armour,
Brandishing their clubs and halberds,
Wielding their cutlasses and swords.
The outside was remarkable enough,
But the inside astonished him.
Here were several mighty pillars,
Round which coiled tawny-bearded dragons, their gold scales gleaming in the sun.
There were long bridges,
Where strutted phoenixes, brilliant of plumage and with bright red crests.

【赏析重点】

（1）分析"金光万道滚红霓，瑞气千条喷紫雾"的中文特点和翻译方法。

（2）分析"碧沉沉，琉璃造就；明幌幌，宝玉妆成"的修辞特点和翻译方法。

（3）分析"金鳞耀日赤须龙""彩羽凌空丹顶凤"的翻译方法。

（三）动作描写

【原典 1　哪吒勇战齐天大圣】

哪吒道："这妖猴能有多大神通，就敢称此名号！不要怕！吃吾一剑！"悟空道："我只站下不动，任你砍几剑罢。"那哪吒奋怒，大喝一声，叫"变！"即变做三头六臂，恶狠狠，手持着六般兵器，乃是斩妖剑、砍妖刀、缚妖索、降妖杵、绣球儿、火轮儿，丫丫叉叉，扑面打来。悟空见了，心惊道："这小哥倒也会弄些手段！莫无礼，看我神通！"好大圣，喝声"变"也变做三头六臂；把金箍棒幌一幌，也变作三条；六只手拿着三条棒架住。这场斗，真是个地动山摇，好杀也。

（第 4 回）

【詹纳尔英译】

"You wicked monkey! How dare you give yourself a title like that, whatever your magic powers may be! Don't worry, all you're getting is my sword." "Give me a few swipes, then," replied Sun Wukong, "I won't move."

"Change," yelled Nezha in a passion, and at once he had three heads and six arms, which made him look most ferocious. In his hands he held six weapons, a demon-beheading sword, a demon-hacking cutlass, a demon-binding rope, a demon-quelling pestle, an embroidered ball, and a fire-wheel and wielding all these he rushed straight at Sun Wukong.

At the sight of him Sun Wukong exclaimed with astonishment, "Well, my boy, you certainly know a trick or two. But just behave yourself and watch what I can do." Our dear Great Sage shouted "Change," and he too had three heads and six arms. He shook his gold-banded cudgel, and it turned into three cudgels, which he gripped with his six hands to ward off Nezha's blows. It was a great fight, and it made the earth shake and the mountains tremble.

【赏析重点】

（1）分析“吃吾一剑”的翻译方法。

（2）分析“丫丫叉叉，扑面打来”的中文特点和翻译方法。

【原典2 悟空智斗牛魔王】

这大圣收了金箍棒，捻诀念咒，摇身一变，变作一个海东青，飕的一翅，钻在云眼里，倒飞下来，落在天鹅身上，抱住颈项眼。那牛王也知是孙行者变化，急忙抖抖翅，变作一只黄鹰，返来海东青。行者又变作一个乌凤，专一赶黄鹰。牛王识得，又变作一只白鹤，长唳一声，向南飞去。行者立定，抖抖翎毛，又变作一只丹凤，高鸣一声。那白鹤见凤是鸟王，诸禽不敢妄动，刷的一翅，淬下山崖，将身一变，变作一只香獐，乜乜（niè niè）些些，在崖前吃草。行者认得，也就落下翅来，变作一只饿虎，剪尾跑蹄，要来赶獐作食。

（第 61 回）

【詹纳尔英译】

Putting away his gold-banded cudgel and saying the words of a spell while making the necessary hand movements, Monkey shook himself and turned into a vulture who soared up into the clouds with his wings beating noisily, then swooped down on the swan, seizing its neck and gouging at its eyes. Realizing that this was Sun Wukong transformed the Bull Demon King braced himself and turned into a golden eagle who gouged, back at the vulture. Then Monkey turned into a black phoenix to chase the eagle, only to be recognized by the Bull King, who turned into a white crane and flew off South with a loud call. Monkey stopped, braced his feathers, and turned into a red phoenix, who called loudly too. At the sight of the phoenix, the king of all the birds whom no bird dared treat with disrespect, the white crane swooped down beside the precipice with a beat of his wings, shook himself, and turned into a river-deer grazing in a timid, stupid way at the foot of the cliff. Monkey spotted him, came swooping down too, and turned into a hungry tiger that came running after the river-deer, swishing his tail hungrily.

【赏析重点】

分析“飕的一翅，钻在云眼里”“长唳一声，向南飞去”“刷的一翅，淬下山崖”的中文特点，对比翻译方法。

（四）历史文化

【原典 1　孙悟空起名】

祖师笑道：“你身躯虽是鄙陋，却像个食松果的猢狲。我与你就身上取个姓氏，意思教你姓‘猢’。猢字去了个兽傍，乃是古月。古者，老也；月者，阴也。老阴不能化育，教你姓‘狲’倒好。狲字去了兽傍，乃是个子系。子者，儿男也；系者，婴细也。正合婴儿之本论。教你姓‘孙’罢。”猴王听说，满心欢喜，朝上叩头道：“好！好！好！今日方知姓也。万望师父慈悲！既然有姓，再乞赐个名字，却好呼唤。”祖师道：“我门中有十二个字，分派起名到你乃第十辈之小徒矣。”猴王道：“那十二个字？”祖师道：“乃广、大、智、慧、真、如、性、海、颖、悟、圆、觉十二字。排到你，正当‘悟’字。与你起个法名叫做‘孙悟空’好么？”猴王笑道：“好！好！好！自今就叫做孙悟空也！”

（第 1 回）

【詹纳尔英译】

The Patriarch smiled and said, “Though you have rather a base sort of body, you look like one of the rhesus monkeys that eat pine seeds, and I ought to give you a surname that fits your appearance and call you Hu (‘Macaque’). The elements that make up the character Hu are ‘animal’, ‘old’ and ‘moon’. What is old is ancient, and the moon embodies the Negative principle, and what is ancient and Negative cannot be transformed. But I think I would do much better to call you Sun (‘Monkey’). Apart from the ‘animal’ element, the character Sun has one part implying male and one part suggesting a baby, which fits in with my basic theories about children. Your surname will be Sun."

When the Monkey King heard this he kowtowed with delight and said, "Great! Great! Now I have a surname. I am eternally grateful to you for your mercy and compassion, master. I beg you to give me a personal name to go with my new surname, then it will be much easier to address me."

"There are twelve words within my sect," said the Patriarch, "which I give as names. You belong to the tenth generation of my disciples." "What are these twelve words?" asked the Monkey King.

"Broad, great, wisdom, intelligence, true, likeness, nature, sea, bright, awakened, complete and enlightenment. If we work out the generations of disciples, then you should have a name with Wu ('Awakened') in it. So we can give you the Dharma-name Sun Wukong, which means 'Monkey Awakened to Emptiness'. Will that do?"

"Marvellous, marvellous," said the smiling Monkey King. "From now on my name will be Sun Wukong."

【赏析重点】

（1）分析"猢字去了个兽傍，乃是古月"的翻译方法。

（2）学习"广、大、智、慧、真、如、性、海、颖、悟、圆、觉"的翻译方法。

【原典2 八卦炉】

那老君到兜率宫，将大圣解去绳索，放了穿琵琶骨之器，推入八卦炉中，命看炉的道人，架火的童子，将火煽起煅炼。原来那炉是乾、坎、艮、震、巽、离、坤、兑八卦。他即将身钻在"巽宫"位下。巽乃风也，有风则无火。只是风搅得烟来，把一双眼熏红了，弄做个老害眼病，故唤作"火眼金睛"。

（第7回）

【詹纳尔英译】

When he reached the Tushita Palace, Lord Lao Zi had the Great Sage untied, took the hook from his collar-bone, pushed him into the Eight Trigrams Furnace, and ordered the priests in charge of it and the fire-boys to fan the fire up to refine him. Now this furnace was made up of the Eight Trigrams-Qian, Kan, Gen, Zhen, Sun, Li, Kun, and Dui—so he squeezed himself into the "Palace of Sun," as Sun was the wind, and where there was wind there could be no fire. All that happened was that the wind stirred up the smoke, which made both his eyes red and left him somewhat blind with the illness called "fire eyes with golden pupils."

【赏析重点】

学习文化概念“兜率宫”“八卦炉”“乾、坎、艮、震、巽、离、坤、兑八卦”“火眼金睛”的翻译方法。

【原典 3 八戒取名】

那怪从新礼拜三藏，愿随西去。又与行者拜了，以先进者为兄，遂称行者为师兄。三藏道：“既从吾善果，要做徒弟，我与你起个法名，早晚好呼唤。”他道：“师父，我是菩萨已与我摩顶受戒，起了法名，叫做猪悟能也。”三藏笑道：“好！好！你师兄叫做悟空，你叫做悟能，其实是我法门中的宗派。”悟能道：“师父，我受了菩萨戒行，断了五荤三厌，在我丈人家持斋把素，更不曾动荤。今日见了师父，我开了斋罢。”三藏道：“不可！不可！你既是不吃五荤三厌，我再与你起个别名，唤为八戒。”那呆子欢欢喜喜道：“谨遵师命。”因此又叫做猪八戒。

（第 19 回）

【詹纳尔英译】

The monster bowed to Sanzang once more and vowed to go to the West with him. Then he bowed to Monkey as his elder brother because he had joined first, addressing him as “elder brother” from then on. “If you wish to earn a good reward by going with me as my disciple, I’ll give you a Buddhist name to call you by.”

“Master,” he replied, “When the Bodhisattva laid her hands upon my head and told me to obey the prohibitions, she gave me a Buddhist name–Zhu Wuneng, Pig Awakened to Power.” “Wonderful, wonderful,” said Brother Monkey with a smile, “I’m called Wukong, Awakened to Emptiness, and you’re called Awakened to Power. That makes us members of the same sect in the Buddhist faith.” “Master,” said Pig, “I have been instructed by the Bodhisattva and I never eat the five stinking foods and the three forbidden meats–wild goose, dog, and snakehead. I’ve eaten vegetarian food in my father-in-law’s house and never touched the stinking foods; but now that I have met you, master, I’m freed from these restrictions.”

“You are not,” Sanzang replied. “You are not to eat the five stinking foods and the three forbidden meats, and I’m giving you another name: Eight Prohibitions, or Bajie.”

“I shall obey my master’s command,” the moron happily replied, and from then on he was known as Zhu Bajie, or Eight Prohibitions Pig.

【赏析重点】

学习文化概念“善果”“受戒”“法名”“五荤三厌”的翻译方法。

第四节　《红楼梦》

A Dream of Red Mansion

一、典籍简介

《红楼梦》描写了一个由盛而衰的贵族大家庭中的爱情婚姻悲剧。小说主人公贾宝玉是荣国府的嫡派子孙，他出身不凡，又聪明灵秀，是贾氏家庭寄予重望的继承人。但他却不愿意接受贵族家庭的生活方式和生活道路。他觉得贵族社会是那样的虚伪、丑恶和腐朽，而纯真美好的东西却存在于包括地位微贱的侍女在内的少女们身上。《红楼梦》是中国古代小说艺术的顶峰。它的艺术成就首先表现在它塑造了众多光彩夺目的人物形象。贾宝玉、林黛玉、薛宝钗，还有王熙凤、史湘云、探春、尤二姐、尤三姐、袭人、晴雯、鸳鸯等等，都是个性鲜明的，就像活动在我们身边的人物一样真切。这些性格内涵极其丰富的人物，在各自不同的地位上生活着；按照各自的生活哲学和思维方式，在贾氏家族内部的极为复杂的人际关系和利害冲突中行动着。不但行为方式和言谈口吻各具特点，就是他们的容貌、衣着和居室布置，也都各有不容混淆的个性特征。读者只要听到说话，或者看到居室陈设，就可以知道他是谁。刻画人物到达如此境界，不仅在中国文学，就是在世界文学中也是少见的。

A Dream of Red Mansion charts the course of prosperity and decline of an aristocratic family. It is a tragedy of love and marriage. The hero of the novel is Jia Baoyu, a direct descendant of the Jia family of the Rong Mansion. An intelligent boy of excellent breeding, he is the heir of the Jia family. However, he has no inclination for the aristocratic way of life, which he finds hypocritical, hateful and corrupt. To him, pure beauty is to be found in young girls, including low-born servant girls. *A Dream of red Mansion* is the peak of the art of the novel in ancient China. Its artistic achievement is displayed first of all in its dazzling array of characters. Jia Baoyu, Lin Daiyu, Xue Baochai, Wang Xifeng, Shi Xiangyun, Tanchun, Second Sister You, Third Sister You, Xiren, Qingwen, Yuanyang and the others all have their distinct personalities and are as true to life as if they were living amongst us. These richly complex characters with their different stations in life and divergent views and philosophies act out an intricate pattern of human relationships and conflicts within the Jia family mansion. Apart from their distinct ways of acting and speaking, and the peculiarities of their appearances, dress and living arrangements, these people all have clear character traits. The reader knows who is who just by their manner of speaking or the layouts of their rooms. Such character delineation is a rare accomplishment not only in Chinese literature but in the whole field of world literature.

《红楼梦》是一部百科全书式的长篇小说。它以一个贵族家庭为中心展开了一幅广阔的社会历史图景。社会的各个阶级和阶层都有真实而生动的表现。封建末世的各种社会矛盾，奴隶和主子的对抗性矛盾，家庭内部的嫡庶的矛盾和各种利害冲突，贵族经济和家庭后继无人的危机，封建主义与具有初步民主主义精神的叛逆倾向的矛盾，等等，都纽结着贯串在情节中。小说对贵族家庭的饮食起居各方面的生活细节，对园林建筑、车轿排场、服饰器用、岁时礼俗、饮食医药等，都有具体细致的描写，具有极其丰富的文化内涵。《红楼梦》文化内涵的博大精深在世界文学史上是罕见的。

A Dream of Red Mansion is an encyclopedic novel. Centered on an aristocratic family, it unrolls a panorama of social history. Every grade and station of Chinese society of that time are presented in a true-to-life fashion. In addition, all the social contradictions which emerged toward the end of the feudal period are threaded through the plot: for instance, the conflict between master and slave, that between the master of the house's legal wife and his concubines the economic crisis in a noble clan in the absence of an heir and that between feudalism and the newly sprouting spirit of democracy. The novel also provides a wealth of details concerning aristocratic households in those days, garden architecture, the equipage of carriages, clothing and ornaments, customs and etiquette, food and drink, medicines, etc. Indeed, the cultural reference content of *A Dream of Red Mansion* is of a kind rarely seen in the history of world literature.

二、作者简介

曹雪芹，清代小说家，清代著名满族文学家。内务府正白旗出身。名沾（音zhān），字梦阮，号雪芹，他出身于一个“百年望族”的大官僚地主家庭，后因家庭的衰败而饱尝了人生的辛酸。在人生的最后阶段，他以坚韧不拔的毅力，历经十年创作了《红楼梦》并专心致志地做着修订工作，死后遗留《红楼梦》前八十回稿子。另有《废艺斋集稿》。

Cao Xueqin, named Zhan, courtesy named Mengruan, with the pseudonym Xueqin, was of Man nationality. He was a famous novelist in the Qing dynasty. He was born to a notable family of landlords and bureaucrats, but later as a result of the declining of his family's fortunes, he suffered various hardships in life. During his later years, with unswerving persistence, he spent ten years writing *Hong Lou Meng* (*A Dream of Red Mansion*) and devoted himself to its editing and proofing. After his death, 80 chapters of the manuscripts were kept. In addition, he also wrote *Fei Yi Zhai Ji Gao* (*Introducing Handicrafts Skills in the Ancient Time*).

三、典籍英译赏析

（一）人物描写

【原典 1　贾宝玉】

黛玉心中正疑惑着："这个宝玉，不知是怎生个惫懒人物，懵懂顽童？"—倒不见那蠢物也罢了。心中想着，忽见丫鬟话未报完，已进来了一位年轻的公子：头上戴着束发嵌宝紫金冠，齐眉勒着二龙抢珠金抹额；穿一件二色金百蝶穿花大红箭袖，束着五彩丝攒花结长穗宫绦，外罩石青起花八团倭缎排穗褂；登着青缎粉底小朝靴。面若中秋之月，色如春晓之花，鬓若刀裁，眉如墨画，面如桃瓣，目若秋波。虽怒时而若笑，即瞋视而有情。项上金螭璎珞，又有一根五色丝绦，系着一块美玉。

（第三回）

【杨宪益英译】

Daiyu was wondering what sort of graceless scamp or little dunce Baoyu was and feeling reluctant to meet such a stupid creature when, even as the maid announced him, in he walked.

He had on a golden coronet studded with jewels and a golden chaplet in the form of two dragons fighting for a pearl. His red archer's jacket, embroidered with golden butterflies and flowers, was tied with a coloured tasselled palace sash. Over this he wore a turquoise fringed coat of Japanese satin with a raised pattern of flowers in eight bunches. His court boots were of black satin with white soles.

His face was as radiant as the mid-autumn moon, his complexion fresh as spring flowers at dawn. The hair above his temples was as sharply outlined as if cut with a knife. His eyebrows were as black as if painted with ink, his cheeks as red as peach-blossom, his eyes bright as autumn ripples. Even when angry he seemed to smile, and there was warmth in his glance even when he frowned.

【霍克斯英译】

'I wonder,' thought Dai-yu, 'just what sort of graceless creature this Bao-yu is going to be?'

The young gentleman who entered in answer to her unspoken question had a small jewel-encrusted gold coronet on the top of his head and a golden headband low down over his brow in the form of two dragons playing with a large pearl.

He was wearing a narrow-sleeved, full-skirted robe of dark red material with a pattern of flowers and butterflies in two shades of gold. It was confined at the waist with a court girdle of coloured silks braided at regular intervals into elaborate clusters of knotwork and terminating in long tassels.

Over the upper part of his robe he wore a jacket of slate-blue Japanese silk damask with a raised pattern of eight large medallions on the front and with tasselled borders.

On his feet he had half-length dress boots of black satin with thick white soles.

As to his person, he had:

a face like the moon of Mid-Autumn,
a complexion like flowers at dawn,
a hairline straight as a knife-cut,
eyebrows that might have been painted by an artist's brush,
a shapely nose, and eyes clear as limpid pools,
that even in anger seemed to smile,
and, as they glared, beamed tenderness the while.

Around his neck he wore a golden torque in the likeness of a dragon and a woven cord of coloured silks to which the famous jade was attached.

【赏析重点】

（1）对比分析“头上戴着束发嵌宝紫金冠，齐眉勒着二龙抢珠金抹额”译文的翻译方法。

（2）分析“二色金百蝶穿花大红箭袖”“五彩丝攒花结长穗宫绦”“石青起花八团倭缎排穗褂”的语义结构特点和翻译方法。

（3）分析“面若中秋之月，色如春晓之花，鬓若刀裁，眉如墨画，面如桃瓣，目若秋波”中的文化特色和翻译方法。

【原典 2 林黛玉】

两弯似蹙非蹙罥烟眉，一双似喜非喜含情目。态生两靥之愁，娇袭一身之病。泪光点点，娇喘微微。闲静似姣花照水，行动如弱柳扶风。心较比干多一窍，病如西子胜三分。

（第三回）

【杨宪益英译】

Her dusky arched eyebrows were knitted and yet not frowning; her speaking eyes held both merriment and sorrow; her very frailty had charm. Her eyes sparkled with tears; her breath was soft and faint. In repose she was like a lovely flower mirrored in the water; in motion, a pliant willow swaying in the wind. She looked more sensitive than Bi Gan, more delicate than Xi Shi.

【霍克斯英译】

Her mist-wreathed brows at first seemed to frown, yet were not frowning;
Her passionate eyes at first seemed to smile, yet were not merry.
Habit had given a melancholy cast to her tender face;
Nature had bestowed a sickly constitution on her delicate frame.
Often the eyes swam with glistening tears;
Often the breath came in gentle gasps.
In stillness she made one think of a graceful flower reflected in the water;
In motion she called to mind tender willow shoots caressed by the wind.
She had more chambers in her heart than the martyred Bi Gan;
And suffered a tithe more pain in it than the beautiful Xi Shi.

【赏析重点】

（1）分析“两弯似蹙非蹙罥烟眉，一双似喜非喜含情目”的语言特点和翻译方法。

（2）分析“泪光点点，娇喘微微”的修辞手法和翻译效果。

（3）对比分析“闲静似姣花照水，行动如弱柳扶风”译文的用词特点。

（4）分析“心较比干多一窍，病如西子胜三分”的文化要素和翻译特点。

【原典 3 王熙凤】

心下想时，只见一群媳妇丫鬟围拥着一个人从后房门进来。这个人打扮与众姑娘不同，彩绣辉煌，恍若神妃神子：头上戴着金丝八宝珠髻，绾着朝阳五凤挂珠钗；项上带着赤金盘螭璎珞圈；裙边系着豆绿宫绦，双衡比目玫瑰佩；身上穿着缕金百蝶穿花大红洋缎窄褙袄，外罩五彩刻丝石青银鼠褂；下着翡翠撒花洋绉裙。一双丹凤三角眼，两弯柳叶吊梢眉，身量苗条，体格风骚，粉面含春威不露，丹唇未启笑先闻。

（第三回）

【杨宪益英译】

While she was still wondering, through the back door trooped some matrons and maids surrounding a young woman. Unlike the girls, she was richly dressed and resplendent as a fairy.

Her gold-filigree tiara was set with jewels and pearls. Her hair-clasps in the form of five phoenixes facing the sun, had pendants of pearls. Her necklet, of red gold, was in the form of a coiled dragon studded with gems. She had double red jade pendants with pea-green tassels attached to her skirt.

Her close-fitting red satin jacket was embroidered with gold butterflies and flowers. Her turquoise cape, lined with white squirrel, was inset with designs in coloured silk. Her skirt of kingfisher-blue crepe was patterned with flowers.

She had the almond-shaped eyes of a phoenix, slanting eyebrows long and drooping as willow leaves. Her figure was slender and her manner vivacious. The springtime charm of her powdered face gave no hint of her latent formidability. And before her crimson lips parted, her laughter rang out.

【霍克斯英译】

Even as she wondered, a beautiful young woman entered from the room behind the one they were sitting in, surrounded by a bevy of serving women and maids. She was dressed quite differently from the others present, gleaming like some fairy princess with sparkling jewels and gay embroideries.

Her chignon was enclosed in a circlet of gold filigree and clustered pearls. It was fastened with a pin embellished with a flying phoenixes, from whose beaks pearls were suspended on tiny chains.

Her necklet was of red gold in the form of a coiling dragon. Her dress had a fitted bodice and was made of dark red silk damask with a pattern of flowers and butterflies in raised gold thread.

Her jacket was lined with ermine. It was of a slate-blue stuff with woven insets in coloured silks.

Her under-skirt was of a turquoise-coloured imported silk crêpe embroidered with flowers.

She had, moreover,
eyes like a painted phoenix,
eyebrows like willow-eaves,
a slender form,
seductive grace;
the ever-smiling summer face
of hidden thunders showed no trace;
the ever-bubbling laughter started
almost before the lips were parted.

【赏析重点】

（1）分析“金丝八宝珠髻”“朝阳五凤挂珠钗”“赤金盘螭璎珞圈”“五彩刻丝石青银鼠褂”“翡翠撒花洋绉裙”的语言特点和翻译方法。

（2）对比分析“一双丹凤三角眼，两弯柳叶吊梢眉”译文的翻译方法。

（二）唱词

【原典1　枉凝眉】

一个是阆苑仙葩，一个是美玉无瑕。若说没奇缘，今生偏又遇着他，若说有奇缘，如何心事终虚化？一个枉自嗟呀，一个空劳牵挂。一个是水中月，一个是镜中花。想眼中能有多少泪珠儿，怎经得秋流到冬尽，春流到夏！

【杨宪益英译】

Vain Longing

One is an immortal flower of fairyland,
The other fair flawless jade,
And were it not predestined
Why should they meet again in this existence?
Yet, if predestined,
Why does their love come to nothing?
One sighs to no purpose,
The other yearns in vain;
One is the moon reflected in the water,
The other but a flower in the mirror.

How many tears can well from her eyes?
Can they flow on from autumn till winter,
From spring till summer?

【霍克斯英译】

Hope Betrayed

One was a flower from paradise,
One a pure jade without spot or stain.
If each for the other one was not intended,
Then why in this life did they meet again?
And yet if fate bad meant them for each other,
Why was their earthly meeting all in vain?
In vain were all her sighs and tears,
In vain were all his anxious fears:
All, insubstantial, doomed to pass,
As moonlight mirrored in the water
Or flowers reflected in a glass.
Row many tears from those poor eyes could flow,
Which every season rained upon her woe?

【赏析重点】

（1）对比曲名“枉凝眉”译文的翻译思路。

（2）对比“阆苑仙葩”“美玉无瑕”译文的用词特点。

（3）分析“秋流到冬尽，春流到夏”的翻译方法。

【原典 2　飞鸟各投林】

为官的，家业凋零；富贵的，金银散尽；有恩的，死里逃生；无情的，分明报应。欠命的，命已还；欠泪的，泪已尽。冤冤相报实非轻，分离聚合皆前定。欲知命短问前生，老来富贵也真侥幸。看破的，遁入空门；痴迷的，枉送了性命。好一似食尽鸟投林，落了片白茫茫大地真干净！

【杨宪益英译】

The Birds Scatter To the Wood

An official household declines,
Rich nobles' wealth is spent.
She who did good escapes the jaws of death,

The heartless meet with certain retribution.
Those who took a life have paid with their own lives,
The tears one owed have all been requited in kind.
Not light the retribution for sins against others;
All are predestined, partings and reunions.
Seek the cause of untimely death in a part existence,
Lucky she who enjoys rank and riches in old age;
Those who see through the world escape from the world,
While foolish lovers forfeit their lives for nothing.
When the food is gone the birds return to the wood;
All that's left is emptiness and a great void.

【霍克斯英译】

The Birds into the Wood Have Flown

The office jack's career is blighted,
The rich man's fortune now all vanished,
The kind with life have been requited,
The cruel exemplarily punished;
The one who owed a life is dead,
The tears one owed have all been shed.
Wrongs suffered have the wrongs done expiated;
The couplings and the sunderings were fated.
Untimely death sin in some past life shows,
But only luck a blest old age bestows.
The disillusioned to their convents fly,
The still deluded miserably die.
Like birds who, having fed, to the woods repair,
They leave the landscape desolate and bare.

【赏析重点】

（1）对比分析“为官的”“富贵的”“有恩的”“无情的”“欠命的”“欠泪的”“看破的”“痴迷的”译文用词特点。

（2）分析“冤冤相报”“分离聚合”的翻译方法。

（3）对比分析“前生”“空门”译文的文化特点。

（三）对联

【原典 1】

孽海情天

厚地高天，堪叹古今情不尽，

痴男怨女，可怜风月债难偿。

【杨宪益英译】

Sea of Grief and Heaven of Love

Firm as earth and lofty as heaven, passion from
time immemorial knows no end;
Pity silly lads and plaintive maids hard put to
it to requite debts of breeze and moonlight.

【霍克斯英译】

Seas of Pain and Skies of Passion

Ancient earth and sky
Marvel that love's passion should outlast all time.
Star-crossed men and maids
Groan that love's debts should be so hard to pay.

【赏析重点】

（1）对比分析横批“孽海情天”译文的语义特点。

（2）对比分析“厚地高天”“痴男怨女”的翻译特点。

【原典 2】

太虚幻境

假作真时真亦假，

无为有处有还无。

【杨宪益英译】

Illusory Land of Great Void

When false is taken for true, true becomes false;
If non-being turns into being, being becomes non-being.

【霍克斯英译】

The Land of Illusion

Truth becomes fiction when the fiction's true;
Real becomes not-real where the unreal's real.

【赏析重点】

对比分析“假”“真”“无”“有”的翻译用词特点。

拓展训练 | Extension Training

1. 课后思考

（1）请用英文概述中国古典小说发展特点。

（2）对比总结四大名著中外译者的翻译策略。

2. 文化外宣汉英翻译

（1）中国古典小说经过了不同的发展阶段，有着鲜明的时代特点：先秦两汉时期的神话传说、史传文学，以及诸子散文中的寓言故事等，是中国古代小说的源头；魏晋南北朝时期出现的文人笔记小说，是中国古代小说的雏形；唐代传奇标志着古典小说的正式形成；宋、元出现的话本小说，为小说的成熟奠定了坚实的基础；明清小说标志着中国古典小说发展的高峰，出现了《三国演义》《水浒传》《西游记》《红楼梦》四大古典名著。“五四”新文化运动之后，现代白话小说创作大量涌现，传播着现代的科学与民主精神。

（2）《红楼梦》详细地记录了都城比邻的两家大院的大家庭生活。在小说的开头，两院都是都城最负盛名的家族。最初极其富裕，有很大的社会影响力。家有女子成为皇妃，最终两家失宠于皇帝，其豪宅被突击搜查和没收。这部小说围绕 30 多个主要人物和 400 多个次要人物，描绘了这一大家庭从显赫到败落的过程。

第四篇 育人处世篇

Early Childhood Education

第十一章　蒙学经典英译

Translation of Children's Classics

一、学习目标

（1）用英文介绍中国古代蒙学教育理念。

（2）掌握中国蒙学教育相关概念汉英翻译。

（3）鉴赏蒙学典籍汉英翻译方法。

二、文化背景

广义上讲，“蒙学”是对我国传统幼儿启蒙教育的统称，包括在儿童智慧开启之际施以的文化知识和伦理道德教育；狭义上讲，专指蒙馆，即“封建社会对儿童进行启蒙教育的学校，教育内容主要是识字、写字和伦理道德教育”。

In a broad sense, “Meng Xue”, or “Teaching for the Ignorant” is a general term for China's traditional elementary education, including cultural knowledge and ethical education at early childhood. In a narrow sense, it specifically refers to “mengguan”, that is, “a school in feudal society that carries out early childhood education of literacy, writing and ethics”.

中国传统蒙学教材在周秦汉魏时期以识字教育为主，在隋唐五代时期注重伦理道德教育，宋元明清时期发展为识字读本、韵语读本、经书读本三轨共存，形成了自身所特有的系列蒙学教材，简称为蒙学“三百千千弟子规”（《三字经》《百家姓》《千字文》《千家诗》《弟子规》）。一方面，这些传统蒙学教材是专为学童编写或选编的启蒙教科书，它通过识字训诂、计算技巧、天文地理、常识典故“教之以事”的方式，让孩童了解礼、乐、射、御、书、数等传统六艺常识，为后面的听说读写打下基础。另一方面，在进行知识教育的同时，这些教材更强调“三纲五常”“孝悌人伦”等封建伦理观念与礼教规范，尤为重视个体德性修养的养成。如宋元明清时期出现的综合性经典蒙学教材《弟子规》《小儿语》等，注重文采斐然的形式表达，具备丰富齐备的知识体系，同时还特别重视教育孩子重义轻利、谦恭有礼等伦理道德观念，告诉初涉世事的孩童如何为人处世、修身慎独。

During the period of Zhou, Qin, Han and Wei dynasties, traditional elementary textbooks focused on literacy education. In the Sui, Tang and Five dynasties, ethical and moral education became the theme of childhood education. In the Song, Yuan, Ming and Qing dynasties, the children's textbooks mainly included three types of literacy books, rhyme books and Confucius classics, such as *San Zi Jing* (*Three-Character Canon*), *Bai Jia Xing* (*The Hundred Family Surnames*), *Qian Zi Wen* (*Thousand-Character Text*), *Qian Jia Shi* (*Poems of One Thousand Writers*), *Di Zi Gui* (*Standards for being a Good Student and Child*), etc. On the one hand, these elementary textbooks especially written for children were used to teach the Six Arts (rites, music, archery, chariot racing, calligraphy and mathematics) and lay a foundation for later listening, speaking, reading and writing. On the other hand, except for knowledge education, these textbook laid more emphasis on feudal ethical concepts and ethical norms such as "Three Fundamental Bonds and Five Constant Virtues" and "filial piety", especially on the cultivation of individual virtue. For example, the classical textbooks of *Di Zi Gui* and *Children's Language* prevailed in the Song, Yuan, Ming and Qing dynasties were written with rhythmic language and had a complete knowledge system. At the same time, another important task was to teach children the ethical and moral conducts of valuing righteousness over profit, being modest and courteous, and how to behave properly in the public and cultivate self-discipline.

小小的蒙学教材蕴含了十分丰富的教育信息，具备多种教育功能，如培养儿童优秀的道德品质、广博的文化知识、扎实的诗文功底。其使用时间之长、范围之广，空前绝后，在中华文明的传承传播过程中建立了重要的历史功勋。同时，大量蒙学典籍也被译介到朝鲜半岛、日本、泰国、越南、马来西亚、印度尼西亚等国家，对周边国家的语言文化产生了深远影响，逐渐形成了"汉字文化圈"。

The traditional elementary education textbooks contain very rich educational information and have a variety of educational functions, such as cultivating children's excellent moral quality, extensive cultural knowledge and fine poetry skills. Most of them were ever used for a long time in China's history, playing an important role in the inheritance and dissemination of Chinese civilization. Meanwhile, a large number of elementary textbooks have also been translated and introduced to the Korean Peninsula, Japan, Thailand, Vietnam, Malaysia, Indonesia and other countries, which has had a far-reaching impact on the language and culture of surrounding countries and contributed to the formation of "Chinese Sphere".

三、文化关键词

蒙学　traditional elementary education
三纲五常　Three Fundamental Bonds and Five Constant Virtues
《三字经》 *San Zi Jing* (*Three-Character Canon*)
《百家姓》 *Bai Jia Xing* (*The Hundred Family Surnames*)
《千字文》 *Qian Zi Wen* (*Thousand-Character Text*)
《千家诗》 *Qian Jia Shi* (*Poems of One Thousand Writers*)
《弟子规》 *Di Zi Gui* (*Standards for being a Good Student and Child*)

第一节　《三字经》

Three-Character Canon

一、典籍简介

《三字经》堪称是在中国广为流传、影响深远的蒙学著作，其作者一般认为是南宋硕儒王应麟（1223—1296）。但实际上早在王应麟之前，《三字经》的雏形就已出现，如宋人项安世曾道："古人教童子多用韵语，如……《三字训》之类。"（《项氏家说》）项安世早生于王应麟一百多年，故《三字训》可看作是《三字经》的前身。不管怎样，鉴于早期的《三字经》叙述历代兴灭仅至宋代，故可断定《三字经》的最早成稿年代应在宋元时期。因此，说《三字经》的作者为宋人王应麟料无大谬。《三字经》问世之后即风靡华夏，成为宋代以后中国广为采用的蒙学读本，可以说，时至今日，未读过《三字经》的汉家蒙童恐怕寥寥无几。《三字经》之所以一经问世便流传不衰，其要有二：一是具有朗朗上口的韵律美感；二是具有言简意赅的教化功用。

The *Three-Character Canon* can be called a most popular and influential enlightening work in China. The author is generally considered to be Wang Yinglin (1223–1296), a learned scholar in the South Song dynasty. As a matter of fact, however, the embryonic form of the *Three-Character Canon* had emerged before Wang Yinglin published it. For instance, Xiang Anshi, a historical figure of the Song dynasty, once said, "The ancient people tended to enlighten their children with rhymed words, such as the *Three-Character Admonition*, etc." (Family Precept of Xiang). Xiang Anshi lived more than a hundred years earlier than Wang Yinglin; the *Three-Character Admonition*, therefore, can be regarded as the predecessor of the *Three-Character Canon*. Anyhow, seeing that the historical account ends with the Song dynasty in its early editions, we know for sure that the earliest edition of the *Three-Character Canon* must have been published during the period between the Song and the Yuan dynasties. Thus, it is plausible to determine that the author of the *Three-Character Canon* was Wang Yingli. The *Three-Character Canon* has become popular all over China as the widely adopted textbook for children immediately following the period of the Song dynasty. So far, so to speak, few Chinese children fail to read the *Three-Character Canon*. The reason why the *Three-Character Canon* has exerted such a lasting influence as soon as it came into being lies in its two features, namely its rhyming beauty, which makes it quite readable, and its instructiveness, which is conveyed in concise wording.

二、典籍英译赏析

【原典 1】

人之初，性本善。性相近，习相远。

【英译】

At the beginning of life.
Man is good in nature.
Human nature is alike.
Habits make them different.

【赏析重点】

对比分析“性相近”“习相远”翻译的句法逻辑差异。

【原典 2】

苟不教，性乃迁。教之道，贵以专。

【英译】

For lack of education,
The nature is in alteration;
And the nurture of the young,
Better be maintained for long.

【赏析重点】

分析“教之道”的翻译方法。

【原典 3】

昔孟母，择邻处。子不学，断机杼。

【英译】

Once Mencius's mother
Chose the best neighborhood for her son;
When her son played truant,
She cut the threads on the loom.

【赏析重点】

学习“断机杼”的文化翻译方法。

【原典 4】

窦燕山，有义方。教五子，名俱扬。

【英译】

Another case is Dou Yanshan*,
Who was wise in family education.
He raised his five sons,
And all of them were blessed with fame.

*Dou Yanshan, a famous historical figure in the period of the Five Dynasties. His real name was Dou Yujun. Since he lived at the foot of Yanshan Mountain, he was also called Dou Yanshan. He had five sons, whom he raised in such a wise way that all of them became high government officials. This is the well-known story of "Five Sons, All Ascend".

【赏析重点】

学习“窦燕山”的文化翻译方法。

【原典 5】

养不教，父之过。教不严，师之惰。

【英译】

Rear children without instructing them,
And the father should be blamed;
Teach in a slack and lazy way,
And the teacher should be criticized.

【赏析重点】

（1）对比分析“养不教”“教不严”的否定句式翻译方法。

（2）分析“父之过”“师之惰”的翻译方法。

【原典 6】

子不学，非所宜。幼不学，老何为。

【英译】

If a pupil plays truant,
It proves to be improper.
If a child fails to learn,
What could he be when getting old?

【赏析重点】

对比分析“子不学”“幼不学”的否定句式翻译方法。

【原典 7】

玉不琢，不成器。人不学，不知义。

【英译】

Without being carved and polished,
A jade can't be a work of art.
If one does not learn,
He'll not know human virtues.

【赏析重点】

分析译文的句法结构转换。

【原典 8】

为人子，方少时。亲师友，习礼仪。

【英译】

When one is young,
He should make the best of his time,
Associating with the good and the wise,
And learning to stand on ceremony.

【赏析重点】

分析“方少时”的语义特点和翻译方法。

【原典 9】

香九龄，能温席。孝于亲，所当执。

【英译】

When Huang Xiang* was nine years old,
He could warm the mat for his father.
Whoever has love for their parents
Should be as kind as such.

*Huang Xiang, a historical figure during the period of East Han. His mother died when he was young. He loved his father so much that during the hot summers he fanned his father to keep him cool and during the cold winter he kept him warm:When he grew up, learned and noble, he became a minister in the government.

【赏析重点】

分析“香九龄，能温席”的文化翻译方法。

第二节 《增广贤文》

Social Wisdom

一、典籍简介

《增广贤文》简称《增广》，它辑自何人，始于何时，至今仍无法找到任何记载。相传是由明朝中期的一位儒生编纂，后经明末清初的士人增补而成。自清朝中后期以来，即风靡全国，影响极大。《增广贤文》的内容以处世立身为中心，涉及社会生活的各方面和各阶层，所有过去士农工商无一不备。它不仅论理精辟，而且语言形式经诗词化处理之后变得既通俗易懂，又朗朗上口，一经成诵，便使人终身不忘，受益匪浅。它的语句或为格言，或为谚语，有的取自古代文献，有的直接取自民间。《增广贤文》阐述的观点绝非仅仅是中国的，大多数观点也适用于整个世界。

So far no record has been found about who compiled *Social Wisdom* and when it was first published. It is said that the contents of the book were first collected and modified by a scholar in the mid Ming dynasty (1368–1644) and then supplemented by scholars in the late Ming and the early Qing (1644–1911) Dynasties. After the mid to late Qing dynasty, the book became popular all over China, creating an extreme influence. The contents of *Social Wisdom* are focused on how to deal with people and conduct oneself. People from various involved aspects and classes of society such as scholars, farmers, workers, businessmen and so on all tried to get a copy of this book to read. Besides its penetrating exposition and argumentation, *Social Wisdom* uses a poetic style that makes the book not only easy to understand, but also easy to read aloud and to remember. This engraves the sentences deeply in your mind, which may benefit you all your life. The sentences of Social wisdom are either maxims or proverbs which come from either historical documents or ordinary people. Most ideas from *Social Wisdom* also apply to the whole world.

二、典籍英译赏析

【原典 1】

钱财如粪土，
仁义值千金。
作事须循天理，
出言要顺人心。
心术不可得罪于天地，
言行要留好样与儿孙。
处富贵地，
要矜怜贫贱的痛痒；

当少壮时，

须体念衰老的酸辛。

【英译】

Money and wealth are pure emptiness,

Humanity and justice are truly priceless.

Behave in accordance with heavenly purposes,

Speak to comply with popular wishes.

Your intentions should not offend heaven and earth;

For the sake of your descendants,

Your words and deeds should set a good example.

If rich and noble,

You should pity the hardships

Of the poor and humble.

When young and vigorous,

You should understand the difficulties

Of the old and feeble.

【赏析重点】

（1）分析“钱财如粪土，仁义值千金”中“粪土”“千金”意象的翻译方法。

（2）分析“天理”“人心”的翻译方法。

【原典2】

诸恶莫作，

众善奉行。

知己知彼，

将心比心。

责人之心责己，

爱己之心爱人。

再三须慎意，

第一莫欺心。

宁可人负我，

切莫我负人。

【英译】

Refrain from doing any evil,
Cherish every chance to do good work.
Know both yourself and others,
To be empathetic to others.
Love others in the way
You are apt to love yourself,
Blame yourself in the way
You are apt to blame others.
Never cheat your conscience,
Always be cautious about your behaviour.
It's better to be wronged
Than to wrong.

【赏析重点】

（1）分析“将心比心”的语义特点和翻译方法。

（2）分析“宁可人负我，切莫我负人”的翻译方法。

【原典3】

毋私小惠而伤大体，
毋借公论而快私情。
毋以己长而形人之短，
毋因己拙而忌人之能。
毋恃势力而凌逼孤寡，
毋贪口腹而恣杀牲禽。

【英译】

Do not cause any damage to the whole
For the sake of a small bounty.
Do not do yourself favors
By pretending to cater to publicity.
Do not envy others' capabilities
Because of your dullness.
Do not contrast others' shortcomings
With your advantages.

Do not rely on any power
To bully the lonely.
Do not willfully kill beasts and birds
For your mouth and belly.

【赏析重点】

（1）分析“私小惠”“借公论”中动词的翻译方法。

（2）分析“毋因己拙而忌人之能”和“毋恃势力而凌逼孤寡”的逻辑差异和翻译方法。

【原典 4】

知足常足，
终身不辱；
知止常止，
终身不耻。
君子爱财，
取之有道；
小人放利，
不顾天理。
悖入亦悖出，
害人终害己。
人非善不交，
物非义不取。

【英译】

If you know when and where to stop,
You can always be free from shame.
If you know how to be content,
You can always be free from humiliation.
If a gentleman loves money,
He makes it in a proper way;
When a villain grabs profit,
He disregards a heavenly reason.
What is unfairly got will be unfairly lost,

A person who harms others
Will harm himself in the end.
Do not associate with people
If they are malevolent.
Do not take things if they are ill-gotten.

【赏析重点】

（1）对比分析不同否定句式的翻译方法。

（2）分析“知足常足”“知止常止”的语义特点和翻译方法。

【原典 5】

但行好事，
莫问前程。
钝鸟先飞，
大器晚成。
千里不欺孤，
独木不成林。

【英译】

Keep performing good deeds,
Do not ask how you will be rewarded.
Dull birds fly first,
Great instruments are forged slowly.
Do not bully one far away from home,
A single tree does not make a forest.

【赏析重点】

（1）对比分析“千里不欺孤”和“独木不成林”两个否定句的逻辑差别和翻译方法。

（2）对比分析“但行好事”和“莫问前程”的结构特点和不同翻译方法。

拓展训练 | Extension Training

1. 思考练习

（1）用英文简要介绍《三字经》《增广贤文》主要内容。

（2）总结分析中国蒙学经典语言特点和翻译策略。

2. 文化外宣汉英翻译

（1）中国有一名古话："兄弟如手足。"意思是兄弟姐妹之间如同手和脚的关系，共同承担着维护、传承、兴旺家族的责任，应该互相帮助，一起努力，彼此成全。兄弟姐妹之间和睦相处，对于一个家庭而言非常重要。孔子曰："孝悌为仁之本。"意思是如果一个家庭能父慈子教，兄弟姐妹之间互相友爱，那么社会就太平了。

（2）中国自古强调尊师重道，正所谓"天地君亲师"，将老师与天、地、君、亲并称，可见老师在中国的重要性。中国最早的专门论述教育、教学问题的论著《学记》中有言："大学之礼，虽诏于天子，无北面，所以尊师也。"意思是教师给君王讲书是不需要行君臣之礼的。古人称老师为"传道授业解惑"者，他们有着丰富的经验，有着广博的知识，既通过自己的言行为学生做好榜样，也通过讲课向学生传授知识。

（3）中国有句名言："言必信，行必果。"意思是一旦承诺了就必须做到。守信是中华民族非常重视的传统美德。古语有云："人无信而不立。"意思是一个人唯有守信用，才能得到别人的信任和尊重，如此才能与别人建立良好的合作关系。一个民族也只有讲信用才能与其他民族和谐相处。中国人向来重视并且努力践行守信这一美德。

（4）五伦是中国古人总结出的五种基本的人伦关系，出自《孟子》，即君臣、父子、兄弟、夫妇和朋友，其中家庭关系占了三伦。孟子认为，君臣之间应有礼义之道，父子之间应有骨肉之亲，夫妻之间应有亲密之爱，兄弟之间应有尊卑之序，朋友之间应有诚信之德，这是处理人与人之间关系的基本道德和行为准则。

第十二章　家训典籍英译

Translation of Family Precepts

一、学习目标

（1）用英文介绍中国家训文化内涵。
（2）掌握中国家训相关概念汉英翻译。
（3）鉴赏家训典籍汉英翻译方法。

二、文化背景

家训文化是中国传统文化特有的文化遗产。作为中国家谱文化的重要组成部分的家训文化，一定程度上代表着中华民族繁衍生息、文明进步的精神“血脉”。迄今已知最早的由汉字记录的家训为商周皇家家训（多半由史官或后人记录），如周公的《诫伯禽书》被认作为最早的家训，周公也被称为“家训开创者”。《诫伯禽书》作为最早的皇家子弟训的代表，其内容丰富完整，堪称古代皇家家庭教育之经典。“诫”的本意是警告，明确告知做事的规矩界限以免犯错误，适用于上对下、长辈对晚辈或平辈之间。与《诫伯禽书》对皇家子弟的训诫有所不同的是，后世使用较多的是适用于长辈对晚辈的平常“家诫”一词，突出了平常家居日用之告诫。这一点在汉代变得非常普遍，自汉代开始大量出现“诫子书”“家诫”。最早有汉代刘向的《诫子歆书》，之后有马援的《诫兄子严敦书》、诸葛亮的《诫子书》和《诫外甥书》等。

The tradition of *Jia Xun* (family precepts or family instructions), as an important part of Chinese genealogy culture, represents the unique heritage of the Chinese history and civilization. So far, the earliest written family rules were found in the royal family instruction of Shang and Zhou dynasties (mostly recorded by historians or later generations). For example, Duke Zhou's *Jie Bo Qin Shu* (Admonitions to Boqin) is recognized as the earliest family rules, and Duke Zhou is also known as the "founder of family rules". As the representative of the earliest rules to the royal children, *Jie Bo Qin Shu* can be called the classic of ancient royal family education. "Jie" (admonition) originally refers to the warnings or counsels about future conduct to avoid making mistakes. It is usually given by elders to younger generations. Different from the *Jie Bo Qin Shu* written to royal children, "*Jia Jie*" (family admonition) used by later generations is more suitable for elders' admonition to younger generations in ordinary families. This became very common in the Han dynasty. Since the Han dynasty, a large number of "*Jiezi Shu*" (admonitions to the children) and "*Jiajie*" (family admonition) have appeared, such as Liu Xiang's *Admonitions to His Son Xin*, Ma Yuan's *Admonitions to His Nephews Yan and Dun*, Zhuge Liang's *Admonitions to His Son* and *Admonitions to His Nephews*.

"训"作为一种文体，指中国古代教导君王治国理政的文辞（字）。也即是说，"训"作为一种教育形式，是指对君王进行的治国理政的教导。"训"专用于对君王的教导，与教导者是否为君王无关。如《伊训》的教导者不是君王，而是大臣伊尹，但教导对象是商王太甲。据考证，复合词"家训"一词在东汉被使用。汉代以降，尤其是魏晋时期，"训"从皇家逐步推广至士族官宦人家，家和训合用以突出其平常家居的意义。南北朝颜之推为家训文化命名，其《颜氏家训》首次以"家训"为书名，作为后世家训的范本而具有里程碑意义。在其带动下，涌现出大量以家训为名的佳作。如南宋陆游的《放翁家训》、朱熹的《紫阳朱子家训》、明代高攀龙的《高氏家训》、清代曾国藩的《曾文正公家训》等。

"*Xun*" (precept), as a literary style, refers to the governance advice presenting to the kings in Chinese history. In other words, "*xun*", as a form of education offering to the kings about the national governance, is especially written to kings, which has nothing to do with the status of instructor. For example, the instructor of *Yixun* (Yi's Precepts) is not the king, but the minister Yiyin. It was written to the King Taijia of Shang dynasty. According to the research, the term "*Jia Xun*" (Family Precepts) was used as early as the Eastern Han dynasty. Since the Han dynasty, especially in the Wei and Jin Dynasties, "*Xun*" was gradually extended from the royal family to the official families of the gentry. "Family" and "*Xun*" were combined together to highlight its significance in ordinary families. Yan Zhitui started the tradition of *Jia Xun* (Family Precepts) in the Northern and Southern Dynasties. His *Admonitions for the Yan Clan* is of milestone significance as a model of family instruction for later generations. Following it, a large number of excellent family instructions have emerged, such as Lu You's *Fangweng's Family Precepts* in the

Southern Song dynasty, *Zhu Zi's Family Precepts* by Zhu Xi, Gao Panlong's *The Family Precepts for the Gao Clan* in the Ming dynasty, *Zeng Wenzheng's Family Precepts* by Zeng Guofan in the Qing dynasty, etc.

中国家训名目繁多，令人叹为观止。除了人们熟悉的"家训"和"家诫"外，一般最为常见的称谓有："家范""家规""家仪""家礼""家语"以及"家约""祖训"等，主要侧重于基本的亲缘关系之内的家族成员，规约性程度不等、形式上没有那么正式。历经漫长的历史发展，传统家训文化的内涵和意义已经变得极为丰富而且多元。中国历史上的家训文化之"家"早已不限于狭义的亲缘组织——家族、宗族，已包括了"扩大的亲缘组织"。同样，家训之"训"也早已不限于狭义的家庭教育，而已广泛涉及饮食起居、修身养性、为人处事、致学求仕等丰富内容。

There is a very large number of family precepts in Chinese history. In addition to the commonly called "*jiaxun*" (family precepts) and "*jiajie*" (family admonitions), people often use other terms like "*jiafan*" (family model), "*jiagui*"(family rules), "*jiayi*" (family rituals), "*jiali*" (family etiquette), "*jiayu*" (family language), "*jiayue*" (family promise) and "*zuxun*" (ancestral precepts). They are mainly used among the family members within the kinship, with varying degrees of conventionality and less formal form. With a long historical development, the connotation and significance of traditional family precepts have become rich and diverse. The tradition of family precepts in Chinese history has not been limited to narrow kinship groups-families and clans, but has included "expanded kinship groups". What's more, the family precepts have long been not limited to family education in a narrow sense, but have extended widely to daily life, self-cultivation, human relationship, academic learning and career pursuit.

三、文化关键词

家训 *Jia Xun* (family precepts /family instructions/family rules)

《诫伯禽书》 *Jie Bo Qin Shu* (*Admonitions to Boqin*)

《颜氏家训》 *Admonitions for the Yan Clan*

《曾文正公家训》 *Zeng Wenzheng's Family Precepts*

《朱子家训》 *Familial Precepts of Master Zhu*

第一节 《颜氏家训》

Admonitions for the Yan Clan

一、典籍简介

《颜氏家训》共七卷二十篇，内容广博，可以分成四部分。第一部分谈论治家之道，包括“序致”“教子”“兄弟”“后娶”“治家”“终制”六篇；第二部分谈论修身治学，包括“风操”“慕贤”“勉学”三篇；第三部分谈论立身处世，包括“名实”“涉务”“省事”“止足”“诫兵”“养生”“归心”“杂艺”八篇；第四部分谈论语言文学，包括“文章”“书证”“音辞”三篇。在第十六篇“归心”中，作者劝诫子孙信佛，为当时兴盛中的佛教张目，并力图证明儒佛本旨是相通的，从而巧妙地维护了儒家思想的正统地位。

Admonitions for the Yan Clan, in seven books and 20 chapters, covers a wide range of subjects. These may be divided into four parts: Part one discusses ways of household management, under which are six chapters Introduction (Ⅰ), Education of the Young (Ⅱ), Brotherhood (Ⅲ), Taking a Second Wife (Ⅳ), Managing a Household (Ⅴ) and My Dying Wish (ⅩⅩ). Part two, which discusses self-cultivation and the pursuit of knowledge, comprises the three chapters of Cultivating Good Manners (Ⅵ), Emulating the Virtuous (Ⅶ) and the Pursuit of Knowledge (Ⅷ). Part three deals with conduct and everyday life. In this part are eight chapters: Name and Reality (Ⅹ), Doing Practical Things (Ⅺ), Keeping Within Bounds (Ⅻ) Resting Content (ⅩⅢ), Shunning a Military Career (ⅩⅣ), Caring for Life (ⅩⅤ), Conversion to Buddhism (ⅩⅥ) and Arts and Hobbies (ⅩⅨ). Part four, composed of the three chapters of On Literary Creation (Ⅸ), Orthographical Notes (ⅩⅦ) and Pronunciation Problems (ⅩⅧ), contains the author's advice on language and literature. In Chapter ⅩⅥ the author encourages his offspring to believe in Buddhism, which gain ground in China at that time, and goes to great lengths to defend its principles. He also takes great trouble to identify Buddhist tenets with Confucian doctrines, while deftly maintaining the established authority of Confucianism.

二、作者简介

颜之推于公元 531 年生于湖北江段，那时中国处于南北朝对峙的局面，统治南方的是南梁，统治北方的是北魏，颜之推出身于仕宦之家，父亲是南梁的官员，能文善书。颜之推 9 岁丧父，家道衰落，一生遭逢离乱，备尝艰辛，几乎被杀害数次；他又博学多才，历经萧梁、北齐、北周、隋四个朝代，这样丰富深刻的人生经历，为他提供了观察人生的众多角度。

Yan Zhitui was born in Jiangling, Hubei, in 531, when China was divided into two political regimes, one in the north and the other in the south what is called the Northern and Southern Dynasties period (420–589). The Southern dynasty at that time was Liang, (502–557), and its northern counterpart was Northern Wei (386–534). Yan's father, a noted writer and calligrapher, served Southern Liang. Yan Zhitui was only nine when his father died and his family came down in the world. His life was a turbulent one, and he escaped death several times by a hair's breadth. He was, however, learned and talented, serving successively, four dynasties—Southern Liang, Northern Qi, Northern Zhou and Sui. Such rich and varied life experiences gave him a unique advantage point from which to view human affairs.

三、典籍英译赏析

【原典 1】

上智不教而成，下愚虽教无益，中庸之人，不教不知也。古者圣王，有“胎教”之法，怀子三月，出居别宫，目不邪视，耳不妄听，音声滋味，以礼节之。书之玉版，藏诸金匮。生子咳提，师保固明孝仁礼义，导习之矣。凡庶纵不能尔，当及婴稚识人颜色、知人喜怒，便加教诲，使为则为，使止则止，比及数岁，可省笞罚。父母威严而有慈，则子女畏慎而生孝矣。

（教子篇）

【今译】

非常聪明的人不用教育就能成才，较为愚笨的人即使教育再多也不起作用，只有绝大多数普通人要教育，不教就不知。古时候的圣王，有“胎教”的做法，怀孕三个月的时候，出去住到别的好房子里，眼睛不能斜视，耳朵不能乱听，听音乐吃美味，都要按照礼义加以节制，还得把这些写到玉版上，藏进金柜里。到胎儿出生还在幼儿时，担任“师”和“保”的人，就要讲解孝、仁、礼、义，来引导学习。普通老百姓家纵使不能如此，也应在婴儿识人脸色、懂得喜怒时，就加以教导训诲，叫做就得做，叫不做就得不做，等到长大几岁，就可省免鞭打惩罚。只要父母既威严又慈爱，子女自然敬畏谨慎而有孝行了。

【英译】

For the wisest, education is superfluous, for the very stupid, it is futile. But for the average man, education is essential for him to acquire knowledge and reason. In ancient times, great kings believed in prenatal education. Their consorts, at three months pregnant, were removed to a special room, where they were exposed to only such things as were considered decent for pregnant women to see or hear. Appropriate diet and music were prepared accordingly. The rules of such decorum were inscribed on a jade plate, which was put away in a golden cabinet. When a prince was two or three years old, his tutors, chosen well in advance, began to give him instructions with regard to filial piety, virtue, etiquette and righteousness. Even though this is not likely to happen in a commoner's family, education of children must begin early when they are barely able to read their parents' gestures and expressions. Gradually they learn to act according to their parents' wishes and can thus be spared corporal punishment even as small children. Loving yet awe-inspiring parents will find their children deferential and dutiful.

【赏析重点】

（1）分析"不教不知也"的翻译方法。

（2）分析"目不邪视，耳不妄听"的语言特征和翻译方法。

【原典 2】

婚姻素对，靖侯成规。近世嫁娶，遂有卖女纳财，买妇输绢，比量父祖，计较锱铢，责多还少，市井无异。或猥婿在门，或傲妇擅室，贪荣求利，反招羞耻，可不慎欤？

（治家篇）

【今译】

婚姻要找清白的配偶，这是当年祖宗靖侯的老规矩。近代嫁娶，就有接受财礼出卖女儿的，运送绢帛买进儿媳妇的，这些人比量门祖家势，计较锱铢钱财、索取多而回报少，这和做买卖没有区别，以至于有的门庭里弄来个下流女婿，有的屋里主管权操纵在恶儿媳妇手中，贪荣求利，招来耻辱，这样的事能不审慎吗！

【英译】

In the matter of marriage, turn to households with high moral standards. This is a family rule laid down by Yan Han, one of our great forefathers. In recent times, however, girls may be bought or sold for a bride-price or for betrothal gifts. The two households concerned focus their consideration on each other's power and position, of today or yesterday, and on the bride-price, for which they haggle in real business fashion, with one side demanding more and the other holding out for less. One should not be surprised if, in such marriages, the son-in-law proves a loathsome wretch, and the daughter-in-law a blatant shrew. So, take care not to plunge into mercenary marriages, for they will bring you humiliation and disgrace instead of honor and gain.

【赏析重点】

（1）学习文化要素“纳财”“输绢”“锱铢”的含义和翻译用词。

（2）分析“贪荣求利，反招羞耻”译文的句式转换方法。

【原典3】

人生在世，会当有业，农民则计量耕稼，商贾别讨论货贿，工巧则致精器用，伎艺则沉思法术，武夫则惯习弓马，文士则讲议经书。多见士大夫耻涉农商，羞务工伎，射则不能穿札，笔则才记姓名，饱食醉酒，忽忽无事，以此销日，以此终年。或因家世馀绪，得一阶半级，便自为足，全忘修学，及有吉凶大事，议论得失，蒙然张口，如坐云雾，公私宴集，谈古赋诗，塞默低头，欠伸而已。有识旁观，代其入地。何惜数年勤学，长受一生愧辱哉！

（勉学篇）

【今译】

人生在世，应当有合适自己的职业，农民则商议耕稼，商人则讨论货财，工匠则精造器用，懂技艺的人则考虑方法技术，武夫则练习骑马射箭，文士则研究议论经书。然而常看到士大夫耻于涉足农商，羞于从事工技，射箭则不能穿铠甲，握笔则才记起姓名，饱食醉酒，恍惚空虚，以此来打发日子，以此来终尽天年。有的凭家世馀荫，弄到一官半职，就自感满足，全忘学习，遇到婚丧大事，议论得失，就昏昏然张口结舌，像坐在云雾之中。公家或私人集会宴欢，谈古赋诗，又是沉默低头，只会打呵欠伸懒腰。有见识的人在旁看到，真替他羞得无处容身。为什么不愿用几年时间勤学，以致一辈子长时间受愧辱呢？

【英译】

A man must engage in some useful occupations. A farmer must plan how to plow and plant; a businessman must know how to bargain and trade; a craftsman must be adroit at making nice products; an entertainer must apply himself to perfecting his skills; a warrior must practise and master archery and horsemanship; a scholar must study and discuss the Confucian classics. Unfortunately, the scholar-officials of today are mostly good for nothing. They belittle and shun commerce and agriculture, they know hardly anything of a craftsman's business. When it comes to archery, they cannot shoot an arrow through a suit of armour. When it comes to writing, they can barely trace their own names. They muddle along all day, frittering their lives away feasting and drinking. Some of them, satisfied with their official posts obtained through familial influence, forget altogether about improving themselves through study. When attending a conference to discuss some matter of grave concern, they are at a loss what to say, nor can they make head or tail of what the others are saying. At an official or family banquet where history is the topic and poetry is improvised, they droop their heads and keep their mouths shut, save for yawning; onlookers with a sense of shame would blush for their sake. However, they could have avoided such disgraceful embarrassment if they had done a few years of diligent study in their younger days.

【赏析重点】

（1）分析"射则不能穿札，笔则才记姓名"的句法特征和翻译方法。

（2）分析"何惜数年勤学，长受一生愧辱哉"句式的翻译处理方法。

【原典4】

铭金人云："无多言，多言多败；无多事，多事多患。"至哉斯戒也！能走者夺其翼，善飞者减其指，有角者无上齿，丰后者无前足，盖天道不使物有兼焉也。古人云："多为少善，不如执一；鼫鼠五能，不成伎术。"

（省事篇）

【今译】

铭刻在金人身上的文字说："不要多话，多话会多失败；不要多事，多事会多祸患。"这个训诫对极了啊！会走的不让生翅膀，善飞的减少其指头，长了双角的缺掉上齿，后部丰硕的没有前足，大概是天道不叫生物兼具这些东西吧！古人说："做得多而做好的少，还不如专心做好一件；鼫既有五种本事，可都成不了技术。"

【英译】

On the back of a Zhou dynasty bronze image was the epigraph "Do not be talkative, for volubility breeds failure; do not be meddlesome for officiousness courts peril." What a golden rule this is to go by!

Of all the creatures in the world, good runners have no wings while good flyers have no forelegs. Those with horns lack front teeth, while those with strong hind legs lack forelimbs. It must be the will of Heaven that no species is favored with more than one advantage.

An ancient saying goes, "Better concentrate on one thing and do it well than to attempt many things with little success. A flying squirrel is said to be equipped with five capabilities: flying, climbing, swimming, burrowing and running, but none is sufficiently developed to be of practical."

【赏析重点】

（1）分析"多言多败""多事多患"的句法特点和翻译方法。

（2）分析"盖天道不使物有兼焉也"中的语义翻译特点。

（3）分析"鼷鼠五能"的翻译方法。

第二节　《朱子家训》

Familial Precepts of Master Zhu

一、典籍简介

《朱子治家格言》，也称《朱柏庐治家格言》，全文 524 字，是中国清代以来一篇影响巨大的家训。《朱子治家格言》内容涉及家庭安全、卫生、饮食、宴客、房田、婚姻、祭祖、读书、教育、理财、交友、纳税、为官、积德等诸多方面的问题，核心是要让人成为一个正大光明、知书明理、生活严谨、宽容善良、理想崇高的人，体现了作者对家庭成员的期望与要求，同时也反映了中国传统文化尤其是儒家的修身齐家之道。

Familial Precepts of Master Zhu, also known as *Familial Precepts of Zhu Bailu* is written by Zhu Yongchun (1627–1698). As one of well-known familial precepts in the Qing dynasty, the 524-Chinese character book touches upon home security, sanitation, banquets, houses and farmland, marriages, sacrifices to ancestors, reading, education, wealth management, friends making, taxpaying, being an official and accumulation of virtues. The core of it lies in teaching people to be upright, learned, kind, tolerant and treat their life earnestly and nurture a high ambition. The book reflects the writer's expectations of and requirements for his family members and also reflects the Confucian way of self-cultivation and regulation of family.

《朱子治家格言》得以广泛流传，除了因其内容集中体现了中国人修身齐家的理想与追求，还因其语言通俗易懂、文体工整精致。通俗易懂则容易被广大民众接受；工整精致则优美动人，便于记忆。

The popularity of *Familial Precepts of Master Zhu* depends on its substance, which reflects Chinese ideals and aspirations for self-cultivation and regulation of family and also on its easy-to-understand language and refined style, which is acceptable and easy to remember by the general public.

二、作者简介

朱用纯（1627—1698），字致一，号柏庐，江苏昆山人，是著名学者、教育家。朱柏庐一生研究程朱理学，主张知行并进，著述丰富，所作《朱子治家格言》以修身、齐家为宗旨，集儒家为人处世方法之大成，三百年来脍炙人口，家喻户晓。

Zhu Yongchun (1627–1698), styled Zhiyi and also known by his literary name Bailu, a famous scholar and educator born in Kunshan, Jiangsu Province. Zhu Bailu devoted his whole life to the study of the Cheng-Zhu school of the neo-Confucianism and advocated the unity of theory and practice. He wrote a range of books. Containing self-cultivation and regulation of families, the 524-Chinese character *Familial Precepts of Master Zhu* epitomizes Confucian principles of conducting oneself in life and has won universal praise and become a household name over the past three hundred years.

三、典籍英译赏析

【原典 1】

黎明即起，洒扫庭除，要内外整洁，既昏便息，关锁门户，必亲自检点。

【今译】

天刚亮就要起床，洒水扫地，打扫庭院，使屋里屋外都要整齐干净；日落后就要休息，锁门关窗，一定要亲自检查。

【英译】

Get up early in the morning, sweep the floor and clean up the yard to keep your house clean and tidy outside and inside. Get into bed after sunset and make sure all the doors and windows are locked.

【赏析重点】

分析“洒扫庭除”的语义特点和翻译方法。

【原典2】

一粥一饭，当思来处不易；半丝半缕，恒念物力维艰。

【今译】

一口粥，一碗饭，要想到它们来得不容易；纵然是半根线半根丝，也要常常想到它们生产出来的艰难。

【英译】

When taking a small bite of congee or having a bowl of rice, remember that every grain comes from hard work. When using even half a cotton thread or half a silk thread, remember that they are not produced easily.

【赏析重点】

分析“一粥一饭，当思来处不易”句法特点和翻译方法。

【原典3】

宜未雨而绸缪，毋临渴而掘井。

【今译】

凡事应该预先做好准备，就像在下雨之前就应把房子修补好，不要口渴了才想到要挖井取水。

【英译】

Make good preparations in advance. Mend your leaky house before raining and don't wait until thirsty to dig a well for water.

【赏析重点】

分析“未雨而绸缪”的语义特点和翻译方法。

【原典4】

自奉必须俭约，宴客切勿流连。

【今译】

自己日常生活所需，应力求节俭朴素，不要铺张浪费。举办宴席、招待客人时，应适可而止，不要频频留客，沉迷其中。

【英译】

Practice economy and seek no extravagance. When entertaining guests, call an end to the dinner in due time and do not frequently persuade your guests to stay.

【赏析重点】

分析“宴客切勿流连”译文的语义增补方法。

【原典5】

器具质而洁，瓦缶胜金玉；饮食约而精，园蔬逾珍馐。

【今译】

饮食器具只要实用干净就好，即使是很普通的瓦罐、碗盘，也胜过金玉做的昂贵器物；饮食虽少但如果精心制作，即使是园子里的蔬菜，也胜过山珍海味。

【英译】

If functional and clean, ordinary food utensils like crocks, bowls and plates are better than expensive tableware made of gold and jade. If exquisitely cooked, home-grown vegetables are more delicious than delicacies.

【赏析重点】

分析“瓦缶胜金玉”译文的语义增补方法。

【原典6】

与肩挑贸易，毋占便宜；见贫苦亲邻，须加温恤。

【今译】

与肩挑货物做小生意的小贩交易，应当体恤他们靠体力谋生不容易，不要斤斤计较，贪小便宜；看见生活穷苦的亲戚或邻居，要给予关怀和救济。

【英译】

Do not haggle with street vendors for they are not easy to run a small business. Provide support to your neighbors and relatives who lead a poor life.

【赏析重点】

分析本句译文的句法结构转换方法。

【原典7】

嫁女择佳婿，毋索重聘；娶媳求淑女，勿计厚奁。

【今译】

嫁女儿要选择贤良的女婿，不要索取贵重的聘礼；娶媳妇应该寻求贤淑女子，不要谋求丰厚的嫁妆。

【英译】

Marry your daughters to men with virtues and do not seek exorbitant bride price. Marry your sons to women with virtues and do not seek a large dowry.

【赏析重点】

（1）分析“嫁女择佳婿”“娶媳求淑女”的句法特点和翻译方法。

（2）学习文化要素“重聘”“厚奁”的含义和翻译用词。

【原典8】

见富贵而生谄容者，最可耻；遇贫穷而作骄态者，贱莫甚。

【今译】

看到有钱、有势的人就表现出巴结讨好的样子，这种行为最是可耻；遇到贫穷的人就作出轻视骄傲的姿态，这种行为最是低贱。

【英译】

The most shameful act is to curry favor with the rich and the powerful. The basest act is to show contempt for the poor.

【赏析重点】

分析“见富贵而生谄容者”“遇贫穷而作骄态者”的句法特点和翻译方法。

【原典9】

勿恃势力而凌逼孤寡，毋贪口腹而恣杀生禽。

【今译】

不可倚仗势力，欺凌压迫孤儿寡妇；不要贪图口腹之欲，而任意杀害牲畜家禽。

【英译】

Never take advantage of your power and position to bully others. Never bully orphans and widows. Never arbitrarily butcher livestock and poultry for the sake of greed.

【赏析重点】

学习“孤寡”“生禽”的语义特点和翻译方法。

【原典 10】

轻听发言，安知非人之谮诉，当忍耐三思；因事相争，焉知非我之不是，须平心暗想。

【今译】

轻易听信他人的议论，未经查证，怎么知道不是对方借机诬陷、挑拨离间呢？应当忍耐，再三思量、查证，以明辨是非、善恶。因事与人相争，怎么知道不是自己的错？必须平心静气地想清楚，不要意气用事。

【英译】

Do not easily believe remarks of others without checking them out. How do you know they are not made by mischief makers? Be patient and make investigations over and over again to tell right from wrong and the good from the evil. How do you know the fault does not lie with your side when quarreling with others? Think it over and do not act on impulse.

【赏析重点】

分析“轻听发言”翻译中的语义增补。

拓展训练 | Extension Training

1. 思考练习

（1）用英文简要介绍《颜氏家训》《朱子家训》主要内容。

（2）总结分析中国家训的语言特点和翻译策略。

2. 文化外宣汉英翻译

（1）中国极其重视亲子关系，尤其强调孝敬父母。古语有云：“百善孝为先。”意思是孝在中国的善良品质之中居于首位，所以中国人衡量一个人品质如何，往往看这个人是否孝敬父母。古代在选官的时候孝敬父母是一项重要的考核标准，汉代更是将《孝经》放在至高的地位上。

（2）中国古代非常重视夫妻关系，有的经书甚至将夫妻关系列为家庭关系中最为重要的关系，认为丈夫应该尊重妻子，妻子应该理解丈夫。春秋时期的政治家、军事家管子曰："分敬而无妒，则夫妇和勉矣。"意思是夫妇之间应该互相尊敬，妻子不要嫉妒，且夫妻可互为老师，时常指点出对方的错误以利于个人品德的修养。中国人常用"琴瑟和谐"来形容夫妻关系。琴与瑟是中国的两种传统乐器，它们在一起合奏的时候，所产生的声音非常和谐，因此被用来比喻夫妻关系。

（3）朋友关系在中国的人际关系中有着重要的地位。中国人喜欢将"师友"并称，老师是长辈，是教授自己知识的人；朋友即有道义之交的同龄人。孔子曰："君子以文会友，以友辅仁。"意思是真正的君子用思想、道义去结交朋友，再通过交友来帮助自己更加仁德。《孝经》有言："士有争友，则身不离于令名。"意思是士人身边有敢于直言劝谏的朋友，就能保持好的名声。

（4）中国一般称朋友为"知音"，这缘于一个故事。古代有一个叫俞伯牙的人，非常善于弹琴，琴艺修养极高。伯牙有一个朋友叫钟子期，非常善于听琴。每次伯牙弹琴，钟子期都能通过琴声了解到他在想什么，想要表达什么。后来钟子期去世了，伯牙便再也不弹琴了，并且把自己视若珍宝的琴也摔碎了。他悲伤地说："我的知音去世了，我也没有必要再弹琴了。"从此，中国人便常用"知音"一词来形容知己朋友。

第五篇

自然科学篇

Science and Technology

第十三章　中医典籍英译

Translation of Traditional Chinese Medicine (TCM)

一、学习目标

（1）用英文介绍中医核心观点。

（2）掌握中医文化概念汉英翻译。

（3）鉴赏中医典籍汉英翻译方法。

二、文化背景

中国医学是一个丰富的宝库，有 5000 多年的历史。早在战国时期（前 475—前 221）就出现了内容系统的医学理论著作《黄帝内经》；汉代（前 206—220）医学家张仲景写成《伤寒论》；明代（1368—1644）的医学家李时珍完成了《本草纲目》。他们把大量的临床实践经验汇集成宝贵的医学资料，对医药学的发展和医药学理论的系统化起到了巨大的推动作用。在中医学方面，中国有“望、闻、问、切”，辨证施治的诊治方法。在针灸、按摩、气功、正骨等方面，有独特的治疗、养生、健身方法。在中药学方面，中国对 3000 多种植物、动物、矿物药材的性能、功效、用法都有详细的研究和记载，并配制成汤剂和丸、散、膏、丹等不同类型的成药。中国的医药学为人们战胜疾病、提高身体素质，做出了巨大的贡献。

With a history of more than 5,000 years, traditional Chinese medicine is a great treasure of medical sciences. *Yellow Emperor's Canon of Medicine*, China scariest and most comprehensive extant treatise on medicine, was compiled during the Warring States period (475 BC–221 BC). In the Han dynasty (206 BC–220 AD) Zhang Zhongjing wrote the *Treatise on Febrile and Other Diseases*, the first medical work containing a fairly thorough description of theory and clinical experience. Li Shizhen, an outstanding pharmacologist of the Ming dynasty (1368–1644) completed his *Compendium of Material Medical*. The theoretical and clinical standpoints of the two medical giants contributed significantly to the development of medical science and the systematization of medical theory In traditional Chinese medicine, which is noted for its dialectical way of diagnosis and treatment, diagnosis is done by means of the four examinations, i.e. wang, or observation (to observe the complexion and fur or the patient's tongue), wén, or auscultation and olfaction (to smell the odours given off by the patient when talking breathing or coughing, and the smell of his excreta), wèn, or inquiry (to ask about the condition of the patient), and qie, or palpation (to feel the patient's pulse). In the areas of acupuncture, massage, qigong and bone-setting traditional Chinese medicine has its unique treatments and ways to keep fit. In the field of traditional Chinese pharmacology the Chinese medical scientists have made in-depth researches into and recorded in details the property, efficacy and usage of over 3,000 kinds of medicinal materials from botanical, zoological and mineral sources. Chinese pharmacy provides not only decoration but also ready-prepared medicines in the form of pills, powder, electuaries and pellets. Traditional Chinese medicine and pharmacology have contributed significantly to mankind in their fight against diseases and their improvement of health.

三、文化关键词

脉　*Mai* (Channel)

精气　*Jingqi* (Essence-Qi)

肾气　*Shenqi* (Kidney-Qi)

五脏　*Wuzang* (Five Zang-Organs)

经络　Jingluo (Channels and Collaterals)

邪风　*Xiefeng* (Evil-Wind)

天干　*Liangan* (the heavenly stems)

地支　*Dizhi* (the earthly branches)

穴位　*Xuewei* (acupuncture point)

标本兼治　treating both manifestation and root cause of disease

调和肝脾　harmonizing liver and spleen

扶正祛邪　strengthening vital qi to eliminate pathogenic factor

清热解毒　clearing heat-toxin

活血化瘀　promoting blood circulation for removing blood stasis

舒筋活络　relieving rigidity of muscles and activating collaterals

润肺止咳　moistening lung for arresting cough

益气活血　benefiting qi for activating blood circulation

补气养血　benefiting qi and nourishing blood

第一节 《黄帝内经》

Yellow Emperor's Canon of Medicine

一、典籍简介

《黄帝内经》，即《素问》与《灵枢》的合称，是中国现存最早的医学典籍，反映了中国古代的医学成就，奠定了中国医学发展的基础，成为中国医药之祖、医家之宗。在中国几千年漫长的历史中，《黄帝内经》一直指导着中国医学的发展，中医学中众多流派的理论观点，莫不源于《黄帝内经》的基本思想。《黄帝内经》不仅为我国医学的发展奠定了基础，而且对国外医学也发挥了重要影响。例如，南北朝至隋唐时期，中医书籍大量传入日本和朝鲜。在很长的一段历史时期，日本和朝鲜的医学都是以《黄帝内经》的思想体系为其理论核心。近年以来，《黄帝内经》引起了西方许多国家的重视，其部分内容相继译成日、英、德、法等国文字。

Yellow Emperor's Canon of Medicine is a free translation of Huangdi Neijing which is composed of two separate books namely *Suwen* and *Lingshu* which are often translated into Plain Conversation and Spiritual Pivot in English respectively. *Yellow Emperor's Canon of Medicine* is the earliest extant medical canon in China that records the achievements of medicine made by Chinese people in ancient times. In the past thousands of years, *Yellow Emperor's Canon of Medicine* guided the development of TCM (traditional Chinese medicine). The so-called various schools of theories in TCM developed in history all originated from the basic theory elucidated in *Yellow Emperor's Canon of Medicine*. *Yellow Emperor's Canon of Medicine* not only laid the foundation for the formation and development of TCM, but also influenced the progress of medicine in other countries around China. For example, from the periods of North-South Dynasties (420–581) to the Sui dynasty (581–618) and the Tang dynasty (618–907) in China, many Chinese books on medicine were brought to Japan and Korea. In quite a long time in Japan and Korea,

Yellow Emperor's Canon of Medicine served as the theoretical core of medicine. In the 20th century *Yellow Emperor's Canon of Medicine* drew attention from many countries in the Western world and some of its content was translated into Japanese, English, German and French.

《黄帝内经》的成书年代，历来有不同的说法。一般认为《素问》成书于周秦之间或战国至两汉时期。《灵枢》的成书年代，根据现有的史料，尚不能确定。从现存《素问》所述来看，其内容大致可以分为 3 个部分。第 1 部分为除运气 7 篇和 2 个附篇外的全部内容，是《素问》成编时的基本内容；第 2 部分为运气 7 篇，即天元纪大论、五运行大论、六微旨大论、气交变大论、五常政大论、六元正纪大论和至真要大论；第 3 部分为《素问》遗篇，即"刺法论"和"本病论"。《灵枢》的内容十分丰富。它以阴阳五行学说为指导，全面论述了人体的生理、病理、诊断、治疗、养生等问题，并叙述了脏腑、精、神、气、血、津液的功能和病理变化，强调了人与自然的密切联系及人体内部协调统一的整体观念，而其最突出的特点则是更翔实地阐述了经络理论和针法。与此相关的内容，占了《灵枢》的 80% 左右。所以《灵枢》是总结汉代以前我国经络学和针刺技术的最重要著述，为针灸学的发展奠定了基础。

There are different opinions over the time when *Yellow Emperor's Canon of Medicine* was compiled. It is generally believed that *Plain Conversation* was compiled in the period between the Zhou dynasty (1064 BC–221 BC) and the Qin dynasty (221 BC–206 BC) or the period between the West Han dynasty (206 BC–230 AD) and the East Han dynasty (25 AD–265 AD). The time when *Spiritual Pivot* was compiled was hard to decide according to historical records. The content of *Plain Conversation* can be divided into three parts. The first part includes seventy two chapters which are the basic contents of *Plain Conversation* when it was first compiled excluding the seven chapters dealing with *Yunqi* (Motion of Qi) theory and two appendices. The second part includes the seven chapters dealing with *Yunqi* (Motion of Qi) theory, namely *Tianyuanji Dalun* (Discussion on the Law of Motions and Changes in Nature), *Wuyunxing Dalun* (Major Discussion on the Changes of Five-Motions), *Liuweizhi Dalun* (Major Discussion on the Abstruseness of the Six Kinds of Qi), *Qijiaobian Dalun* (Major Discussion on the Changes of Qi-Convergence), *Wuchangzheng Dalun* (Major Discussion on the Administration of Five-Motions), *Liuyuan Zhengji Dalun* (Major Discussion on the Progress of the Six Climatic Changes) and *Zhizhenyao Dalun* (Major Discussion on the Most Important and Abstruse Theory). The third part is the so-called appendices which refer to the seventy-two and seventy-three chapters that were lost in history even before Wang Bing's time. *Spiritual Pivot*, based on the theory of *Yin* and *Yang* and *Wuxing* (Five Elements), describes physiology, pathology, diagnosis and treatment of the human body as well as how to cultivate health. It discusses the physiological functions and pathological changes of *Zangfu* (Viscera), *Jing* (Essence), *Shen* (Spirit or mind), *Qi*, blood and body fluid, emphasizing the importance of harmonic relationship between man and nature, fully and accurately elucidating the theory of *Jingluo* (Channels and Colla terals) and the techniques of acupuncture. In fact about four-fifths of the content is related to acupuncture. For this reason, *Spiritual Pivot* is regarded as the most important classic that has summarized the theory of *jingluo* (Channels and Collaterals) and the techniques of acupuncture before the Han dynasty.

二、典籍英译赏析

【原典 1】

黄帝曰：余闻上古有真人者，提挈天地，把握阴阳，呼吸精气，独立守神，肌肉若一，故能寿敝天地，无有终时，此其道生。

【今译】

我听说上古时代有称为真人的人，掌握了天地阴阳变化的规律，能够调节呼吸，吸收精纯的清气，超然独处，令精神守持于内，锻炼身体，使筋骨肌肉与整个身体达到高度的协调，所以他的寿命同于天地而没有终了的时候，这是他修道养生的结果。

【李照国英译】

Huangdi asked, "I am told that there were so-called *Zhenren* (immortal beings) in ancient times [who could] grasp the law of nature. They followed the principles of *Yin* and *Yang*, inhaling fresh air, cultivating their spirit and keeping their muscles integrated. So their life expectancy was as long as that of the earth and the heavens. This is their *Dao* (the art of preserving health) of life."

【Paul U. Unschuld (文树德), Hermann Tessenow (田和曼) 英译】

Huang Di:
"I have heard,
in high antiquity there were true men.
They upheld [the patterns of] heaven and earth and
they grasped [the regularity of] *yin* and *yang*.

They exhaled and inhaled essence *qi*.
They stood for themselves and guarded their spirit.
Muscles and flesh were like one.
Hence,
they were able to achieve longevity, in correspondence with heaven and earth.
There was no point in time when [their life could have] come to an end.
Such was their life in the Way.

【赏析重点】

（1）对比分析文化关键词“真人”“精气”“肌肉”的翻译选词。

（2）对比分析“故能寿敝天地，无有终时，此其道生”译文的句式转换。

【原典 2】

中古之时，有至人者，淳德全道，和于阴阳，调于四时，去世离俗，积精全神，游行天地之间，视听八达之外，此盖益其寿命而强者也，亦归于真人。

【今译】

中古的时候，有称为‘至人’的人。他们具有淳厚的道德，能调和阴阳四时的变化，避开世俗的干扰，积蓄精气，集中精神，游行于广阔的天地自然之间，视听于八方之外。这是他们延长寿命和强健身体的方法。这种人也归属于‘真人’。

【李照国英译】

In the middle ancient times, there were so-called *Zhiren* (perfect person) who possessed supreme morality and the tenets of cultivating health, abiding by [the changes of] *Yin* and *Yang*, adapting [themselves] to the changes of seasons, abandoning secular desires, avoiding distraction and roaming around on the earth and in the heavens. So they could see and hear [things and voices] beyond the eight directions. Such a practice and self-cultivation enabled them to keep fit and prolong their life. [These people were] similar to the *Zhenren* (immortal beings).

【Paul U. Unschuld（文树德）, Hermann Tessenow（田和曼）英译】

At the time of middle antiquity,
there were the accomplished men.
They were of pure virtue and they were entirely in accord with the Way.
They adapted themselves to [the regularity] of *yin* and *yang* and
they lived in harmony with the four seasons.
They left the world and they departed from the common.

They accumulated essence and preserved their spirit.
They roamed between heaven and earth and
their vision as well as their hearing went beyond the eight reaches.
This way, they added to their lifespan and were strong.
They, too, may be counted among the true men.

【赏析重点】

（1）分析“去世离俗，积精全神”的结构特点和翻译方法。

（2）分析“八达”的含义和翻译用词特点。

【原典 3】

其次有圣人者，处天地之和，从八风之理，适嗜欲于世俗之间，无恚嗔之心，行不欲离于世，被服章，举不欲观于俗，外不劳形于事，内无思想之患，以恬愉为务，以自得为功，形体不敝，精神不散，亦可以百数。

【今译】

其次有称为圣人的人，他们能够安处于天地平和之气之中，适应于八风的活动规律，使自己的嗜欲同世俗相适应，没有恼怒怨恨之情，其行为不偏离世俗社会的一般准则，穿着装饰普通纹彩的衣服，举止却不比照世俗的习惯，在外不使形体因事物而劳累，在内无思想负担，以安静、愉快为目的，以悠然自得为满足，因此他的形体不衰惫，精神不耗散，可以活到百岁左右。

【李照国英译】

The third kind of people was known as Shengren (sages) who were capable of living in a harmonic environment between the earth and the heavens and adapting [themselves] to the wind from the eight different directions. [In daily life they] could properly tackle their interest and desire and their mind was free from anger and discontentment. [They] did not try to draw themselves away from secular customs, and also worn luxurious clothes. But they never followed the behavior of ordinary people. Physically, they tried not to exhaust their body; mentally, they freed themselves from any anxiety, regarding peace and happiness as the target of their life and taking self-contentment as the symbol of achievement. [As a result] their body was seldom susceptible to decline and their spirit was never subject to exhaustion. That was why they could live over one hundred years.

【Paul U. Unschuld（文树德），Hermann Tessenow(田和曼）英译】

Next, there were the sages.

They lived in harmony with heaven and earth and
they followed the patterns of the eight winds.

They accommodated their cravings and their desires within the world and the common and their heart knew no anger.

In their activities they had no desire to disassociate themselves from the world; in their clothing and bearing they had no desire to be observed by the common people.

Externally, they did not tax their physical appearance with any affairs;
internally, they did not suffer from any pondering.
They made every effort to achieve peaceful relaxation and
they considered self-realization as success.
Their physical body did not deteriorate and
their essence and their spirit did not dissipate.
They, too, could reach a number of one hundred [years].

【赏析重点】

（1）分析文化关键词“八风”“恚嗔”的翻译用词特点。

（2）分析“外不劳形于事，内无思想之患”句式特点和翻译方法。

【原典 4】

是故多食咸，则脉凝泣而变色。多食苦，则皮槁而毛拔。多食辛，则筋急而爪枯。多食酸，则肉胝皱而唇揭。多食甘，则骨痛而发落。此五味之所伤也。故心欲苦，肺欲辛，肝欲酸，脾欲甘，肾欲咸，此五味之所合也。

【今译】

所以过食咸味，则使血脉凝涩不畅，而且面色发生变化。过食苦味，则使皮肤枯槁，毫毛脱落。过食辛味，则使筋脉劲急，爪甲枯干。过食酸味，则使肌肉粗厚而唇缩。过食甘味，则使骨骼疼痛而头发脱落，这些是由于饮食五味的偏食所造成的损害。所以心喜苦味，肺喜辛味，肝喜酸味，脾喜甘味，肾喜咸味，这就是五味与五脏之气相合的对应关系。

【李照国英译】

Excessive taking of salty [food] stagnates the blood vessels and change the countenance. Excessive taking of bitter [food] makes the skin dry and body hair lose. Excessive taking of pungent [food] causes cramp of musculature and dry nails. Excessive taking of sour [food] leads to wrinkled thickness of the muscles and chap the lips.

Excessive taking of sweet [food] results in pain of bones and loss of hair. These are the impairments caused by excessive [taking of] the five kinds of flavors. Thus the heart is desirous of bitter [flavor], the lung is desirous of pungent [flavor], the liver is desirous of sour [flavor], the spleen is desirous of sweet [flavor]and the kidney is desirous of salty [flavor]. These are the relationships between the five flavors and the Five Zang-Organs.

【Paul U. Unschuld（文树德），Hermann Tessenow（田和曼）英译】

Hence, if one consumes large quantities of salty [food],
then the [contents of the] vessels will congeal so that [their flow] is impeded
and the complexion changes.
If one consumes large quantities of bitter [food],
then the skin will desiccate and the body hair is plucked out.
If one consumes large quantities of acrid [food],
then the sinews become tense and the nails dry.
If one consumes large quantities of sour [food],
then the flesh hardens and shows wrinkles and the lips peel.
If one consumes large quantities of sweet [food],
then the bones will ache and the hair on the head falls off.
These are the harms resulting from the five flavors.
Hence,
the heart longs for bitter [flavor].
The lung longs for acrid [flavor].
The liver longs for sour [flavor].
The spleen longs for sweet [flavor].
The kidneys long for salty [flavor].
This is what the five flavors conform with. {The qi of the five depots}.

【赏析重点】

（1）对比分析“皮槁而毛拔”“筋急而爪枯”译文的用词差异。

（2）对比分析“此五味之所合也”译文的语义差异。

第二节 《本草纲目》

Compendium of Material Medical

一、典籍简介

《本草纲目》是一部药物学著作，作者为明代伟大的医药学家李时珍。该书是我国中药史上最完整最全面的一部医学书籍，几乎列出了所有人们认为有医疗功效的植物、动物及其他物质。经过参阅 800 余部医学著作以及 30 年的实地考察学习，李时珍最终于 1578 年完成该书第一稿。神农氏是我国神话中的一位伟人，他教会了人民农耕及使用草药，李时珍因这部医学著作和其他众多成就常被后人比作神农。

Bencao Gangmu , also known as *The Compendium of Material Medical* (a book on Chinese herbal medicine) , is a material medical work written by the great medical and pharmaceutical expert in the Ming dynasty, Li Shizhen. It is regarded as the most complete and comprehensive medical book ever written in the history of traditional Chinese medicine in China. It almost lists all the plants, animals, minerals and other objects that were believed to have medicinal properties. Li Shizhen completed the first draft of the book in 1578, after conducting readings of 800 other medical reference books and carrying out 30 years of field study. For this and many other achievements Li Shizhen has often been compared to Shennong, a great man in the Chinese mythology who taught people about agriculture and herbal medicine.

《本草纲目》共五十二卷，开篇为目录及 1160 幅手工插图，第一卷到第四卷是序例和用于治疗最常见疾病的药草单，第五卷到第五十二卷是该书的主要部分，记载了 1892 种不同种类的药物，其中 374 种是李时珍自己新增加的。该书收录了约 11096 首治疗普通疾病的方剂，其中 8160 首由李时珍自己拟定或收集。全书近 200 万字，分为 16 部、60 类。每种药物分列释名、气味、主治、疗效和附方等。《本草纲目》改进了中药的分类方法，格式比较统一，叙述也比较科学和缜密，此外，对提高动植物生物学分类的可靠性和科学价值也具有很大意义。该书纠正了前人对药物和疾病性质的很多错误理解。他还增加了很多新药，在某些药物中加入自己的发现。

Bencao Gangmu has 52 volumes in total. At the very beginning is the table of contents and l, 160 hand-drawn illustrations. Volumes l to 4 are an index and a comprehensive list of herbs that would treat the most common illnesses. Volumes 5 to 52 form the main content of the text, recording l, 892 distinct medicines, of which 374 were added by Li himself. There are some 11,096 prescriptions to treat the common illnesses, of which 8,160 were compiled or collected by Li. The text is written in almost 2 million Chinese characters, classified into 16 divisions and 60 orders. For every medicine there are explanations of the names, detailed descriptions of the odor, medical function,effects, side recipes etc. *Bencao Gangmu* improved the classification of traditional Chinese medicine, complying with a uniform format, and the language was comparatively scientific and precise; besides, it played a very significant role in promoting the credibility and scientific values of the biological classification of both plants and animals. The work corrected many false understandings of the nature of the medicines and illnesses. Li also included many new herbs and added his own discovery in certain drugs.

《本草纲目》不仅是一部药物学著作，还涉及生物学、化学、地理、矿物学、地质学、历史和天文学等方面内容。该书先后被翻译成 20 多种语言，在世界范围内广为流传，直至现在仍在作为一部重要的医学著作刊印使用。

Bencao Gangmu is more than a pharmaceutical work, for it contains information covering the topics in biology, chemistry, geography, mineralogy, geology, history, astronomy etc. It has been translated into more than 20 languages and spread all over the world. Even now it is still in print and used as a great medical work.

二、作者简介

李时珍（1518—1593），字东璧，号濒湖。湖广蕲州（今湖北蕲春）人。明代卓越的医药学家，世界文化史上伟大的自然科学家。李时珍精通医术，钻研医典，万里跋涉，采方问药，历时 27 年写成了举世闻名的中医药著作《本草纲目》。被达尔文誉为 16 世纪的“中国百科全书”。此书收录 1892 种药物，其中新增药物 374 种。药物插图 1100 余幅，11000 多个药方。他采用比较科学的方法对药物进行分类，每种药物后面附有用法和方剂，就药论治，按证寻药，创立了本草学的新体系。

Li Shizhen(1518–1593), styled Dongbi, literary name Binhu, a native of Qizhou (present Qichun Town, Hubei Province), was a prominent pharmacist in the Ming dynasty and a great natural scientist in the cultural history of the world.

He had consummate medical skill and made intensive study of medical classics. After trekking over a long distance to cull medicinal herbs, he wrote the world-famous monumental masterpiece *Bencaogangmu* (Compendium of Materia Medica) after 27 years of hard work.

Acclaimed as the "Chinese Encyclopedia" of the 16th century by Darwin, it included indications and prescriptions of 1,892 medicinal herbs, among which 374 were newly added. There were more than 1,100 medicine illustrations and over 11,000 recipes. In the course of compiling the work, Li Shizhen made his endeavors all the way throughout the country to pick up specimens in the wild and to search and collect folk recipes. His classifications of medicine were based on fairly scientific approaches.

三、典籍英译赏析

【原典 1　西瓜】

瓜瓤

〔气味〕甘、淡，寒，无毒。

瑞曰：有小毒。多食作吐利，胃弱者不可食。同油饼食，损脾。

时珍曰：按《延寿书》云：北人禀浓，食之犹惯；南人禀薄，多食易至霍乱，冷病终身也。又按：《相感志》云：食西瓜后食其子，即不噫瓜气。以瓜划破，曝日中，少顷食，即冷如水也。得酒气、近糯米，即易烂。猫踏之，即易沙。

〔主治〕消烦止渴，解暑热（吴瑞）。疗喉痹（汪颖）。宽中下气，利小水，治血痢，解酒毒（宁原）。含汁，治口疮（震亨）。

〔发明〕颖曰：西瓜性寒解热，有天生白虎汤之号。然亦不宜多食。时珍曰：西瓜、甜瓜皆属生冷。世俗以为醍醐灌顶，甘露洒心，取其一时之快，不知其伤脾助湿之害也。

皮

〔气味〕甘，凉，无毒。

〔主治〕口、舌、唇内生疮，烧研噙之（震亨）。

【英译】

XIGUARANG

Pulp of watermelon

Endosperm vulgaris

[Quality and Taste]

It is sweet, plain, cold and nontoxic.

Wu Rui: It is slightly toxic, and overeating causes vomiting and diarrhea. People with a debilitated stomach should not have the fruit. If it is eaten together with fried cake, it causes damage to the spleen.

Li Shizhen: The book *Yanshou Shu:* "People in the north have strong build and are used to Xigua. But people in the south are generally debilitated and cannot stand too much Xigua. If it is overeaten, it may trigger cholera and the patient will probably be troubled with a cold ailment all his life."

The book *Xianggan Zhi*: "After eating Xigua, eat the seed of the melon. In this way, retching can be avoided. Cut open Xigua and expose it in the sun. After a short while, the juice is as cool as water. When the melon is exposed to wine or kept close to Nuomi/oryza glutinosae/polished glutinous rice, it easily rots. When a cat steps on the melon, its pulp becomes granular."

[Indications]

Wu Rui: It relieves restless and quenches thirst. It disperses summer heat.

Wang Ying: It treats a sore throat.

Ning Yuan: It relieves chest obstruction and brings down adverse ascending gas. It facilitates urination. It stops dysentery with bloody discharge. It detoxifies alcoholism.

Zhu Zhenheng: Hold the juice of Xiguain the mouth. It helps dissolve aphtha.

[Explication]

Wang Ying: Xigua is cold in quality and eliminates Heat. It is called a natural Baihu Tang. But anyway, do not eat too much of it.

Li Shizhen: Both Xigua and Tiangua are cold in quality. People cherish the melon as it is like sweet dew, refreshing one's heart for a time. But people do not know it damages the Spleen as it is strengthening the pathogenic Humidity.

XIGUAPI

Watermelon peel

Exocarpium citrulli

[Quality and Taste] It is sweet. cool and nontoxic.

[Indications] Zhu Zhenheng: It is good for treating aphtha in the oral cavity, tongue and lip. Burn the drug and grind it into powder. Hold the drug in the mouth

【赏析重点】

（1）分析"禀浓""禀薄"语义特征和翻译用词。

（2）分析"消烦止渴，解暑热""宽中下气，利小水"句中动词翻译的特点。

【原典2　桑】

桑椹

一名文武实。

〔主治〕单食，止消渴（苏恭）。利五脏关节，通血气。久服不饥，安魂镇神，令人聪明，变白不老。多收暴干为末。蜜丸日服（藏器）。捣汁饮，解中酒毒。酿酒服，利水气消肿（时珍）。

【英译】

SANGSHEN

Mulberry fruit

Fructus mori

It is also called Wenwushi

[Indications] Su Gong: Take the drug independently. It quenches thirst in diabetes.

Chen Cangqi: It tonifies the Five Viscera, facilitates the movement of joints and motivates the circulation of blood and qi. Long-term use makes one no longer hungry（even without eating normal food）. It pacifies the soul and mind, and increases wisdom. It helps turn white hair black and keeps one looking young. Collect the drug and dry it in the sun; then grind it into powder. Make pills with honey and take it daily.

Li Shizhen: Pound the fresh fruit to get juice. Drink the juice to dissolve alcoholism. Brew wine with fruit. Such wine works to eliminate fluid retention and swelling.

【赏析重点】

（1）分析文化关键词“五脏”“血气”“魂”“神”的翻译用词。

（2）分析“多收暴干为末”译文句法转换。

拓展训练 | Extension Training

1. 思考练习

（1）用英文简要介绍《黄帝内经》《本草纲目》的主要内容。

（2）总结医学典籍的翻译方法和翻译策略。

2. 文化外宣汉英翻译

（1）在春秋战国时期，中国的医药学理论就已经基本形成，出现了阴阳学说、五行学说、藏象学说和经络学说等中医理论，确立了“望、闻、问、切”（即四诊法）的诊断方法，以及砭石、针刺、艾灸、汤药等四大治疗方法。两千多年的发展过程中，出现了诸多医学典籍，它们至今仍然发挥着重要作用。

（2）针灸是针与灸的合称，在经络学说理论的指导下，通过刺激经络上的穴位，使气运行正常，从而达到治愈的目的。针、灸两种方法可同时使用。针的前身是砭石。砭石是一种经过磨砺而成的锥形或楔形的小石器，古人用其按摩以缓解疼痛。以针刺激体表的穴位，可以起到治病的作用。灸法的产生是在火的使用以后。最初是用各种树枝点燃来施灸，后来发展为用艾草施灸。艾灸就是将用艾草加工成的艾绒、艾条或艾炷点燃，熏烤人体穴位，产生温热的刺痛来缓解病痛。艾灸在中国应用得很早，许多医学著作里都有记载。

（3）气的含义可以概括为三个方面：一是中国古代哲学概念，指构成宇宙万物的实在本元，也是构成人类形体与化生精神的实在元素。二是构成人体、维持人体生命活动的物质、能量、信息的总称。人体生命之气随其性质有阳气、阴气之分，随其转化有元气、宗气、营气、卫气之别，随其功能活动有胃气、心气、肝气、肾气、肺气、脾气、脏腑之气等的称谓。三是指导致人体发病的因素，即邪气。

（4）阴阳失调即阴阳之间失去平衡协调的简称。是指在疾病的发生发展过程中，由于各种致病因素的影响，导致机体阴阳双方失去相对的平衡与协调，从而出现阴阳偏盛或偏衰、阴阳互损、阴阳格拒、阴阳亡失等一系列病理变化。阴阳失调主要体现为寒、热性症候的变化。另外，中医学认为，各种致病因素作用于人体，都必须通过机体内部的阴阳失调才能形成疾病，所以，阴阳失调也是对人体各种功能性和器质性病变的高度概括。

第十四章　数学典籍英译

Translation of Ancient Chinese Mathematics

一、学习目标

（1）用英文介绍中国古代数学成就。

（2）掌握中国古代数学特色文化概念汉英翻译。

（3）鉴赏中国古代数学典籍汉英翻译方法。

二、文化背景

在中国古代，数学叫作“算术”，又称“算学”。数学是儒家学者必须掌握的六艺（六艺即六项基本才能，分别为礼、乐、射、御、书、数）之一。春秋时期，人们就已经开始应用十进位制记数法，并谙熟九九乘法表、整数四则运算。

In ancient China, mathematics was called arithmetic, which was included as one of the Six Arts (six basic arts, i.e. rites, music, archery, charioting, calligraphy and mathematics) that a confucianist should mastered. In the Spring and Autumn Period (770 BC–476 BC) Chinese people started to apply the decimal system and mastered the multiplication table and integer arithmetic.

从春秋时期开始，中国古代数学不断发展，出现了许多优秀的数学家，他们结合自身研究和历史经验撰写了一批重要的数学著作。刘徽的《九章算术》是中国历史上第一部系统完整的数学著作，成书于西汉时期。《九章算术》被后世奉为十大算学经典之首，它对中国数学体系的影响与古希腊数学著作《几何原本》对西方数学体系的影响不相上下。祖冲之（429—500）是南北朝时期著名数学家、科学家。《缀术》是祖冲之的数学著作，代表了当时数学领域的最高水平。在唐代时，《缀术》被列入国子监数学教科书“算经十书”之中。祖冲之在前人成就的基础上，通过割圆术的方法，得出圆周率的数值在 3.1415926 和 3.1415927 之间，这意味着圆周率的数值被精确到了小数点后第 7 位。祖冲之成为世界上第一位将圆周率值计算到小数第 7 位的科学家，比欧洲人早了 1100 多年。人们为了纪念他的贡献，把他的计算结果命名为“祖率”。

From the Spring and Autumn Period (770 BC–476 BC), with the continuous development of mathematics in ancient China, many excellent mathematicians appeared. And based on their studies and experiences, they wrote several classic books of great significance. *Nine Chapters on the Mathematical Art* written by Liu Hui in the Western Han dynasty (206 BC–25 AD) is the first book systematically giving an introduction on mathematics. It is considered as the top masterpiece among Ten Great Books on Mathematics and has exerted equal influence on the western mathematics development with the book *Euclid's Elements* of ancient greek. Zu Chongzhi (429–500) was a prestigious mathematician and scientist in the Southern and Northern Dynasties (420–589). *Zhui Shu*, a classic written by Zu Chongzhi, represented the highest level in mathematics at that time. In the Tang dynasty (618–907), this book was listed in the textbook on mathematics, *Ten Computational Canons*, by the Imperial College. Based on the previous achievements accomplished by ancestors, Zu Chongzhi calculated the value of π is between 3.1415926 and 3.1415927 by cyclotomic method, which means the accuracy of π had been put further to the seventh decimal place. Zu Chongzhi also became the first scientist who calculated the value of π to the seventh decimal place, which was 1,100 years in advanced of European scientists. In honor of Zu Chongzhi and his accomplishment, his result of π is called Zu Lǜ . Zu Chongzhi's study on the value of π satisfied the demand of productive labor at that time.

三、文化关键词

算术　arithmetic

算筹　counting rods

算盘　abacus

十进位制　decimal system

九九乘法表　multiplication table

整数四则运算　integer arithmetic

《九章算术》 *Nine Chapters on the Mathematical Art*

《周髀算经》 *The Arithmetical Classic of the Gnomon and the Circular Pacths of Heaven*

第一节　《九章算术》

Nine Chapters on the Mathematical Art

一、典籍简介

《九章算术》是中国古代数学专著，是“算经十书”中最重要的一种。《九章算术》大约于东汉初年（公元1世纪）成书，它的出现标志着中国古代数学体系的形成。

The *Jiuzhang Suanshu* (*Nine Chapters on the Mathematical Art*) is the longest suviving and one of the most important in the Ten Great Books on Mathematics. The book was finished in the early Eastern Han dynasty(about lst century), indicating the formation of ancient Chinese mathematical system.It became the criterion of mathematical learning and research for mathematicians of later generations ever since then.

后世的古代数学家，大都是从《九章算术》开始学习和研究数学的，许多人曾为它做过注释，其中最著名的有刘徽（263）、李淳风（656）等人。唐宋两代都由国家明令规定为教科书。1084年由当时的北宋朝廷进行刊刻，是世界上最早的印刷本数学书。《九章算术》在隋唐时期就已传入朝鲜、日本，现在它已被译成日、俄、德、英、法等多种文字。《九章算术》分为九章，收有246个数学问题及解法与步骤。

Afterwards, the *Jiuzhang Suanshu* has been annotated by many mathematicians, the most famous ones including Liu Hui (263) and Li Chunfeng (656). During the Tang dynasty and Song dynasty, it was officially declared to be the national mathematical textbook. The edition published by the Northern Song government in 1084 was the earliest mathematical book in the world. The book was introduced to Korea and Japan during the Sui and Tang dynasties. Now, it has been trans lated into several languages, including Japanese, Russian, German, English and French. The book has nine chapters containing 246 questions with their solutions and procedures. Here is a brief description of each chapter.

《九章算术》的数学成就如下：

（1）提出用分数进行运算的完整法则，比欧洲早1400多年。

（2）提出整套的比例理论，比欧洲早了1400多年。

（3）介绍了开平方、开立方的方法，其程序与现今程序基本一致，比西方早了数百年。

（4）采用分离系数的方法表示线性方程组，比西方早了 1600 年。

（5）提出了正负数，比西方早了 6 个世纪。

（6）提出了勾股数问题的通解公式，比西方早了 3 个世纪。

（7）提出了各种多边形、圆、弓形等的面积公式。

The book's major achievements are as follows:

1. Devising a systematic treatment of arithmetic operations with fractions, 1,400 years earlier than the Europeans.

2. Dealing with various types of problems on proportions, 1,400 years earlier than the Europeans.

3. Devising methods for extracting square root and cubic root, which is quite similar to today's method, several hundred years earlier than the Western mathematicians.

4. Developing solutions for a system of linear equations, about 1,600 years earlier than the Western mathematicians.

5. Introducing the concepts of positive and negative numbers, more than 600 years earlier than the West.

6. Developing a general solution formula for the Pythagorean problems (problems of Gou gu) , 300 years earlier than the West.

7. Putting forward theories of calculating areas and volumes of different shapes and figures.

二、典籍英译赏析

【原典 1】

今有田广十五步，从十六步。问为田几何。

答曰：一亩。

方田术曰：广从相乘得积步。以亩法二百四十步除之，即亩数。百亩为一顷。

【今译】

已知某块田地宽 15 步，长 16 步。问这块田地的面积是多少？

答：这块田地面积为 1 亩。

方形（含长方形、正方形）田地的算法是：长宽相乘得其面积——平方步数。以亩法 240 平方步数除所得面积——平方步数，即为亩数。100 亩为 1 顷。

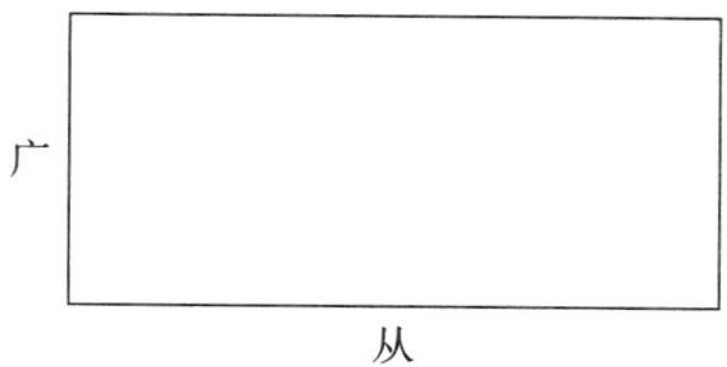

【Lam Lay Yong 英译】

Now there is a field, width 15 *bu* and length 16 *bu*. Find [the area of] the field.

Answer says: 1 *mu* 亩 .

Method of *fang tian* says: The width and length in *bu* are mutually multiplied (*xiang cheng* 相乘) to give the area in *bu*. With [one] *mu* as divisor, divide (*chu* 除) by 240 *bu* to obtain the quantity in *mu*. 100 *mu* is equivalent to 1 *qing* (顷).

【赏析重点】

分析“以亩法二百四十步除之”的逻辑语义和翻译方法。

【原典 2】

今有三分之一，五分之二。问合之得几何。答曰：十五分之十一。

又有三分之二，七分之四，九分之五。问合之得几何。答曰：得一、六十三分之五十。

又有二分之一，三分之二，四分之三，五分之四。问合之得几何。答曰：得二、六十分之四十三。

合分术曰：母互乘子，并以为实，母相乘为法，实如法而一。不满法者，以法命之，其母同者，直相从之。

【今译】

现有$\frac{1}{3}$，$\frac{2}{5}$，问相加得多少？　答：$\frac{11}{15}$。

又有$\frac{2}{3}$，$\frac{4}{7}$，$\frac{5}{9}$，问三数相加得多少？　答：$1\frac{50}{63}$。

又有$\frac{1}{2}$，$\frac{2}{3}$，$\frac{3}{4}$，$\frac{4}{5}$，问四数相加得多少？　答：$2\frac{43}{60}$。

分数相加的法则是：以诸分母与诸分子交互相乘，所得诸乘积相加之和作为被除数，而以诸分母相乘之积作为除数。以除数去除被除数，若除之不尽，则以余数为分子，除数为分母，得一分数。若诸分数之分母相同，则可以用分子直接相加。

【Lam Lay Yong 英译】

Now there are $\frac{1}{3}$ and $\frac{2}{5}$. Find their sum (*he* 合).

Answer says: $\frac{11}{15}$.

Next there are $\frac{2}{3}$, $\frac{4}{7}$ and $\frac{5}{9}$. Find their sum.

Answer says: $1\frac{50}{63}$.

Next there are $\frac{1}{2}$, $\frac{2}{3}$, $\frac{3}{4}$ and $\frac{4}{5}$. Find their sum.

Answer says: $2\frac{43}{60}$.

Method of adding fractions (*he fen* 合分) says: Multiply mutually each numerator and the other denominator(s) (*mu hu cheng zi* 母互乘子), and let the sum [of the products] be the *shi* 实 (dividend). Multiply the *denominators* and let [the product] be the *fa* 法 (divisor). Divide the *shi* by the *fa* (*shi ru fa er yi* 实如法而一). When the remaining [shi] is less than the *fa*, assign it to the *fa* (*yi fa ming zhi* 以法命之) [to form a fraction].

【赏析重点】

分析“实如法而一”的语义特征和翻译方法。

【原典 3】

今有兔先走一百步，犬追之二百五十步，不及三十步而止。问犬不止，复行几何步及之。

答曰：一百七步七分步之一。

术曰：置兔先走一百步，以犬走不及三十步减之，余为法。以不及三十步乘犬追步数为实，实如法得一步。

【今译】

今有兔先跑 100 步，狗追到 250 步时，差 30 步停下了。问狗不停下来，再走几步能追上兔?

答：再走 $107\frac{1}{7}$步。

算法：将兔先跑的 100 步减去狗所差的 30 步，余数作除数。用所差的 30 步乘以狗追的步数作被除数，除数除被除数得所求的步数。

【Lam Lay Yong 英译】

Now there is a rabbit which walks 100 *bu* before it is chased by a dog. When the dog has gone 250 *bu*, it stops and is 30 *bu* behind [the rabbit]. If the dog does not stop, find how many more *bu* it would have to go before it reaches [the rabbit].

Answer says: $107\frac{1}{7}$ *bu*.

Method says: Put down the distance walked by the rabbit, 100 *bu*, and subtract the distance 30 *bu* of the dog behind [-the rabbit]; let the remainder be the *fa*. Multiply the distance in bu that the dog has gone by the 30 *bu* of the dog behind [the rabbit] to form the *shi*. Divide the *shi* by the *fa* to obtain [the distance] in *bu*.

【赏析重点】

（1）分析“以犬走不及三十步减之”的逻辑特点和翻译方法。

（2）分析“复行几何步及之”译文的句法特点。

第二节　《周髀算经》

The Arithmetical Classic of the Gnomon and the Circular Paths of Heaven

一、典籍简介

《周髀算经》是中国历史上最早的一部数学典籍，也是一部天文学著作。成书时间在公元前 5 世纪与公元 2 世纪之间，唐代被收入“算经十书”，并被列为《十经》的第一部。该书包括许多重要的数学内容，还对天体方位作了测定。《周髀算经》中周公与商高之间的对话涉及 246 个问题，每个问题都以相应数学算法得到解决。其中谈到了勾股定理（亦称毕达哥拉斯定理）及其在测量上的应用，记载了大禹如何运用勾股定理治理水灾、加深河床、测量高低。这是世界上关于勾股定理最早的文字记录之一。

The oldest mathematical classic in China, *Zhou Bi Suanjing* or *The Arithmetical Classic of the Gnomon and the Circular Paths of Heaven*, is an astronomy text as well. It is thought to have been compiled sometime between 500 BC and 200 AD. During the Tang dynasty, the book was listed as the first of all the texts included in *Ten Great Books on Mathematics*. It contains some important mathe matical sections and measures the positions of the heavenly bodies. *Zhoubi Suanjing* is a collection of 246 problems encountered during the conversations between the Duke of Zhou and Shang Gao. Each question has stated their numerical answer and corresponding arithmetic algorithm. The author of the *Zhoubi Suanjing* writes that Emperor Yu quells floods, deepens rivers and streams, surveys high places and low places by using the *Gougu* rule. And this book contains one of the first recorded proofs of the *Gougu* rule, or the Pythagorean Theorem in the world.

二、典籍英译赏析

【原典 1】

荣方曰："周髀者何？"

陈子曰："古时天子治周，此数望之从周，故曰周髀。髀者，表也。"

【今译】

荣方问："周髀是什么？"

陈子答："从前周天子治理天下，数学、天文学的原理，是以周代王城（今河南洛阳）为测望的基地，故称为周髀。髀，就是表竿的意思。"

【英译】

Rong Fang asked "What is meant by [the term] *zhou bi*?". Chen Zi replied "In ancient times the Son of Heaven ruled from *Zhou* 周. This meant that quantities were observed at *Zhou*, hence the term *zhou bi*. Bi 髀 means *biao* 表 gnomon."

【赏析重点】

分析"数望之从周"的逻辑结构和翻译方法。

【原典 2】

平矩以正绳，偃矩以望高，覆矩以测深，卧矩以知远，环矩以为圆，合矩以为方。方属地，圆属天，天圆地方。方数为典，以方出圆。

【今译】

利用矩的直角边和重垂线，可确定水平面。把矩仰立放，可测高度。把矩倒置，可测深度。把矩卧放与地面平行，可测水平距离的长度。把矩环旋一周，可以得到圆形。将两矩相合，可得方形。方的数理应用于观测地，圆的数理应用于观测天，所以称天圆地方。以方的数理为基础，以处理方的方法推导出圆之数理。

【英译】

The level trysquare is used to set lines true. The supine trysquare is used to sight on heights. The inverted trysquare is used to plumb depths. The recumbent trysquare is used to find distances. The rotated trysquare is used to make circles, and joined trysquares are used to make squares. The square pertains to Earth, and the circle pertains to Heaven. Heaven is a circle, and Earth is a square. The numbers of the square are basic, and the circle is produced from the square.

【赏析重点】

（1）学习“正绳”“望高”“测深”“知远”“为圆”“为方”词组的动词翻译。

（2）分析“以方出圆”的翻译方法。

【原典3】

数之法，出于圆方。圆出于方，方出于矩。矩出于九九八十一。故折矩，以为句广三，股修四，径隅五。既方之外，半其一矩。环而共盘，得成三、四、五。两矩共长二十有五，是谓积矩。

【今译】

数学的方法来源于圆和方的数理特性。圆可由方的数理特性推导，方可由矩的直角数理特性推导，矩的数理原理出于乘除法则。所以将矩形对角一折为二得两个相等直角三角形，直角三角形的勾（即短边）等于三，股（即长边）等于四，那么径（即弦，斜边之长）就等于五。在直角三角形之外，以径（斜边）为边作正方形，取半个长方形。环绕正方形一周，共同形成一方盘。由此推导，得以成立三四五数理关系（今称为勾股定理）。两个矩形共长二十五。这种推导法就是所谓的积矩法。

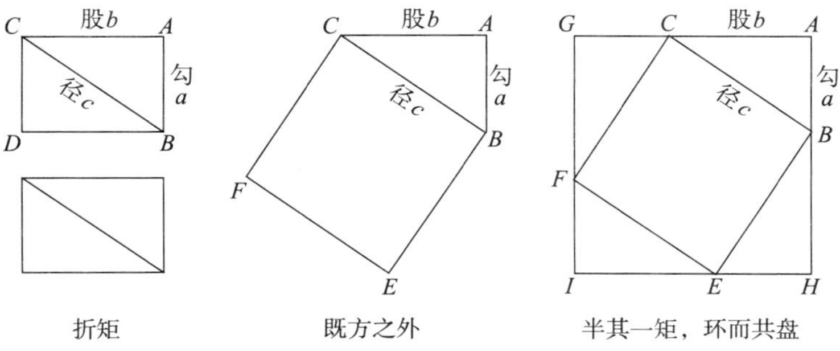

折矩　　既方之外　　半其一矩，环而共盘

【英译】

The patterns for these numbers come from the circle and the square. The circle comes from the square, the square comes from the trysquare and the trysquare comes from [the fact that] nine nines are eighty-one. Therefore fold a trysquare, so that the base is three in breadth; the altitude is four in extension and the diameter is five aslant. Having squared its outside, halve it [to obtain] one trysquare. Placing them round together in a ring, one can form three, four and five. The two trysquares have a combined length of twenty-five. This is called the accumulation of trysquares.

【赏析重点】

（1）分析"句广""股修""径隅"的翻译方法。

（2）分析"环而共盘"的逻辑语义和翻译方法。

【原典 4】

日夏至南万六千里，日冬至南十三万五千里，日中无影。以此观之，从南至夏至之日中十一万九千里。北至其夜半亦然。凡径二十三万八千里，此夏至日道之径也，其周七十一万四千里。从夏至之日中，至冬至之日中十一万九千里。北至极下亦然。

【今译】

夏至，太阳在离测量点南边 16000 里处的天空上；冬至，太阳在离测量点南边 135000 里处的天空上；在正当中午时，竖立的表竿没有日影。由此看来，从极下向南到夏至正午的无日影之地 119000 里，直径共 238000 里，这是夏至日道的直径。其周长 714000 里。从夏至正午的无日影之地到冬至正午的无日影之地 119000 里，向北到极下也是同样距离。

【英译】

16,000 *li* south [of Zhou] on the day of the summer solstice, and 135,000 *li* south on the day of the winter solstice, there is no shadow at noon. From this we can see that from the pole south to noon at the summer solstice is 119,000 *li*, and it is the same distance north to midnight. The diameter overall is 238,000 *li*, and this is the diameter of the solar path at the summer solstice. Its circumference is 714,000 *li*. From the summer solstice noon to the winter solstice noon is 119,000 *li*, and it is the same distance north to the subpolar point.

【赏析重点】

分析“日夏至南万六千里”的句法特点和翻译方法。

拓展训练 | Extension Training

1. 思考练习

（1）用英文简要介绍《九章算术》《周髀算经》主要内容。

（2）总结分析数学常用概念表达翻译方法。

2. 文化外宣汉英翻译

（1）春秋战国时期，中国古人不但发明了十进位制，还发明了九九乘法表。九九乘法表，又称“九九表”“小九九”，是中国古代筹算中进行乘法、除法、开方等运算的基本计算规则。后来，九九乘法表向东传入朝鲜、日本，经过丝绸之路向西传入印度等国，直到公元 13 世纪欧洲才开始使用九九乘法表。

（2）在中国民间传说中，算盘是远古时代黄帝手下一个叫隶首的人发明的。由于人们在日常生产和生活中都需要计算，却没有方便的计算工具，隶首就想出了一个办法：到河滩捡回不同颜色的石片，给每块石片都打上眼，用细绳逐个穿起来。每 10 个或 100 个石片中间穿一个不同颜色的石片，这样清算起来就省事多了。此后，他又想到一个更加实用的办法，把石片每 10 颗一穿，穿成 100 个数，放在一个大泥盘上，在上边写清数位，如十位、百位、千位、万位。这就是算盘的雏形。

（3）我国古代为建立度量衡标准始终做着不懈的努力，并且积累了丰富的经验。传出土于殷墟的三支骨尺，长度皆在 16 厘米左右，正好是中等身高人拇指尖至食指尖间一拃的长度，与“布手知尺”相吻合。古人深知用人体作长度标准误差很大的道理，因此一直在寻找一种复现性较好的自然物来定义一尺的长度。《淮南子 · 天文训》中说：“十二粟而当一寸。”《说文》十发为程。十程为分。《孙子算经》中说：“蚕吐丝为忽，十忽为秒，十秒为毫，十毫为厘，十厘为分等，说法各异然而都难以与汉尺度相符。”

第十五章　农业典籍英译

Translation of Chinese Agricultural Classics

一、学习目标

（1）用英文介绍中国古代农业成就。

（2）掌握中国农业文化概念汉英翻译。

（3）鉴赏中国农业典籍汉英翻译方法。

二、文化背景

中国是世界上最早发展农业的国家之一，在新石器时代早期就已经出现了人工种植的稻谷。重视农业是古代君主治理国家的基本思想。古代劳动人民也在实践的基础上不断总结耕种的经验。在漫长的历史发展中出现了许多先进的农业生产工具和技艺，杰出的农学家及农业著作，以及功绩卓著的水利灌溉工程等。

China is one of the earliest countries that developed agriculture in the world and at the latest, the artificial cultivation of rice appeared in the early phase of the Neolithic Age (approx. 10,000–4,000 years ago). The ancient imperial emperors attached great importance to agriculture and regarded it as the basic concept of governing a nation. At the same time, the ancient Chinese labouring people continually summarized experiences in cultivation based on their agricultural practices, and numerous advanced agricultural tools and techniques, outstanding agriculturists and famous books of agriculture as well as famous and meritorious water conservancy irrigation projects emerged in a long history of development.

农作物的播种、收获等都受到太阳光照的影响，根据季节的变化而变化。早在春秋战国时期，古人就已经确定了夏至、春分、秋分、冬至四个节气，并认识到夏至这天的白日最长、夜晚最短，冬至则是白日最短、夜晚最长，春分、秋分为昼夜等分。秦汉时期，根据太阳在公转轨道上的位置，将一年分割为平均的二十四份，并冠以不同的名字。公元前 104 年，中国第一部历法《太初历》正式把二十四节气列入历法。二十四节气中的“气”，是指气候，节气是指一个季节的开始。二十四节气分别为：立春、雨水、惊蛰、春分、清明、谷雨、立夏、小满、芒种、夏至、小暑、大暑、立秋、处暑、白露、秋分、寒露、霜降、立冬、小雪、大雪、冬至、小寒、大寒。

The sowing and harvest of crops are decided by sun exposure and change according to different seasons. As early as the Spring and Autumn Period and Warring States Period (770 BC–221 BC), ancient Chinese people had determined the 4 earliest Solar Terms as the Summer Solstice, Spring Equinox, Autumn Equinox and Winter Solstice. They also realised that on the Summer Solstice, the daytime is the longest with the shortest night while on the winter Solstice, people experience the longest night and shortest daytime, and on the Spring Equinox and Autumn Equinox, the lengths of daytime and night are the same. During the Qin and Han dynasties (206 BC–220 AD), in terms of the changing position of the sun on the orbit, one year time could be divided into 24 Solar Terms with respective name. In 104 B.C., the first calendar in China named as Taichu Calendar officially regulated the 24 Solar Terms. The Qi in the 24 Solar Terms is referred to the climate and the Solar Term means the beginning of a season. The 24 Solar Terms are the Beginning of Spring, Rain Water, Waking of Insects, Spring Equinox, Pure Brightness, Grain Rain, Beginning of Summer, Lesser Fullness of Grain, Grain in Beard, Summer Solstice, Lesser Heat, Greater Heat, Beginning of Autumn, End of Heat, White Dew, Autumnal Equinox, Cold Dew, Frosts Descent, Beginning of Winter, Lesser Snow, Greater Snow, Winter Solstice. Lesser Cold and Greater Cold.

二十四节气按照春、夏、秋、冬的季节变化来排列，每个节气都有与之相对的农事安排，因此二十四节气是指导耕种、田间管理、秋收等农业生产的重要历法。在从事农业生产时，人们要以十四节气为农业气候历，不违背农时（适宜于从事耕种、收获的时节），耕种收获，应时劳作。

The 24 Solar Terms are put in order according to spring, summer, autumn and winter, and in each term corresponding farming work should be arranged. This is also the reason why this is important to guide people to manage the cultivation, crop growth and autumn harvest. In terms of agricultural production, people should treat the 24 Solar Terms as the agricultural schedule without violating the proper farming season (the season that is suitable for cultivation and harvest), in order to plant and reap crops in season.

在中国古代“重农”思想的影响下，农业得到了广泛的发展，同时还出现了许多优秀的农学家，以及集合了当时最为先进的农学技术的农学专著。贾思勰（生卒年不详）是北魏时期杰出的农学家。他出身农民家庭，从小就很喜欢读书，尤其重视对农业生产技术知识的学习和研究。他撰写了涵盖农、林、牧、副、渔等方面的农学专著《齐民要术》。书名中的“齐民”，指普通百姓，“要术”指谋生方法。宋应星（1587—？），明代科学家。他对中国各地的农业和手工业做了广泛的社会调查，虚心向当地的群众请教，收集了丰富的资料，所撰写的《天工开物》于 1637 年刊行。《天工开物》内容丰富，不仅囊括了农业，还对手工业、工业等方面进行了系统的总结，构成了一个完整的科学技术体系。英国的达尔文称此书为“权威著作”，李约瑟则称此书为“17 世纪早期的重要工业技术著作”。

In ancient China, influenced by the thought of valuing agriculture, the agriculture was widely developed. There were many outstanding agriculturists as well as numerous famous books of agriculture collecting the most advanced agricultural techniques at that time. Jia Sixie (unknown years of birth and death) is an outstanding agriculturist of the Northern Wei dynasty (386–534). He was born in a farmers' family and loved reading from childhood, especially concentrating on the study and research on agricultural techniques and knowledge. He wrote the famous book *Main Techniques for the Welfare of the People* (*Qi Min Yao Shu*), covering the areas of agriculture, forestry, animal husbandry, side-line production and fishery. With regards to the book name, *Qi Min* means ordinary people and *Yao Shu* refers to the way to make a living. Song Yingxing (1587–?), a scientist in the late Ming dynasty (1368–1644), conducted a social survey on the agricultural and handicraft industries in many places of China, studied from local peoples experience and gathered rich troves of data. The *Exploitation of the Works of Nature* (Tian Gong Kai Wu) was presumed in 1637. *The Exploitation of the Works of Nature* not only covers the agricultural industry, but also gives a systematic summary of the handicraft industry as well as other industries. It overall constructs a complete framework of scientific and technological development in China at that time. It was considered “an authoritative work” by Charles Darwin and claimed as “a great work of industrial technologies in the early 17th century” by Joseph Needham.

三、文化关键词

五谷（麻、菽、麦、稷、黍） Five Grains (sesamum,beans, wheat, panicum millet and glutinous millet)

耕 loosening the soil by ploughing

耙 breaking the soil into fine particles by harrowing

耘 hand weeding

舂 foot-operated pounding mills

牛车 ox-powered waterwheel

踏车 man-powered waterwheel

桔槔 counterweight lever

辘轳 pulley wheel

瓷窑 porcelain kiln

鸟铳 bird pistol

牛碾 ox-drawn rolling mill

打枷 separating beans from the pods by beating with a flail

纺纬 spinning wheel for making yams

弹棉 bowing of cotton fibres

淘洗铁砂 concentrating iron ore by washing

瓦坯脱桶 separating tiles from the mold

瓷坯汶水 dipping thoroughly dried wares in water

瓷器过釉 dipping clayware in liquid glaze

升炼水银 sublimation and condensation of mercury ore

双纤独轮车 the single-wheeled cart drawn by two mules or horses

第一节 《齐民要术》

Main Techniques for the Welfare of the People

一、典籍简介

《齐民要术》是迄今保存最为完整的我国古代农学著作，由北魏时期官员贾思勰所著。有人认为《齐民要术》成书于东魏武定二年，即公元 544 年，还有记载说该书的完成时间在公元 533 和 544 年间。该书正文分十卷，共九十二篇，收录了中国1500年前农艺、园艺、造林、蚕桑、畜牧、兽医、配种、酿造、烹饪、贮藏以及治荒等方面的知识。书中援引古籍近200部，所引的重要农学著作如《氾胜之书》《四民月令》等汉晋重要农书现已失传，因此后人只能从此书了解当时的农业运作。该书自出版后，长期受中国历朝政府重视，传遍海外后亦常被认为是研究古物种变化的经典，达尔文研究进化论时曾参考一部中国古代百科全书，有说此书正是《齐民要术》。《齐民要术》可解作平民谋生方法，也可解为治理民生的方法。

Qimin Yaoshu (also *Main Techniques for the Welfare of the People*) is the most completely preserved of the ancient Chinese agricultural texts, and was written by the Northern Wei dynasty official Jia Sixie. The book is believed to have been completed in the second year of Wu Ding of Eastern Wei, namely in 544, while another account gives the completion between 533 and 544. The text of the book is divided into 10 volumes and 92 chapters, and records 1,500-year-old Chinese agronomy, horticulture, afforestation, sericulture, animal husbandry, veterinary medicine, breeding, brewing, cooking, storage, as well as remedies for barren land. The book quoted nearly 200 ancient books. Important agricultural books such as *Fansheng Zhishu* and *Simin Yueling* from the Han and Jin dynasties are now lost, so future generations can only understand the operation of agriculture at the time from this book. Since the publication of the book, historical Chinese governments have long attached great importance to it. Since the book spread overseas, it has also often been considered a classic to study changes in the ancient species. When Charles Darwin was researching the theory of evolution, he made reference to an encyclopedia of ancient China. It is said that the book he referred to was in fact *Qimin Yaoshu* .The book's name *Qimin Yaoshu* can be explained as techniques by which civilians make their livelihood, and also be explicated as techniques to harness the people's livelihood.

二、作者简介

贾思勰（生卒年不详），青州益都（今山东寿光市）人。北魏时期大臣，中国古代杰出的农学家。曾任高阳太守，著有综合性农书《齐民要术》。系统地总结了秦汉以来我国黄河流域的农业科学技术知识，其取材布局，为后世的农学著作提供了可以遵循的依据。该作品不仅是我国现存最早和最完善的农学名著，也是世界农学史上最早的名著之一，对后世的农业生产有着深远的影响。该著作由耕田、谷物、蔬菜、果树、树木、畜产、酿造、调味、调理、外国物产等各章构成，是中国现存的最早的、最完整的大型农业百科全书。

Jia Sixie, born in Yidu, Shandong province, was an agronomist in the Northern Wei dynasty. Being a Taishou (governor, literally "Warden Major") of the District of Gaoyang, he was proficient in agricultural science and systematized dryland agricultural technology during the revival of agriculture in North China. He wrote *Qimin Yaoshu* (*Main Techniques for the Welfare of the People*) which is composed of farming, grain, vegetables, fruit trees, trees, livestock, brewing, seasoning, conditioning, foreign products and other chapters. It is the earliest and most complete large-scale agricultural encyclopedia in China.

三、典籍英译赏析

【原典 1】

凡种谷，雨后为佳；遇小雨，宜接湿种；遇大雨，待萝①生。小雨，不接湿，无以生禾苗；大雨，不待白背，湿辗，则令苗瘦。萝若盛者，先锄一遍，然后纳种②，乃佳也。

【注释】

①萝：杂草，亦作“秽”。

②纳种：即下种。本书用“纳”字的例子很少，多数是借用“内”字。

【今译】

种谷子，都以雨后下种为好；下过小雨，趁湿时种；下大雨，等杂草发芽后再种。雨下得小，不趁湿时下种，禾苗不容易生出；雨大了，如不等地面发白湿着就去辗压，禾苗会瘦弱。杂草如果很多，先锄一遍，然后下种，才合适。

【英译】

In sowing spiked millets, it is better to follow a rain. If a light drizzle, catch up the damp; if a heavy shower, wait till weeds sprout. For, in drizzles, the seed corn would not sprout unless sown with enough wetness; after a heavy rain, when the surface was not yet tolerably dry (to appear pale) treading will make (the ground stickly and) the seedlings will be weak. If weeds should grow to unwonted height, hoe them down before sowing.

【赏析重点】

（1）分析“雨后为佳”的逻辑结构和翻译方法。

（2）分析“小雨，不接湿，无以生禾苗”的逻辑衔接特点和翻译方法。

【原典 2】

凡五果[①]，花盛时遭霜，则无子。常预于园中，往往[②]贮恶草生粪。天雨新晴，北风寒切，是夜必霜。此时放火作煴[③]，少得烟气，则免于霜矣。

【注释】

①五果：按习惯，是指桃、李、梅、栗、枣；但事实上应是泛指各种果树说的。因为梅花开时不可能有霜害，枣花却只在晚霜后才开花。

②往往：随时。

③煴：郁烟，看不见火焰的燃烧而产生出来的许多烟。

【今译】

各种果树，花开得旺盛时遇到结霜，便不能结实。应当随时在园里积蓄一些杂草、烂叶、生牲口粪，作为准备。雨后新晴，吹着北风，寒气增加很急，夜间必定结霜。这时放火烧草，作成暗火，生出一些烟，就可保护果树，不受霜的侵害。

【英译】

If a frost occurs when fruit-trees are in blossom, no fruit will be formed. Always keep some combustibles such as hewn weeds or stable refuse in the orchards. Whenever a day breaks clear after a period of rain, and the northerly wind blows sharply cold, it is the signal for a frosty night. Set a smothered fire to the dirt heap in the evening so as to make it smoking (but not blazing). This will prevent frost injuries.

【赏析重点】

（1）分析“天雨新晴，北风寒切”的结构特点和翻译方法。

（2）分析“少得烟气”的语义特点和翻译方法。

【原典 3】

凡栽一切树木，欲记其阴阳，不令转易。阴阳易位则难生。小小栽者，不烦记也。大树髡之；不髡风摇则死。小则不髡。

【注释】

髡：本义是将头发剪短。此处用在树木，便是剪去一部分枝条。

【今译】

凡属移栽树木，都要记下它的阴面阳面，照原有位置栽下不要换。改换了原有的阴阳面，就不容易成活。很小很小的树苗，移栽时可以不必记。大树，要把枝叶剪去；不剪掉，风吹摇动，根不牢固，就会死掉。小的就不必剪。

【英译】

In transplantation, take good care to maintain a tree in its original relationship to sun and shade. Negligence often leads to failure of survival. With smaller trees this trouble and all anxieties may be dispensed. Always poll bigger treesor they might be shaken to death by wind. Smaller trees may do well without polling.

【赏析重点】

（1）分析“欲记其阴阳”的文化语义特点和翻译方法。

（2）分析“不髡风摇则死”的逻辑结构和翻译方法。

【原典4】

常留腊月、正月生羔为种者，上；十一月、二月生者，次之。非此数月生者，毛必焦卷，骨髓细小。所以然者，是逢寒遇热故也。其八、九、十月生者，虽值秋肥，然比至冬暮，母乳已竭，春草未生，是故不佳。

【今译】

将腊月、正月的羊羔留来作种，最好；十一月、二月的，次一等。不是这几个月生的，毛不润泽顺直，骨架也小。原因是出生之后逢寒遇热的结果。八、九、十月生的，母羊虽然在秋肥中，但到冬天母羊奶用完了，青草没有出生，小羊便长不好。

【英译】

Lamb or kids born in the first or last months of the year are the best; next, those in the 1th or 2nd months. Litters of other months will have singed pillage and small stature due to the influence of cold and hot seasons. Birth in the 8th, 9th and 10th months certainly coincides with the autumn fattening of the dams; but owing to the incidence of weaning time into late winter when no green fodder is available, the growth of the young animals is handicapped. Therefore the youngs are not very good.

【赏析重点】

（1）分析“逢寒遇热”的结构特点和翻译方法。

（2）分析“母乳已竭，春草未生”结构特点和翻译方法。

【原典5】

肉酱法：牛、羊、獐、鹿、兔肉，皆得作。取良杀新肉，去脂细剉，晒曲令燥熟捣。

大率：肉一斗，曲末五升，白盐二升半，黄蒸一升。

曝干，熟捣，绢簁。

盘上和令均调，内瓮子中。泥封日曝。寒月作之，宜埋之于黍穰积中。

【今译】

做肉酱的方法：牛肉、羊肉、獐肉、鹿肉、兔肉，都可以做。取活杀的新鲜好肉，去掉脂肪，斫碎。干了的陈肉不合用。连脂肪做，酱就嫌腻。曲要晒干燥，捣细，用绢筛筛。

一般的比例：一斗肉，五升曲末，二升半白盐，一升黄蒸。

晒干，捣细，绢筛筛过。

在盘子里拌和均匀，放进瓮里。瓮口用泥封上，搁在太阳下面晒着。如果冷天做，要埋在黍糠堆里面。

【英译】

For meat-chiang: beef, mutton, venison, hare (or meat of any game)will do; always use good, freshly slaughtered meat. Pick away fats, and mince finely. (Meat aged or dried is no good; fat makes the product over unctuous.) Dry some wine starter in sunshine, when very dry, pound fine and sift. Take 10 parts of finely-chopped meat, 5 of starter powder, 2.5 of white table salt, 1 of yellow mould (vid supra) pounded fine when dry and sift (as with wine starter). Mix well in a pan, then move into a pottery jar, seal with mud and bake in sunshine. If made in winter days, bury the jar in millet chaff (to keep warm).

【赏析重点】

（1）分析“晒曲令燥熟擣”的语义逻辑特点和翻译方法。

（2）分析“曝干，熟捣，绢簁”的翻译方法。

第二节 《天工开物》

The Exploitation of the Works of Nature

一、典籍简介

《天工开物》是中国古代百科全书式的科技著作，论述了农业和手工业两大领域内 30 个生产部门的技术，分上中下三卷，共 18 章，插图 123 幅。每章首有“宋子曰”一段作为引言，对全章内容作提要性叙述。上卷主要记述谷物栽培及农具、水利机械，养蚕与丝织技术，植物染料与染色技术，制盐技术与工具，甘蔗种植与制糖技术。中卷记述砖、瓦及白瓷的烧炼技术，冶炼与铸造技术，舟车结构与使用方法，锻造铁器的工艺，烧制石灰、采煤等技术，植物油脂提炼工艺，造纸技术。下卷记述金银等各种金属矿石的开采与冶炼技术，冷兵器的制造工艺，朱砂研制，制墨，酒曲制造，珍珠、宝石等的开采工艺等。

Tian Gong Kai Wu, or *The Exploitation of the Works of Nature*, is an ancient Chinese encyclopedia in science and technology. It involves two major fields-agriculture and handicrafts. It can be divided into three parts, consisting of 18 chapters, along with 123 figures and illustrations. Every chapter begins with the words "Songzi Says" which introduces the major contents of each chapter. Volume Ⅰ discusses such topics as grain cultivation and farming tools, water conservancy machinery, salt making and the tools used, sugar cane plantation and sugar making, oil and fat refining, silkworm raising and silk making, dyestuff and dye making. Volume Ⅰ mainly discusses the techniques of metallurgy and casting, the mining of gold and silver and other metal ores and the smelting techniques, the arts and techniques of forging iron and metal articles, methods of making bricks and tiles, and the calcination of stones, sulphur and the mining of coal. Volume Ⅲ focuses on techniques of paper making, cinnabar refining and ink making, structuring boats and carts and the methods of using them, the methods of making gunpowder and incendiary weapons, yeast making and the mining of pearls and gems.

二、作者简介

宋应星（1587—约 1666），字长庚，明朝后期出生于江西省奉新县。宋应星自幼聪颖好学，记忆力过人，不及十岁便会作诗。他博览群书，兴趣广泛，十三经传、宋代理学、历史乃至诸子百家均有涉猎，对音乐、天文、医药、弈棋、绘画以及自然科学亦十分喜爱。

Song Yingxing (born in 1587 and died approximately in 1666), styled himself Changgeng, was a native of Fengxin County, Jiangxi Province living in the late Ming dynasty. In childhood, he already showed his talent and his eagerness to learn. He had a very good memory and could write poems when he was less than ten years old. He had a wide range of interest and read extensively, including such books as the Thirteen Confucian Classics, Philosophy of the Song dynasty, history books and books on different schools of thought. In addition, he was fond of music, astronomy, medicine, games of chess, painting and natural science.

1616—1631 年，宋应星多次远游应试科举，均落第而归。科举及第的目标虽未实现，长途旅行却打开了眼界，增长了社会见闻。宋应星的足迹遍及京师、江西、湖北、安徽、江苏、山东、河南、河北、浙江等省的许多城市和乡村。沿途他在田间、作坊调查到不少农业和手工业的技术知识、操作过程，并对操作实态作了素描，记下不少笔记，为日后撰写《天工开物》积累了第一手资料。

Between 1616 and 1631, Song Yingxing travelled very long distances to take the imperial public examinations many times, but unfortunately he failed in each examination. Although he was not successful in these examinations and did not achieve his goal, the experience of the long travels broadened his horizon and enriched his social experience and knowledge. Song Yingxing, on his journey to the capital, travelled to many cities and rural areas in many provinces such as Jiangxi, Hubei, Anhui, Jiangsu, Shandong, Henan, Hebei and Zhejiang. In the course of travelling up north, he visited the fields and workshops for the purpose of accumulating knowledge about agriculture, handicrafts and the operational processes. He also made plentiful sketches of the actual operational processes and took many notes. All this enabled him to acquire firsthand materials for the writing of his works *Tian Gong Kai Wu*.

三、典籍英译赏析

【原典 1】

凡攻治小米，扬得其实，舂得其精，磨得其粹。风扬、车扇而外，簸法生焉。其法篾织为圆盘，铺米其中，挤匀扬播。轻者居前，簸弃地下；重者在后，嘉实存焉。凡小米舂、磨、扬、播制器，已详《稻》《麦》之中。唯小碾一制在《稻》《麦》之外。北方攻小米者，家置石墩，中高边下，边沿不开槽。铺米墩上，妇子两人相向，接手而碾之。其碾石图长如牛赶石，而两头插木柄。米堕边时随手以小扫上。家有此具，杵臼竟悬也。

【今译】

小米是这样加工的：扬净后得到实粒，舂后得到小米，磨后得到小米粉。除去风扬、车扇两法外，还有一种簸法。簸法是用篾条编成圆盘，把谷子铺在上面，均匀地扬簸。轻的扬到前面，就从箕口丢弃地下。重的留在后面，那就是饱满的实粒了。小米加工用的舂、磨、扬、播等工具，已经详述于《攻稻》《攻麦》两节中。只是小碾这个工具，在《攻稻》《攻麦》两章节没有谈到。北方加工小米，在家里安置一个石墩，中间高，四边低，边沿不开槽。碾石是长圆形的，好像牛拉的石磙子，两头插上木柄。碾时，把谷子铺在墩上，妇女两人面对面，相互用手交接碾柄来碾压。米落到碾的边沿时，就随手用小扫帚扫进去。家里有了这种工具，就用不着杵臼了。

【英译】

Farmers winnow to get millets, pound them to get grains and grind them to get powder. Besides winnowing in the wind and using a winnower, there is another method, that is, shaking the millets with winnowing riddles. These bamboo strips are woven into an oblong pan like a riddle. Pour the millets into the pan and shake them into the air. The lighter particles will fly to the front and fall to the ground, and the heavy particles that remain behind are the good full kernels. The methods for pounding, grinding and winnowing are the same as those for other grains and have been described in the section on rice and wheat. In addition, a small rolling mill is used to process millet in North China. A stone frustum whose center is higher than the edges is placed in the house. Millet is spread on the frustum, two women sit face to face and hold a stone roller to press and grind the millets in turn. The roller is cylindrical in shape and is much the same as the roller driven by an ox, but there are wooden handles on both ends. At the same time, when the millets fall to the edge, the millets should be immediately swept to the top with a small brush. There is no need to use any mortar and pestle when a household has such a stone roller at home.

【赏析重点】

（1）分析“轻者居前，簸弃地下；重者在后，嘉实存焉”的句式特点和翻译方法。

（2）分析“中间高，四边低”的翻译方法。

【原典2】

凡小麦，其质为面。盖精之至者，稻中再舂之米；粹之至者，麦中重罗之面也。小麦收获时，束稿击取，如击稻法。其去秕法，北土用扬，盖风扇流传未遍率土也。凡扬不在宇下，必待风至而后为之。风不至，雨不收，皆不可为也。

【今译】

小麦是面粉原料。稻谷加工后最精者是舂过两次的精米，小麦加工后最上品是重复罗过的细白面粉。收获小麦时，手握一把麦秆击取，其法如同击稻。去麦秕，在北方用扬场的方法，因为风车没有遍布全国各地。扬麦不能在屋檐下，必待风至而后为之。风不来、雨不停都不能扬麦。

【英译】

Wheat is the raw material for flour. The finest rice is obtained from the processing of unhusked rice by pounding it twice, while the top-quality wheat flour is obtained from the processing of wheat by sifting repeatedly. The way of reaping wheat by hand is the same as reaping rice. People in the north winnow wheat by hand, for the winnower is not widely used. Farmers can not winnow wheat under the eaves, and they have to wait till it is windy. Winnowing can't be done when there is no wind and when it is raining.

【赏析重点】

（1）分析“稻中再舂之米”“麦中重罗之面”的语义特点和翻译方法。

（2）分析“风不至，雨不收”的句式特点和翻译方法。

【原典3】

凡豆菽刈获，少者用枷，多而省力者仍铺场，烈日晒干，牛曳石赶而压落之。凡打豆枷，竹木竿为柄，其端锥圆眼，拴木一条长三尺许，铺豆于场，执柄而击之。凡豆击之后，用风扇扬去荚叶，筛以继之，嘉实洒然入禀矣。是故舂磨不及麻，碾不及菽也。

【今译】

豆类收获后，量少的用连枷脱粒，如果量多，省力的办法仍然是铺在晒场上，在烈日下晒干，用牛拉石磙来脱粒。打豆的连枷，是用竹竿或木杆作柄，柄的前端钻个圆孔，拴上一条长约三尺左右的木棒。把豆铺在场上，手执枷柄甩打。豆打落后，用风车扇去荚叶，再筛过，就可得到饱满的豆粒入仓了。所以说，芝麻用不着舂和磨，豆类用不着碾和磙。

【英译】

After the reaping of the beans, farmers use a nail to get the beans from the stalks. When there is a large amount of the beans, they spread the stalks on the ground, let them dry in the sun, and then roll the beans off by using an ox-drawn stone roller. The flail is constructed by using a bamboo or wooden pole as the handle, by drilling a round hole in one end and tying another crabstick about three *chi* long. Spread the stalks on the ground and beat them with a flail. After that, farmers use a winnower to get rid of the remaining pods. Then after sifting in a sifter, the beans can be stored in a barn. Therefore, sesame seeds do not need to be pounded and ground and beans don't need to be ground.

【赏析重点】

（1）分析“多而省力者仍铺场”译文的逻辑结构调整。

（2）分析“筛以继之，嘉实洒然入廪矣”的逻辑特点和翻译方法。

【原典4】

宋子曰，天有五气，是生五味。润下作咸，王访箕子而首闻其义焉。口之于味也，辛酸甘苦经年绝一无恙。独食盐禁戒旬日，则缚鸡胜匹，倦怠恹然。岂非天一生水，而此味为生人生气之源哉？四海之中，五服而外，为蔬为谷，皆有寂灭之乡，而斥卤则巧生以待。孰知其所以然？

【今译】

宋子说，大自然有五行之气，由此产生五味。五行中的水湿润而流动，具有盐的咸味。周武王访问箕子时，才首先得知关于五行的道理。人们吃的辣、酸、甜、苦四种味道的食物，经年缺少其中之一，都平安无事。唯独食盐，十日不吃，便身无缚鸡之力、疲倦不振。这不正好说明大自然产生水，而水中的盐质是人的活力的源泉吗？四海之内、边荒以外，都有不能种植蔬菜五谷的不毛之地，但食盐却巧妙地到处都出产，以待人取用。其原因何在呢？

【英译】

Songzi says that there are five elements in nature, water, fire wood, metal and earth, which are the basic elements of everything. They give birth to five tastes: salty, bitter, sour, spicy and sweet. Among the five elements water is wet; it flows and tastes salty. When King Wu of the Zhou dynasty visited Qizi, a sage at that time, he learned about the five elements. People can survive even they do not eat food which they tastes either spicy, sour, sweet and bitter for as long as a year. However they cannot do without salt. If people do not eat salt for ten consecutive days, they will become so weak and tired that they can not even tie up a chicken. This proves that water is the creation of Nature, and the salt in water is the life-giving source for human beings. There exist large areas of bare and barren lands where crops and vegetables are not grown, but surprisingly, salt is produced and obtainable everywhere.

【赏析重点】

（1）分析“天有五气，是生五味”的翻译方法。

（2）分析“岂非天一生水，而此味为生人生气之源哉”的句式翻译方法。

拓展训练 | Extension Training

1. 思考练习

（1）用英文简要介绍《齐民要术》《天工开物》主要内容。

（2）总结分析《齐民要术》《天工开物》英文翻译方法和翻译策略。

2. 文化外宣汉英翻译

（1）在人类发展的历史长河中，中国作为四大文明古国之一，在自然科学和工程技术领域曾取得过辉煌的成就。中华民族的科学发现和技术发明几乎涵盖了所有的学科领域，特别是以天、算、农、医为代表的科学体系和以四大发明为代表的技术成就，在人类发展的历史进程中曾产生过深刻的影响，其中有的还远播到世界各地，或为当地人民所直接采用，或激发了他们进行相关的研究并产生了自己的发明。

（2）中国科学院外籍院士、英国著名科学史家李约瑟（Joseph Needham，1900—1995）曾指出，在古代和中古代科学技术发明的许多重要方面，中国人成功地走在那些创造出著名“希腊奇迹”的传奇式人物的前面，和拥有古代西方世界全部文化财富的阿拉伯人并驾齐驱，并在公元 3 世纪到 13 世纪之间保持了一个西方所望尘莫及的科学知识水平。

（3）立冬是冬季的开始，人们要加强三麦（小麦、大麦、元麦）和油菜的冬前管理，保证壮苗越冬。立冬之后是小雪节气，气温已经降到零摄氏度以下，开始出现降雪，但雪量不大，人们要加强越冬作物的田间管理，保证秋种作物的生长。大雪节气的雪量要比小雪节气大，中国有“瑞雪兆丰年”的俗语，覆盖大地的积雪越多，越能冻死害虫，为越冬作物创造良好的越冬环境。冬至，太阳直射南回归线，北半球地区的白昼最短，黑夜最长，也就意味着进入一年中最寒冷的阶段。

（4）清明时节草木萌动，天气逐渐变得温暖、清澈，故名。在农事安排上，有“清明前后，种瓜种豆”的俗语。清明不仅是二十四节气之一，也是中国传统节日，这一天人们要扫墓祭祖、外出踏春。谷雨是春季最后一个季节，古人有“雨生百谷”的说法，因此得名，此时的降雨对五谷的生长十分有利。

第十六章　地理游记典籍英译

Translation of Human Geography of Ancient China

一、学习目标

（1）用英文介绍中国古代地理主要成就。

（2）掌握中国古代地理文化概念汉英翻译。

（3）鉴赏中国地理典籍汉英翻译方法。

二、文化背景

“地理”一词最早出现在《易经》当中，有“仰以观于天文，俯以察于地理”的记载。“上知天文、下知地理”也逐渐成为古人对博学多识的人的一种描述。中国古代地理学起步很早，在地图制作、学术著作等方面有突出成就，在先秦时期中国人就已经撰写了地理学著作《山海经》。

Dili, the word meaning geography in Chinese, first appeared in *The Book of Changes*, which had a record of “looking up to observe astronomy and looking down to survey geography (*Dili*)”. Knowing both astronomy and geography then gradually became ancient peoples description to knowledgeable persons. Ancient Chinese geography started very early and had outstanding achievements in map-making, academic works and other aspects. Before the Qin dynasty (221 BC–206 BC) Chinese people had written a geography book, *The Book of Mountains and Seas*.

殷商时期，随着最原始的文字甲骨文的出现，古人对地理的发现得以用文字的方式记录下来。在这一时期，已经出现了“南”“北”等文字。周代，人们对于地理更加重视，出现了司徒、司马等官职，其中司徒主要从事土地和农业生产的管理工作。

In the Shang dynasty (1600 BC–1046 BC) with the advent of the most primitive writing Oracle, the ancients were able to record geography (*Dili*) by writing. During this period, characters about south, north and other words were appeared. In the Zhou dynasty (1046 BC–221 BC) more attention was attached to geography by setting up official positions, such as, Situ, an official in charge of the management of land and agricultural production.

战国时期，魏国人假借大禹之名撰写了《尚书 · 禹贡》，其中首次提出“九州”这个地理概念，即以山脉、河流为标志，将国家分为九个行政区，对九个行政区的疆域、山脉、河流、植被、土壤、少数民族、交通等内容进行了简要描述。齐国人邹衍在九州概念的基础上，提出了“大小九州”的地理学概念。他认为中国之内有九州，为小九州，中国之外也有九州，为大九州，而中国只占天下的八十一分之一。

During the Warring States Period (475 BC–221 BC) people of the State of Wei wrote the article *Shang Shu Yu Gong* in the name of Yu the great (an emperor of ancient China). This article put forward the geographical concept of Nine States (Jiuzhou), a poetic name for the first time in the history of China. The Nine States referred to ancient China's nine administrative regions marked by mountains and rivers. The article briefly described the boundaries, mountains, rivers vegetation, soil, minorities, traffic and other features of the nine administrative regions. Based on this concept of Nine States, Zou Yan from the State of Qi put forward the geographic concept of the Big and Small Nine States. He believed that there were nine small states inside China while there were nine big states outside China, and that China took one eighty-first of the world.

唐代是中国历史上经济、文化等方面大繁荣的鼎盛时期之一，随着国内外交流愈加紧密，人们对地理的认识也从本国扩展到周边国家。从 801 年开始，在宰相、地理学家贾耽的主持下，历时 17 年，中国古代最早的世界地图——《海内华夷图》问世。贾耽在裴秀制图六体的基础上，采用古今对照、双色绘画的方式绘制了该地图。同时，佛教在中国逐渐推广，也为古代地理的发展作出了重要贡献，其中最具代表性的事件为玄奘西行印度、鉴真东渡日本。

The Tang dynasty (618–907) is one of the most prosperous heydays for economy, culture and other aspects in Chinese history. With closer domestic and international exchanges, people's knowledge of geography at the time expanded from China to neighboring countries. From the year of 801 and under the auspices of the prime minister and geographer Jia Dan, it took 17 years to finish ancient China's earliest world map, *Map of China and Other Countries*. On the basis of Pei Xiu's Six Elements of Map, Jia Dan drew this map by means of ancient-modern comparing and two-color painting. Meanwhile, the gradual spread of Buddhism in China also made important contributions to the development of ancient geography. The most representative cases include Xuanzang's westward journey to India and Jianzhen's eastward voyage to japan in the Ming dynasty (1368–1644).

明代，郑和带领船队下西洋，不仅是中国航海史上的壮举，更是一次伟大的地理大发现。从明代永乐三年（1405）至宣德八年（1433），郑和奉命率领船队七下西洋。据《明史·郑和传》记载，郑和下西洋共经过 30 多个国家或地区，包括东南亚的爪哇、泰国、苏门答腊、印度半岛南端，以及非洲东岸的红海、麦加等地。郑和航海的探索比西方著名海上探险家达·伽马、哥伦布等人早了 80 多年，代表了中国古代海上探索的最高成就。

Zheng He and his fleet's voyage to the western seas was not only a feat of China's maritime history, but also a great geographical discovery. From 1405 to 1433, Zheng He received orders to lead fleets to western seas for 7 times. According to history of the Ming dynasty: *Biography of Zheng He*. Zheng He's voyages went by more than 30 countries or regions including Java, Thailand, Sumatra and the southern tip of the Indian Peninsula in Southeast Asia, as well as Red Sea, Mecca and other places in the east coast of Africa. Zheng He's maritime exploration, which represents the highest achievements of maritime exploration in ancient China is 80 years earlier than that of Vasco de Gama, Christopher Columbus and others the famous western maritime explorers.

三、文化关键词

海内华夷图　Map of China and Other Countries

郑和航海图　Compass Map of Zhenghe's Nautical Chart

郑和下西洋　Zheng He led voyages to the western seas

《水经注》 *Commentary on the Waterways Classic*

《大唐西域记》 *The Great Tang Records on the Western Regions*

《梦溪笔谈》 *Brush Talks from Dream Brook*

第一节 《徐霞客游记》

The Travel Diaries of Xu Xiake

一、典籍简介

《徐霞客游记》主要是一部地理学著作，它以日记为主包括名山游记 17 篇和《浙游日记》《江右游日记》《楚游日记》《粤西游日记》《黔游日记》《滇游日记》等。不算散佚的，目前可考的游记资料约 60 万字，都是徐霞客去世后由他人整理而成，称为《徐霞客游记》。《徐霞客游记》是我国最早的一部详细记录旅行者考察地理环境的游记，也是世界上最早的一部记述岩溶地貌并详细考证和探析岩溶地貌成因的著作。

The Travel Diaries of Xu Xiake is primarily a work of geography, which was written mainly in the form of the diary including 17 travel diaries of Great Mountains in China, and other diaries which kept records of his travel in Zhejiang Province, the area west to Chang Jiang, the State of Chu, Guangxi Province, Guizhou Province, and Yunnan Province. Excluding the lost materials, the present materials of his travel diaries have 600,000-odd Chinese characters, which was collected and compiled into book form posthumously by others, and was named *The Travel Diaries of Xu Xiake*. It is the first travelogue in China to record minutely the geographical features and environment along the way where he travelled, and it is also the first one in the whole world to document the topographic features of the karst and rectify detailedly and investigate the contributing factors of the topographic features of the karst.

该书一改传统地理学著作的纂写体例，系统地观察自然、描述自然，开辟了地理学的新方向。它既是系统考察我国地质、地貌的地学名著，又是描绘中华风景资源的旅游鸿篇，也是文字优美的文学佳作，在国内外均具有较为深远的影响。

Unlike the traditional style of the geographical writings, it opens up a new direction of the geography with his systematic observation and description of the nature. It is not only a geographical masterpiece which systematically investigates the geology and topographic features of China, but also a travelling masterwork which describes the landscape resources of China, and also a literary gem with fine and proper expressions, all of which have a far-reaching impact both at home and abroad.

二、作者介绍

徐霞客，名宏祖（原为弘祖，因避乾隆之名“弘历”之讳而改），字振之，号霞客，后以号行世，明代南直隶江阴（今属江苏江阴市）人，出生于万历十四年十一月二十七日（公元 1587 年 1 月 5 日），是我国明代杰出的旅行家、地理学家、史学家和文学家，巨著《徐霞客游记》是其代表作。

Xu Xiake, whose given name is Hongzu (宏祖) (it is originally Hongzu (弘祖), but it has been changed into Hongzu (宏祖) because Emperor Qianlong's name Hongli (弘历) has the same Chinese character Hong (弘), so Hong is a taboo at that time) and who styled himself as Zhenzhi (振之), better known by his artistic name Xiake (霞客) (Mistlike Traveler), was born in Jiangyin County (in present-day Jiangsu Province) of Nan Zhili on January 5,1587 (the 27th day of the 11th lunar month of the 14 years during Emperor Wanlis /Bj Reign). His masterpiece, *The Travel Diaries of Xu Xiake* best illustrates that he is an outstanding traveler geographer, historian and man of letters.

作为旅行家，徐霞客放弃了科举，弃绝了仕途，少怀周游全国之志。徐霞客先后游历了大半个中国，足迹遍及华东、华北、中南、西南各地区，据陈函辉的《霞客徐先生墓志铭》、丁文江的《徐霞客先生年谱》和徐霞客本人的游记可知，徐霞客历时 34 年游览五岳，深入西南边疆，足迹遍及全国 16 个省、自治区和 3 个直辖市，对长江的源头、石灰岩的地质地貌、自然环境的地区差异以及植物的分布，均有详尽考察、真实记述和科学论证。徐霞客无论是对地学，抑或是史学，还是文学，均有杰出贡献。

As a traveler, Xu Xiake gave up taking the imperial examination and abandoned the hope of taking the official career because he dreamed of travelling the whole country in his childhood. Xu Xiake travelled extensively around the whole country including the east, west, central south, and southwest areas. According to the *Epitaph for Xu Xiake* by Chen Hanhui, The Chronological Biography of Xu Xiake by Din Wenjiang (丁文江), and *Xu Xiake's own Travel Diaries*, it could be known that Xu Xiake spent 34 years in travelling Wu YUE, the Five Great Mountains in China and going deep into the frontiers of Southwest China, his feet covering 16 provinces and 3 municipalities directly under the Central Government of China. He examined closely, recorded truly, and rectified scientifically the source of Chang Jiang, geological and topographic features of the limestone, the regional differences of the natural environment, and the distribution of the plants. Because of his

Travel Diaries, Xu Xiake was deemed to have brilliant contribution to the geography, historiography, and literature.

三、典籍英译赏析

游天台山日记
Tiantai SHAN

【原典 1】

四月初一日早雨。行十五里，路有歧，马首西向台山，天色渐霁。又十里，抵松门岭，山峻路滑，舍骑步行。自奉化来，虽越岭数重，皆循山麓；至此迂回临陟，俱在山脊。而雨后新霁，泉声山色，往复创变，翠丛中山鹃映发，令人攀历忘苦。

【今译】

四月初一日，早上一直下雨。前行十五里，路旁有岔道，勒马从西面向天台山进发，天色逐渐转晴。又走了十里路，抵达松门岭下。山高路滑，只好舍弃骑马，步行前进。从奉化来的道路，虽然经过数重山岭，都是顺着山麓；到这里后，无论迂回、曲折或临水、登高，都在大山脊上面。雨后新晴，秀美的山色中叮咚的流泉声随处可闻，反复地变化出新的景观，绿树丛中怒放的红杜鹃花相互辉映，令人忘却了攀登跋涉的辛苦。

【英译】

The 1 Day of the 4 Lunar Month, 1613 in Chinese Calendar. It rained in the morning, but we still set out. After fifteen *li* we came to a fork in the road where we directed our horses to the west which could lead to Tiantai SHAN (天台山). As we went on, the weather gradually cleared up. Ten more *li*, and we reached Songmen Ling (松门岭) (岭 , a ridge), where the mountain was steep and the road was slippery, so we went down from our horses and walked forward. Since I left Fenghua (XIAN)(奉化县). I had left behind several mountains, but all the time I had been traveling at the foot of the mountains. Now I had to advance by a circuitous route on the ridges. The rain had just stopped and the sky was clearing up. I was intoxicated by the magnificent scenery: the gurgling of the spring water, the beauty of the mountains, the shifting of the scenery, and the full bloom of the azaleas on the verdant hillsides. As far as the eve could see, all was pleasing, which made me forget the laborious climb.

【赏析重点】

（1）分析“行十五里，路有歧，马首西向台山”译文的结构组合特点。

（2）分析“泉声山色，往复创变，翠丛中山鹃映发，令人攀历忘苦”结构特点和翻译方法。

【原典2】

又十五里，饭于筋竹庵。山顶随处种麦。从筋竹岭南行，则向国清大路。适有国清僧云峰同饭，言此抵石梁，山险路长，行李不便，不若以轻装往，而重担向国清相待。

【今译】

又前行十五里路，在筋竹庵里休息、用饭。山顶上到处都种有麦子。从筋竹岭向南走，就是通往国清寺的大路。恰好有国清寺僧人云峰同桌吃饭，他说：从这条路到石梁，山险岭峻，路途漫长，不方便携带行李。不如轻装前往，而让担夫将重的行李先担去国清寺等待。

【英译】

I walked on and covered another fifteen *li*. Then I decided to have a rest and have a meal at Jinzhu *An*（筋竹庵）(庵 *AN*,a Chinese Covent). The wheat was grown everywhere at the top of the mountains. Then we proceeded southward from Jinzhu LING（筋竹岭）to Guoqing MIAO（国清庙）(庙 *MIAO*, a temple for enshrining and worshiping the sages). While I was having the meal, I encountered a monk named Yunfeng（云峰）from Guoqing MIAO who happened to be eating lunch, too. He told me that it was such a long and dangerous journey from here to Shi Liang（石）(Stone Bridge) that it was inconvenient to carry baggage and suggested that I set off with light packs and a porter be called to lug my heavy belongings to Guoqing MIAO in advance to await my arrival.

【赏析重点】

（1）分析“适有国清僧云峰同饭”译文的结构调整。

（2）分析“言此抵石梁，山险路长，行李不便”的结构特点和翻译方法。

游黄山日记徽州府

Huang SHAN

【原典1】

余如言登顶，则天都、莲花并肩其前，翠微、三海门环绕于后，下瞰绝壁峭岫，罗列坞中，即丞相原也。顶前一石，伏而复起，势若中断，独悬坞中，上有怪松盘盖。余侧身攀踞其上，而浔阳踞大顶相对，各夸胜绝。

【今译】

我照他所说的登上光明顶，只见天都、莲花两峰在前方并肩而立，翠微、三海门在后面环绕，向下鸟瞰，极陡峭的山崖和峻峭的山岭，罗列于大山坞中，那就是丞相原了。光明顶前的一巨石，低伏一段后又重新峙立，其势就如中断一样，孤独地悬空于山坞中，石上有怪异的松树盘根错节地覆盖着。我侧身攀登到巨石上坐着，浔阳叔翁则坐在光明大顶上与我相对，各自夸耀景致的极为优美。

【英译】

I followed his suggestion and reached Guangming ding, where I saw Tiandu FENG and Lianhua FENG standing side by side in the front and Cui FENG（翠峰）and Sanhai MEN（三海门）encircling the backside. Looking down, we could see extremely high precipices and perpendicular peaks lying side by side on Chengxiang YUAN（丞相原）(原 YUAN, a ravine). A huge rock stood in front of Guangming DING, falling and then rising abruptly, as if it were broken in half from the middle. It lay detached over the ravine, with grotesque pine trees growing all over it. I climbed the rock sideways and perched while my uncle squatted at the top of Guangming DING opposite to me, each applauding this superb view.

【赏析重点】

（1）分析“顶前一石，伏而复起，势若中断”的结构特点和翻译方法。

（2）分析“余侧身攀踞其上”的语义逻辑和翻译方法。

【原典2】

下崖，循而东，里许，为石笋矼。矼脊斜亘，两夹悬坞中，乱峰森罗，其西一面即接引崖所窥者。矼侧一峰突起，多奇石怪松。登之，俯瞰壑中，正与接引崖对瞰，峰回岫转，顿改前观。

【今译】

走下接引崖，顺小路往东行一里多路，就是石笋矼。石笋矼山脊倾斜连绵，两夹崖壁悬于山坞中，乱峰森罗万象，它西边的一面就是在接引崖上所窥视的地方。石笋矼侧面一山峰突起，上面很多奇石怪松。登上山峰顶，俯瞰山谷中，正好与接引崖对视，峰回山转，顿改前观。

【英译】

After coming down from Jieyin YA, I headed eastward along a path for about one *li*. I reached the ridge Shisun GANG which stretched on in a slanting way, with its two cliffs on opposite sides suspending over a col. The ridge was surrounded by clusters of peaks, and its western side was what I had seen from Jieyin YA. A peak rose abruptly from one side of the ridge, with grotesque rocks and pine trees on it. I climbed to its top to take a view of the ravine down below, and I found that this place was just opposite to Jieyin YA. Since the viewpoint had changed, the twisting and winding peaks and mountains presented a new look different from what I had previously seen.

【赏析重点】

（1）分析"下崖，循而东，里许"的句式特点和翻译方法。

（2）分析"矼脊斜亘，两夹悬坞中"译文的结构重组。

（3）分析"峰回岫转，顿改前观"的增译翻译方法。

第二节 《大唐西域记》

The Great Tang Records on the Western Regions

一、典籍简介

《大唐西域记》，简称《西域记》，为唐代著名高僧玄奘口述，门人辩机执笔编集而成。《大唐西域记》共十二卷，成书于唐贞观二十年（646 年），为玄奘游历印度、西域旅途 19 年间之游历见闻录，其中包括了新疆至南印度一百四十多个国家的风土人情，提供了大量印度史料，在四库全书之中为史部地理外纪类。

The *Da-Tang-Xi-Yu-Ji* (大唐西域记, *The Great Tang Records on the Western Regions*), is a narrative of monk Xuanzang's nineteen-year journey through Chang'an to India describing the geography, land and maritime transportation routes, climate, local products, peoples, languages, history, politics, economic life, religion, culture, and customs of 110 countries, regions, and city-states from what is now Xinjiang to Sri Lanka. Compiled in 646 by Bianji from dictation by Xuanzang, the records required over a year of compiling and editing, and contains more than 120,000 Chinese characters in twelve volumes.

该书的内容十分丰富，不但记载了东起中国新疆、西至伊朗、南到印度半岛南端、北到吉尔吉斯斯坦、东北至孟加拉国这一广阔地区的历史、地理和风土人情，还对各地宗教寺院的状况和佛教的故事做了详细的记载。《大唐西域记》对研究中亚和南亚地区的地理、风貌具有非常重要的参考意义和价值。印度著名的那烂陀寺遗址，就是根据该书提供的线索发掘和复原的。

The book is rich in content. It records the histories, geographies and customs of a vast area stretching from China's Xinjiang in east to Iran in west the southern tip of the Indian Peninsula in south, Kyrgyzstan in north, and Bangladesh in northeast. Also, it has detailed records to the status of religious temples and the tales about Buddhism in various places. It has a very important reference value for the study on the geographies and customs of Central and South Asian regions. The famous ruins of Nalanda Monastery in India has been found and rebuilt on the basis of the clues offered by this book.

二、作者简介

玄奘（602—664），唐朝著名的三藏法师，汉传佛教史上最伟大的译经师之一，中国佛教法相唯识宗创始人。俗姓陈，名祎，出生于河南洛阳洛州缑氏县（今河南省偃师市南境）。他是中国著名古典小说《西游记》中心人物唐僧的原型。主要成就：汉传佛教史上最伟大的译经师之一；中国佛教法相唯识宗创始人。

Xuan Zang (602–664) was the famous Tripitaka Master of the Tang dynasty, the greatest translator of Sanskrit Buddhist texts into Chinese, and was the founder of the Vijnanavada sect of Chinese Buddhism. His family name was Chen and his given name was Hui. He was born in Goushi county, Luoyang city, Henan province (what is now in the south of Yanshi city, Henan province). He was the basis for the one of the key characters Tang Seng (monk of the Tang dynasty) in the popular epic novel *Journey to the West*. Major achievements: The greatest translator of Sanskrit Buddhist texts into Chinese and the founder of the Vijnanavada sect of Chinese Buddhism.

三、典籍英译赏析

【原典 1】

屈支国。东西千余里。南北六百余里。国大都城周十七八里。宜糜麦有粳稻出蒲萄石榴。多梨柰桃杏。土产黄金铜铁铅锡。气序和风俗质。文字取则印度。粗有改变。

【今译】

屈支国之疆域东西一千多里，南北六百多里。大都城方圆十七八里。土质宜于种植黍子、麦子，出产粳稻、葡萄、石榴，盛产梨、花红、桃子、杏子。矿产为金、铜、铁、铅、锡。气候四季温和，民风淳厚朴实。书面文字效法印度，稍加修改。

【塞缪尔·比尔英译】

The country of K'iu-chi is from east to west some thousand li or so; from north to south about 600 *li*. The capital of the realm is from 17 to 18 *li* in circuit. The soil is suitable for rice and corn, also (a kind of rice called) keng-t'ao;① it produces grapes,② pomegranates, and numerous species of plums, pears, peaches, and almonds, also grow here. The ground is rich in minerals – gold, copper, iron, and lead, and tin.③ The air is soft, and the manners of the people honest. The style of writing (literature) is Indian, with some differences.

① A rice which is not glutinous (Jul.), i.e., common rice.

② The grape in Chinese is pu-ta'u; this is one of the products which the earth is said to have produced naturally, and on which men (all flesh) fed for a period; those who took little retaining their whiteness of colour, those who ate greedily turning dark-coloured. (See in the Chung-hu-mo-ho-ti-king, k. i. fol. 3). The similarity between this word pu-ta'u and the Greek botrus has been pointed out by Mr. Kings mill.

③ The mistake in the text of "ming" for "yuen" is pointed out by M. Julien.

【赏析重点】

（1）分析"宜糜麦有粳稻出蒲萄石榴"译文的结构转换；

（2）分析"文字取则印度，粗有改变"的翻译方法。

【原典 2】

管弦伎乐特善诸国。服饰锦褐断发巾帽。货用金钱银钱小铜钱。王屈支种也。智谋寡昧迫于强臣。其俗生子以木押头。

【今译】

器乐歌舞，独擅盛场，尤胜各国。衣饰多用彩绸、毛布，头发剪短，束戴帻帽。通用货币为金钱、银钱、小铜钱。国王为屈支土著，才智平庸，谋略不足，受制于干练的权臣。其地风俗，用木板箍扎初生婴儿的头部，以使头形扁薄不圆。

【塞缪尔·比尔英译】

They excel other countries in their skill in playing on the lute and pipe. They clothe themselves with ornamental garments of silk and embroidery.① They cut their hair and wear a flowing covering (over their heads). In commerce they use gold, silver, and copper coins. The king is of the K'iu-chi race; his wisdom being small, he is ruled by a powerful minister. The children born of common parents have their heads flattened by the pressure of a wooden board.②

① The symbol "ho" sometimes means "embroidered work done by puncturing leather"–Medhurst. This seems more applicable to the passage than the other meaning of felt or coarse-wool.

② This is a well-known custom among some tribes of North American Indians.

【赏析重点】

（1）分析“管弦伎乐特善诸国”的语义逻辑特点和翻译方法。

（2）分析“服饰锦褐断发巾帽”译文的结构转换。

【原典3】

伽蓝百余所。僧徒五千余人习学小乘教说一切有部。经教律仪取则印度。其习读者。即本文矣。尚拘渐教食杂三净。洁清耽翫（wán）人以功竞。

【今译】

境内有佛寺百多所，僧人五千多，均研习小乘教的说一切有部。佛经教义与戒律仪轨都效法印度，故学习者直接阅读印度原文。僧徒依然滞溜于渐教阶段，兼食三种净肉。不过人人洁身自好，钻研佛典，互相以修行之功效竞胜。

【塞缪尔·比尔英译】

There are about one hundred convents (saṅghārāmas) in this country, with five thousand and more disciples. These belong to the Little Vehicle of the school of the Sarvāstivādas (Shwo-yih-tsai-yu-po). Their doctrine (teaching of Sūtras) and their rules of discipline (principles of the Vinaya) are like those of India, and those who read them use the same (originals). They especially hold to the customs of the "gradual doctrine", and partake only of the three pure kinds of food. They live purely, and provoke others (by their conduct) to a religious life.

【赏析重点】

（1）分析“僧徒五千余人习学小乘教说一切有部”译文的结构转换。

（2）分析“其习读者。即本文矣”的语义特点和翻译方法。

【原典 4】

从此北行三十余里，至那烂陀（唐言施无厌）僧伽蓝。闻之耆旧曰：此伽蓝南庵没罗林中有池，其龙名那烂陀，傍建伽蓝，因取为称。从其实议，是如来在昔修菩萨行，为大国王，建都此地，悲愍众生，好乐周给，时美其德，号施无厌，由是伽蓝因以为称。

【今译】

从这里向北行走三十多里，抵达那烂陀（唐语谓“施无厌”）寺。听年老长者说：这座佛寺之南的庵没罗林中有个水池，池中之龙名叫那烂陀，由于旁边建有佛寺，所以即用它来命名。其真实含义是：当初如来修习菩萨行，生为大国国王，在此建立都城，慈悲怜悯众生，喜欢周济穷人，人们赞其德行，称他为施无厌，佛寺遂得此名。

【塞缪尔·比尔英译】

Going north from this 30 li or so, we come to Nālanda saṅghārāma.① The old accounts of the country say that to the south of this saṅghārāma, in the middle of an āmra (An-mo-lo) grove, there is a tank. The Nāga of this tank is called Nālanda.② By the side of it is built the saṅghārāma, which therefore takes the name (of the Nāga). But the truth is that Tathāgata in old days practised the life of a Bodhisattva here, and became the king of a great country, and established his capital in this land. Moved by pity for living things, he delighted in continually relieving them. In remembrance of this Virtue he was called③ "charity without intermission"; and the saṅghārāma was called in perpetuation of this name.

① Nālanda has been identified with the village of Baragaon, which lies seven miles north of Rājgīr (Cunningham, Anc. Geog., p. 468).

② According to I-tsing the name Nālanda is derived from Nāga Nanda (see J. R. A. S., N.S., vol. xiii. p. 571). For a description of this temple of Nālanda see "Two Chinese Buddhist Inscriptions found at Buddha Gayā," J. R. A. S., N.S., vol. xiii. l. c. See also Abstract of Four Lectures, p. 140.

③ So I understand the passage. It has no reference to the Nāga. The word Nālanda would thus appear to be derived from na+alam+da, "not giving enough," or "not having enough to give."

【赏析重点】

（1）分析“悲愍众生，好乐周给”的结构特点和翻译方法。

（2）学习文化关键词“菩萨行”、“施无厌”的翻译方法。

【原典 5】

僧徒数千，并俊才高学也，德重当时，声驰异域者，数百余矣。戒行清白，律仪淳粹，僧有严制，众咸贞素，印度诸国皆仰则焉。

【今译】

那烂陀寺内有僧人几千名，都是才能出众，学识渊博之人，德操为人所重，声誉传布国外者，共有一百多人。他们恪守戒规，品行清白教律纯粹，制度严格，僧众全都信仰坚定，印度各国都仰慕他们，将其作为学习榜样。

【塞缪尔·比尔英译】

The priests, to the number of several thousands, are men of the highest ability and talent. Their distinction is very great at the present time, and there are many hundreds whose fame has rapidly spread through distant regions. Their conduct is pure and unblamable. They follow in sincerity the precepts of the moral law. The rules of this convent are severe, and all the priests are bound to observe them. The countries of India respect them and follow them.

【赏析重点】

（1）分析“声驰异域者，数百余矣”译文的句法转换。

（2）分析“戒行清白，律仪淳粹”的结构特点和翻译方法。

拓展训练 | Extension Training

1. 思考练习

（1）用英文简要介绍《梦溪笔谈》《徐霞客游记》《大唐西域记》主要内容。

（2）总结分析地理风土人情英文翻译方法和翻译策略。

2. 文化外宣汉英翻译

（1）“四大发明”这一说法最早由英国科学家、历史学家李约瑟提出，指的是中国的造纸术、印刷术、指南针和火药。英国哲学家培根也曾说过：“印刷术、火药、指南针这三种发明已经在世界范围内把事物的全部面貌和情况改变了。”“四大发明”的出现，不仅推动了中国历史、文化、经济等方面的发展，甚至推动了全世界的进步。

（2）中国是世界上最早养蚕的国家，古人以蚕茧抽丝织绸，漂絮后，席上会留下一些残絮，经晒干之后，称之为“方絮”。这种纸张十分粗糙，不能用来写字，因此纸并没有在文化传播上发挥积极的作用。东汉（25—220）时，蔡伦对造纸术进行了改进，选用树皮、麻头破布、旧渔网等方便获得的原料，经过浸、捣等工序制成纸浆，再经过抄、烘等步骤，将纸浆风干之后，就制造出了更适合书写的纸张。造纸术作为中国最伟大的发明之一，充当了人类文明、科技传播的“使者”。造纸术首先传入与中国毗邻的朝鲜和越南，随后传到了日本，而后又传入了阿拉伯，再经阿拉伯地区传入欧洲。到 19 世纪，中国的造纸术已传遍世界各国。

（3）指南针是人们判别方向的重要工具，世界上最早的指南针—司南在战国时期（前 475—前 221）便已出现。“司南”是用天然磁石制成的，样子像一把汤勺，可以放在平滑的底盘（方形的金属盘）上，并且可以自由旋转。当它静止的时候，勺柄就会指向南方。除了司南，北宋时期（960—1127）还出现了一种更为便捷的指南工具——指南鱼。指南鱼由薄铁片制成，一般两寸长、五分宽，鱼的腹部略下凹，像一只小船，磁化后浮在水面，就能指示南北。由于液体的摩擦力比固体小，转动起来比较灵活，所以指南鱼比司南更灵敏、更准确。

拓展训练参考译文

第一篇　哲学思想篇

第一章　儒家经典英译

文化外宣汉英翻译

（1）Confucianism was the most important thought among the early philosophies and one of the most influential schools of thought in the Chinese history. In Chinese Confucianism is called Ru Jia (literally school of scholars). Before the Spring and Autumn Period, Ru (scholar) originally referred to a funeral or ritual master. Gradually Ru became a profession specialized in ritual ceremonies. Over a period of several hundred years by the Western Zhou Dynasty (1046 BC–771 BC) the position of Ru was rising along with the society's more emphasis on rituals and rites. Confucius, known as Kongzi in Chinese, founded the orthodox Confucianism based on his study and innovation of the past rituals and rites. Mencius carried forward and further developed Confucianism. Later Xunzi improved and perfected Confucius methodologies.

（2）Benevolence or humaneness (Ren) is the core virtue of Confucianism representing Confucius' highest ideal and ethical standard.Confucian ethics are characterized by the promotion of virtues including humaneness (Ren), righteousness (Yi), propriety (Li), knowledge (Zhi), integrity (Xin), forgiveness (Shu), loyalty (Zhong), piety (Xiao) and filial respect (Ti). Humaneness advocates love and kindness for each other. Righteousness means fairness and justice, which Confucius regarded as the first thing people need to follow in their conduct. Mencius interpreted the concept of righteousness further and promoted it as another core virtue of Confucianism. Proper etiquettes (Li) actually refer to rites of the Zhou Dynasty which Confucius wanted to restore. Xunzi deepened the concept of propriety suggesting that only by following proper etiquettes in individual and social conduct could the ruler maintain people's obedience and stability of the state. Knowledge (Zhi) refers to both wisdom and knowledge. Learnedness, inquiring, deliberation and determination to act are all attributes of Zhi. Confucianists believed that only people with wisdom and knowledge can eventually achieve the goal of governing with benevolence. Therefore Confucianism pays special attention to education and training of talented people.Integrity (Xin) includes honesty and trustworthiness and advocates the ethic of keeping one's promise and practicing what is preached.Forgiveness (Shu) means understanding and tolerance, not enforcing one's own will to others. Loyalty (Zhong) represents Confucius' teachings about helping others as much as you can and treating friends with honesty and trust.Mencius extended the meaning of Zhong to dedicating oneself to teaching others. Piety (Xiao) means devotion and reverence to parents and filial respect (Ti) refers to love for one's brothers and sisters.

（3）Confucius wished to establish a society where the world belonged to all under heaven. Politically he advocated rule of benevolence and emphasized that the ruler must treat his people with human-heartedness and govern with ethical principles so that people would willingly and sincerely submit to the rule. Rulers must rule with moral standards,be kind to their people, reduce compulsory labor service and let people live and work in peace and contentment; and they should not punish people, but educate them in order to maintain social stability and development. Confucius systematically explored the relationship between wealth and morality. His belief that wealth is something that all people desire, but has to be acquired in the proper way shows that Confucius placed morality before wealth. He also argued that only by making the people prosperous could the state become rich.In terms of aesthetics, Confucius emphasized the unity of beauty and kindness, namely the harmony between the content and form. Additionally he advocated "poetry learning" to achieve transformation of social politics through literature and art.

第二章　道家经典英译

文化外宣汉英翻译

（1）The core of Lao Zi's thought is Tao,which represents the movement and law of the universe. He thinks that all the matters of the universe are derived from Tao, which gives a basis for the universe existence. Reversibility is the basic motion of Tao; that is, two opposite sides that forms a contradiction will turn in their opposite directions; the basic nature of Tao is to let things take their own course naturally. The doctrine of Tao is the theoretical foundation of Lao Zi thought. Lao Zi believes in fatalism, apathy, and inertia, and the conquest of hardness with softness, retreat as a way of advance, and winning of the weak over the strong.

（2）Daoism contrasts "action" to "non-action." "Action" generally means that the rulers impose their will on others or the world without showing any respect for or following the intrinsic nature of things. "Non-action" is the opposite of "action," and has three main points: 1) through self-control containing the desire to interfere; 2) following the nature of all things and the people; and 3) bringing into play the initiative of all things and people. "Non-action" does not mean not doing anything, but is a wiser way of doing things.Non-action leads to the result of getting everything done.

（3）Laozi applied "Tao" to elucidating the origin and evolvement of the universe. Moreover, Laozi maintained that the characters and law of "Tao" could be applied to guide people's thinking and behavior, which should be in conformance with the nature. Laozi believed that what appears soft and weak can actually defeat what is hard and strong,inasmuch as what looks fragile is hard in nature. Proficient in the philosophy of Laozi,Zhuangzi was an inheritor and promoter of Taoism. Zhuangzi, whose given name was Zhou, once worked as an official in charge of painting work at the town of Meng in the Song State. In the book bearing his name, Zhuangzi succeeded to and developed Laozi's viewpoint that "Tao is defined by nature" and claimed that everything exterior can be equated with self,and life and death are equal. What Zhuangzi had been pursuing is a spiritual realm of absolute freedom.Since there are so many similarities between Laozi and Zhuangzi in terms of thinking, descendants usually mention them comparably.

第二篇　历史战争篇

第三章　编年史书英译

文化外宣汉英翻译

（1）The Zhenguan period (627 AD–649 AD) of the Tang Dynasty enjoyed great prosperity in the reign of Emperor Li Shimin, or Emperor Taizong of Tang. It is called Golden Years of Zhenguan by historians.The Kaiyuan years (713 AD–741 AD), in which Li Shimin's great grand-son, Emperor Li Longji,or in Chinese Tang Xuan Zong was on the throne, saw the peak of the flourish and prosperity of the Tang Dynasty. It is known as Peace and Prosperity of the Kaiyuan Years. Emperor Taizong held that "the key to politics is to use the right persons." With the courage and insight of a statesman, he recruited a great number of intelligent and capable men. All of his prime ministers were men of outstanding ability: Fang Xuanling excelled at planning; Du Ruhui was noted for his decisiveness; Wei Zheng was a brave admonitor; Li Jing was accomplished with both the pen and the sword, either as a general or a prime minister. Those people played an im elopment and prosperity of the Zhenguan Years.

（2）Xun Zi, a Chinese thinker from the late Warring States Period,once said, "A monarch is a boat and the common people he rules are the water.Water can either support the boat or capsize the boat." Emperor Taizong of the Tang dynasty, who viewed history as a mirror, was greatly impressed by Xun Zi's view.He quoted this view many times during his discussions with his ministers and officials with regard to national matters. In an article titled On System of Government,he said, "Monarchs are boats and common people are the water. Water can carry the boats and can also capsize the boats." For a long time, Emperor Taizong of the Tang dynasty had adhered to the governing strategies based on people-oriented policy and not disturbing farming.He once preached to his chief of staff that doing so is not only out of "sympathy with the people", but also to "maintain sustainable wealth and prosperity". Based on these tenets, Emperor Taizong of the Tang dynasty prioritized the stability of the country above all of his policies during his reign and sought development in stability, while being always prepared for danger during times of peace. These measures finally steered the country out of the chaotic situation since the final years of the Sui dynasty and sailed into a state of great peace and order.

（3）Nurturing the people means to provide the people with necessities of life and educate them. According to *The Book of History*, this is what constitutes good governance. To reach this goal,the ruler must manage well the"six necessities and three matters, "the six necessities being, metal wood, water, fire, land, and grain, and the three matters being fostering virtue, proper use of tesources, and ensuting people's livelihood. This concept of governance, which focuses on promoting both economic and ethical progress, is people-centered.

第四章　兵法典籍英译

文化外宣汉英翻译

（1）Sun Wu establishes the thought that army is the first and foremost thing of a state. He thinks that military affairs, being related to the life and death of the state and people, should be so tackled as to achieve political purposes. So, the ruler should deal with military affairs from the point of view of politics. He thinks there are five factors in the military affairs which are the most important: "Dao", "Tian", "Di", "Jiang", "Fa". "Dao" refers to the strate gy trying to win over masses to support the war; "Tian" refers to the change of the nature; "Di" refers to the topographic condition; "Jiang" refers to the quality of the military commander; "Fa"refers to the rules and regulations. He especially stresses "Dao" and "Jiang", asserting that a commander must "know" how to deal with military affairs from the point of view of politics and make decisions and strategies accordingly.

(2) *Master Sun's Art of War* is full of dialectic thought, in which he stresses a mutual relation between "Jiang", "Tian" and "Di", and puts forward a systematic theory that unites climatic, geographical and human factors into one. He says, "One who knows his own strength and that of the enemy is invincible in battle; where there is a knowledge of the climate and geography, there will be a complete victory." He also puts an emphasis on mutation, saying "The army is like water...Just as water has no certain form, an army has no certain battle formation.The spirit of military operation lies in an accordance with the enemy's changes." He thinks that commanding an army is full of crafts. He also reveals special military laws that the army's victory lies in feigning, and that interests constitute the motivation of war,which shows the tendency to utilitarianism values.

(3) As one of the four great classical novels in China, *Romance of the Three Kingdoms* has a famous story: Fire at Chibi (Red Cliff), which describes one of the most prestigious battles in ancient Chinese history: Battle of Chibi. It happened in 208, the joint army of Sun Quan and Liu Bei tried to resist the large army led by Cao Cao. This battle is a perfect example of the implementation of Master Sun's Art of War. Despite their numerical disadvantage, the joint army depending on their rich experience in water battle avoided the direct confrontation and applied the fire attack to bum down Cao Cao's warships and finally won the battle.

第三篇　文学艺术篇

第五章　先秦诗歌英译

文化外宣汉英翻译

(1) In *The Book of Songs*, the content is divided into three categories according to

style and tune: *feng* (ballad), *ya* (court hymn), and *song* (eulogy). Ballads are music from different regions,mostly folk songs.Court hymns,divided into *daya* (major hymn) and *xiaoya* (minor hymn), are songs sung at court banquets or grand ceremonies. They are mostly the works by lettered noblemen. Eulogies are ritual or sacrificial dance music and songs, most of which praise the achievements of ancestors. Court hymns and eulogies are highbrow songs while ballads are lowbrow ones. Therefore, ballads, court hymns, and eulogies not only refer to the styles of *The Book of Songs* but also classify the songs into highbrow and lowbrow categories. Later on *fengya* generally referred to anything elegant.

（2）These are the three ways of expression employed in *The Book of Songs*: a narrative (*fu*) is a direct reference to anlobject or an event, an analogy (*bi*) metaphorically likens one thing to another, and an association (*xing*) is an impromptu expression of a feeling, a mood or a thought,or using an objective thing as metaphor for sensibilities. Confucian scholars of the Han dynasty summarized and formulated this concept of narrative, analogy and association,which later became the basic principle and method in classical Chinese literary creation.

第六章　汉魏晋诗英译

文化外宣汉英翻译

（1）Originally, *yuefu* (poems were written in the Han dynasty) was a government office set up by the imperial court to train musicians, collect folk songs and ballads, compose music, and match musical instruments to it. It later came to refer to folk songs and ballads collected, matched with music, and played by court musicians. Poems of this style represented a new creation of ancient folk songs and ballads in the years after *The Book of Songs* was compiled, and equaled *The Book of Songs* and *Odes of Chu* in importance. About 50 to 60 yuefu poems have been handed down to this day. They truthfully depicted various aspects of society at the time and revealed genuine emotions, thus creating a literary tradition reflecting ordinary people's sentiments. In particular, *yuefu* poems were noted for their vivid depiction of women's life. All poems that could be chanted or were written with *yuefu* themes were collectively called yuefu poems in later times.

（2）The Jian'an literary style, also known as the Han-Wei literary style, refers to the literary style from the Jian'an era (196–220) of the Han dynasty to the early Northern Wei dynasty, featuring powerful expression of passion,anxiety,and indignation. The final years of the Han dynasty saw political turmoil, incessant wars, and displacement of people. Leading literary figures like Cao Cao, Cao Pi, and Cao Zhi, and the "Seven Masters," i.e., Kong Rong, Chen Lin, Wang Can, Xu Gan, Ruan Yu, Ying Yang, and Liu Zhen, as well as female poet Cai Yan,inherited the realistic tradition of the folksongs of the Han dynasty. In their writings, they dealt with subjects such as social upheaval, the suffering of the people, and the aspiration of individuals, expressing their creative spirit and resolve to pursue a noble cause. Their works demonstrate strength, courage and determination to overcome great odds. With a melancholy and powerful style that was magnificent, unique, and distinctive of its age. Jian'an literature emerged as a uniqye genre and came to be viewed by later gegerations as an outstanding titerary style with Jian'an poetry particularly highly regarded.

（3）*Yijing* (aesthetic conception) refers to a state where the scene described in a literary or artistic work reflects the sense and sensibility intended. *Jing* originally meant perimeter or boundary. With the introduction of Buddhism into China during the late Han, Wei and Jin dynasties, the idea gained popularity that the physical world was but an illusion, and that only the mind was real in existence. So *jing* came to be seen as a realm that could be attained by having sensibllities of the mind. As a literary and artistic term, *jing* has several meanings. The term *yijing* was originally put forward by renowned Tang poet Wang Changling. It describes an intense aesthetic experience in which one's perception of an object reaches a realm of perfect union with the implication denoted by the object. Aesthetic appreciation in the mind is characterized by "projecting meaning into a scene"and "harmonizing one's thought with a scene." In contrast with the term *yixiang*（意象）, *yijing*（意境）fully reveals the implication and the heightened aesthetic sense that an artistic work is intended to deliver. The concept is extended to include other notions such as sentiment and scene, actual and implied meanings,or mind and object. It also raises literary and artistic works to a new realm of aesthetic appreciation. After evolving through several dynasties, this concept developed into an important criterion to judge the quality of a literary or artistic work, representing an accomplishment drawing on classical writings through ages.It has also become a hallmark for all outstanding literary and artistic works. The term also represents a perfect union between foreign thoughts and culture and those typically Chinese.

第七章　唐诗英译

文化外宣汉英翻译

（1）Tang poetry refers to poetry written in or about China's Tang dynasty (618–907) and follows a certain style, often considered as the Golden Age of Chinese poetry. According to a compilation, the Quantangshi included almost 50,000 Tang poems written by over 2,200 authors.During the Tang dynasty, poetry continued to be an important part of social life at all levels of society. Scholars were required to master poetry for the civil service examinations,but the art was theoretically available to everyone. This led to a large record of poetry and poets, a partial record of which survives today.Two of the most famous poets of the period were Du Fu and Li Bai.

（2）*Jintishi* (new stylistic poetry), or regulated verse developed from the 5th century onwards. By the Tang dynasty, a series of set tone patterns had been developed, which were intended to ensure a balance between the four tones of Middle Chinese in each couplet: the level tone, and the three oblique tones (rising, departing and entering). The Tang dynasty was the high point of the jintishi. Wang Wei and Cui Hao were notable pioneers of the form, while Du Fu was its most accomplished exponent. The basic form of *jintishi* is *lüshi*, with eight lines. In addition to the tonal constraints, this form required parallelism between the lines in the second and third couplets.The lines in these couplets had to contain contrasting content, with the characters in each line usually in the same part of speech. Another form is the *jueju*, or quatrain which followed the tonal pattern of the first four lines of the *lüshi*.This form does not require parallelism.

（3）Poetry of the Prime Tang Dynasty refers to the poetic creation and achievements during the Kaiyuan (713–742) and Tianbao (742–756) reign periods of Emperor Xuanzong of the Tang dynasty, as compared with poetic writing in the early Tang, mid-Tang, and late Tang periods. This period, marked by good governance, prosperity, and stability, was a golden era for the great Tang empire before it was disrupted by the An Lushan and Shi Siming Rebellion. There was cultural infusion between the north and south, and travels to and from the outside world were frequent. All this made it possible for artistic creation to blossom. Of all the four periods of poetic creation, i.e., the early Tang, the prime Tang, the mid-Tang and the late Tang, the prime Tang was the shortest, but its artistic attainment was most remarkable.This period produced legendary poet Li Bai and poetic genius Du Fu as well as a galaxy of outstanding poets such as Zhang

Jiuling, Meng Haoran, Wang Wei, Wangchangling and Wang Zhihuan. These poets extolled natural scenery, expressed noble aspirations, and depicted real life. Their writing style was both vigorous and unrestrained. They were broad in vision and were adept at using fresh, natural language,and their poems were full of power,vigor and an enterprising spirit. Their poems represented the highest attainment in classical Chinese poetry. This period also saw the thriving of the natural landscape school and the frontier school in poetry writing.

第八章　宋词英译

文化外宣汉英翻译

（1）The themes of the Ci-poems were relatively more concentrated than the ones of Tang Poetry. The poet of graceful school mostly depicted the love romance, sorrow of separation. travels and folk customs, feasts and entertainment, etc., while the poet of heroic school expanded the range to some political subjects including patriotism, nostalgia and history-retrospect, etc. In the Southern Song dynasty, although writers added more and more themes referring to daily life into their Ci-poems, the most distinguished subject was still the emotion-expression, especially the love romance. Besides, the patriotic and philosophical themes were also depicted profoundly. Additionally, Ci-poems of object-description and acknowledgement could also rival the poetry.

（2）The poets and Ci-poems of the Song dynasty are generally divided into two writing styles, heroic school and graceful school. Graceful school,mild and implicit, with a main feature of emphasizing the content on romance affairs, has an exquisite and deliberate structure, harmonious rhythm and mellow and graceful wording.possessing a delicate beauty. While heroic school, bold and indulgent, with a main feature of wide range of subject and grand disposition, mostly involves some poetic expression and sentence structure, with some formal words and phrases, mostly concentrating on narration. The graceful school strictly follows the rhythm regulation, stresses the collocation of Ci-poem and music,and has a relatively fixed range of themes. However, the heroic school tends to break the fetter of music, improvises freely and expands the content to a broader realm including politics and philosophy.

（3）*Yixiang* (imagery) refers to a typical image in literary works, which embodies the author's subjective feelings and unique artistic conceptions. *Yi*（意）literally means an author's feelings and thoughts, and *xiang* (象) refers to the image of a material object in the external world, an artistic image reflecting the author's thoughts and feelings. In literary creation, imagery often refers to those images in nature with which an author's feelings and thoughts are associated. Emphasizing the harmonious relationship between beauty in both form and content, it is a mature state of literary creation.

第九章 元曲英译

文化外宣汉英翻译

(1) In Chinese literature, *qu* or *yuanqu* consists of *sanqu* and *zaju*. Along with *shi* and *ci*, the former comprises Chinese poetry. The latter is a form of Chinese opera. *Qu* became popular during the late Southern Song dynasty,and reached its highest popularity in Yuan dynasty, therefore it is often called *yuanqu*. Both *sanqu* and *ci* are lyrics written to fit a particular melody, but *sanqu* differs from *ci* in that it is more colloquial, and is allowed to contain *chenzi* ("filler words" which are additional words to make a more complete meaning). *Sanqu* can be further divided into *xiaoling* and *santao*, with the latter comprising of more than one melody.

(2) The Classical Prose Movement of the late Tang dynasty and the Song dynasty in China advocated clarity and precision rather than the florid piantien or parallel prose style that had been popular since the Han dynasty. Parallel prose had a rigid structure and came to be criticized for being overly ornate at the expense of content. The aim of the gucen stylists was to follow the spirit of pre-Han prose rather than to imitate it directly. They used elements of colloquial language to make their writings more direct. The first great promoters of the movement were Han Yu and Liu Zongyuan who were not only great writers but also great theorists, providing the foundation of the movement. Both were enthusiastic to promote the movement and were keen to teach young people, so the movement could develop.

第十章 古典小说英译

文化外宣汉英翻译

(1) Traditional Chinese fiction has evolved through different stages, with distinctive features for each period. The myths, legends and historical biographies of the pre-Qin and Han dynasties, and the fables in the works of the earlier Chinese thinkers were the sources of traditional Chinese fiction. The literary sketches by men of letters in the Wei,

Jin, Northern and Southern dynasties were embryonic forms of traditional fiction. The legendary tales of the Tang dynasty marked the eventual emergence of Chinese fiction. The story-tellers' prompt-books in the Song and Yuan dynasties laid the foundation that allowed traditional fiction to reach maturity. The novels of the Ming and Qing dynasties marked the peak in the development of pre-modern fiction. That period is famous for producing four great Chinese classical novels, namely, *Romance of the Three Kingdoms, Journey to the West, Outlaws of the Marsh and A Dream of the Red Chamber*. During and after the New Culture Movement and the May 4th Movement around 1919, a large amount of modern vernacular fiction appeared, bringing forth a message of science and democracy of the modern age.

(2) *A Dream of Red Mansions* itself is a detailed, episodic record of the lives of the extended family, which occupies two large adjacent family compounds in the capital. Their ancestors were made Dukes and, at the beginning of the novel, the two houses still comprised one of the most illustrious families in the capital. Originally extremely wealthy and influential, with a female member made an imperial concubine, the family eventually fell into disfavor with the emperor, and had their mansions raided and confiscated. The novel is a charting of the family's fall from the height of their prestige, centering around some 30 main characters and more than 400 minor players.

第四篇　育人处世篇

第十一章　蒙学经典英译

文化外宣汉英翻译

(1) China has an old saying that "brothers are like hands and feet", meaning siblings should live in concord like hands and feet. Siblings in a family take the common responsibility of making the family sustainable and prosperous and passing down the family culture. They should help each other, work together and facilitate each other's success. It is very important for them to live in harmony in a family. Confucius said The filial piety and fraternal duty are the foundation of benevolence", meaning that in families, if parents are benign children well educated and siblings love each other, our society will be in harmony.

(2) China has emphasized respecting teachers and honoring their teachers since

old times. Among the five major objects called "Tian, Di, Jun, Qin, Shi"(Heaven, Earth, Monarch, Parents and Teacher) worshiped by Chinese confucianists, teachers are ranked equally with heaven, the earth, monarchs and parents, which shows the importance of teachers in China. As was recorded in *About Learning*, Chinas earliest works about education and teaching issues particularly, teachers didnt subject to the ritual between rulers and subjects while tutoring the emperor. They were called by ancients as those who impart knowledge, display skill and solve doubts. With rich experience and profound learning, they set a good example for students through their words and deeds, and also imparted knowledge to students through lectures.

(3) "Be truthful in speech and firm in action" is a well-known saying in China, meaning that one should have credit. Credit is a traditional virtue that Chinese people lay great importance upon. As the old saying goes, "A man without credit would not establish a firm foothold." It means that only with credit can a man win trust and respect from others and establish good cooperative relationship with others. Only with credit, likewise, can a nation live in harmony with other people. Chinese people have always attached importance to this virtue and try hard to practice it.

(4) The five cardinal relationships from *Mencius* were five basic human relationships in ancient China, namely, the relationships between rulers and their subjects, between parents and children,between siblings, between husbands and wives and between friends. Three of them deal with the family relationships. Mencius held that there should be doctrine of propriety and righteousness between the rulers and his subjects:there should be love between parents and children; there should be affection between husbands and wives; there should be order between brothers; and there should be credibility and integrity between friends. These were the basic ethics and codes in dealing with human relationships.

第十二章　家训典籍英译

文化外宣汉英翻译

(1) China has always attached great importance to the relationship between parents and children, with particular emphasis on filial piety. As the old saying goes, "Filial piety is the most important of all virtues." It means that filial piety ranks first in Chinese virtues. In this sense whether a person has good quality or not can be seen from whether

he is filial to his parents. In selecting officials in ancient times, filial piety was also an important evaluation criterion. In the Han dynasty (206 BC–220 AD) *Book of Filial Piety* was even highly praised.

(2) China attached great importance to the relationship between husbands and wives in ancient times. Some classics even ranked it as the most important one in family relationships, holding that the husband should respect his wife while the wife should understand her husband. The politician and militarist Guan Zi in the Spring and Autumn Period (770 BC–476 BC) once said that husbands and wives should respect each other. The wife should not to envy the husband. Instead she and her husband could teach each other, and often pointed out each others mistakes to facilitate their self-cultivation morally. In China, the term Harmony of Qin and Se (marital harmony) is often used to describe the relationship between husbands and wives, Qin and Se, two raditional Chinese musical instruments were likened to the relationship between husbands and wives because their ensemble can produce very harmonious sound.

(3) Relationship among friends plays an important role in China's ethics. Chinese people like to call teachers and friends in pair, in which teachers are the elder who impart knowledge, while friends are peers who share common morality and goals. As was said by Confucius, a true gentleman made friends with thoughts and morality, and then improved his virtues through making friends. *Classic of Filial Piery* also reads, "If a commendable person has friends who are not afraid of speaking up advices, he can maintain a good reputation."

(4) In China, bosom friends are called Zhiyin. There is a story about it. In ancient times, there was a man called Yu Boya, who was very good at playing Qin (a seven-stringed plucked instrument) and had achieved great accomplishment in this aspect. Boya had a friend named Zhong Ziqi, who was very good at appreciating the music played by Qin. Every time Boya played the Qin. Ziqi could understand what he was thinking about and what he wanted to express in his music. After Zhong Ziqi died, Boya never played Qin again.What's more, he broke his precious Qin. He said in sorrow. "There is no need to play Qin any more since my Zhiyin passed away." Since then, Chinese people often refer to their bosom friends as Zhiyin.

第五篇　自然科学篇

第十三章　中医典籍英译

文化外宣汉英翻译

（1）In the Spring and Autumn Period (770 BC–476 BC) and Warring States Period (475 BC–221 BC) the theory of traditional Chinese medical science already established, including the Theory of yin and Yang, Five-element Theory, visceral Manifestation Theory and the Meridian and Collateral Theory. It founded the four main diagnosis methods, i.e. observation, auscultation and olfaction, inquiry and palpation, and the four therapeutic methods including Bian-stone (a small cone or wedge stone implement formed through stone grinding), used by the ancient Chinese to remit pain by massage acupuncture, moxibustion and decoction. After a development stretching over two thousand years, it appeared numerous medical canons which still inspire people with great significance.

（2）The acupuncture-moxibustion therapy is a combination of acupuncture and moxibustion. It is a traditional therapy operated under the instruction of the Meridian and Collateral Theory. Through stimulating the acupoints, it can channel the Qi in formal movement, thereby curing diseases. Acupuncture and moxibustion can be performed at the same time. The predecessor of the acupuncture needle was Bian-stone which was a small cone or wedge stone implement formed through stone grinding, used by the ancient Chinese to remit pain by massage. They should be used based on the specific condition to stimulate the corresponding acupoints in order to achieve the best treatment effect. The moxibustion therapy emerged after people knew how to use fire. Initially, people did moxibustion with various lit branches, and then, wormwood. Moxibustion is to light the moxa wool, moxa stick or moxa cone made from wormwood to fumigate and roast acupuncture points of the human body for the purposes of relieving pain and making people feel comfortable. Moxibustion has been used in China for a very long time and recorded in many medical publication.

（3）The concept of qi includes three levels of meaning: 1) an ancient philosophical concept, referring to the origin of everything in the universe and the substantial element that constitutes the soma and psyche; 2) the substance, energy, and information that constitute the human body and maintain the life activities. Qi of human can be divided into yin qi and yang qi based on the nature; original qi, pectoral qi, nutrient qi, and defense qi based on the transformation; stomach qi, heart qi, liver qi, kidney qi, lung qi, spleen qi and visceral qi based on its function; and 3) qi refers to pathogenic qi, a type of qi that causes diseases.

(4) Yin-yang disharmony is a brief way to refer to the loss of balance between yin and yang. Specifically, it denotes that during the development and progression of a disease, the relative balance and coordination between yin and yang is disrupted due to various pathogenic factors, which results in a series of pathological changes including relative exuberance or debilitation, mutual impairment, mutual repelling, and collapse of yin and yang. The breakdown of balance between yin and yang primarily manifests itself as cold or heat patterns. In addition, traditional Chinese medicine believes that pathogenic qi will not cause illnesses until the yin-yang balance of the human body is broken. Therefore, in this sense, the term is also a general statement denoting various functional and organic disorders.

第十四章　数学典籍英译

文化外宣汉英翻译

(1) In the Spring and Autumn Period (770 BC–476 BC) and Warring States Period (475 BC–221 BC) the ancient Chinese not only invented the decimal system but also created the multiplication table which is also called nine-times table. With a history of more than 2,000 years, it is the basic calculation rule for the operations of multiplication, division and radication in rod arithmetic. Later the multiplication table was introduced eastward into North Korea, Japan and westward along the Silk Road into India and other countries. The European didn't employ the multiplication table until 13th century.

(2) According to the legend, abacus was created by a servant of the Yellow Emperor, Li Shou in ancient China. Due to the absence of a convenient tool for daily calculation, Li Shou found a method: he collected stone chips of different colors along the river shoal and strung them together with thin thread. Between each ten or hundred chips, he added a stone chip of different colors. As thus, counting became more easy and convenient. Then, he came up a more practical approach which was to strung ten chips together as one set and made it to a hundred sets and put them on a hug clay plate market with digits such as the tens, the hundreds, and the thousands which was the primitive abacus.

（3）Ancient Chinese people tried continuously to find applicable standards for the measurement, and accumulated many experiences in this process. It was said that three gu chi（骨尺 bone rulers) were unearthed from the Yin Ruins（殷墟）, and each had a length of 16 cm, which was equal to 1 zha（拃 span) of a man of medium height. This verified the old words saying "measuring chi with spans"（丈手知尺）. They were aware that discrepancies would occur when using human body as standards, so they never stopped trying to find natural objects with precision to define the Chinese mathematical foot, which serve as asurement. In the *Huai Nan Zi / Tian Wen Xun*（《淮南子・天文训》）, it is said thatl cun（寸）is equal to the total length of 12 millets. In the *Shuo wen*（《说文》）, 10 times of the diameter of a piece of hair（发）on the ponytail is equal to 1 cheng (fi), and 10 cheng was equal to 1 fen（分）. In the *Sun Zi Suan Jing*（《孙子算经》）, the length of silk from a silk worm at one time represents 1 hu（忽）, where 10 hu（忽）was equal to 1 miao（秒）; 10 miao（秒）was equal to 1 hao（毫）;10 hao（毫）was equal to 1 li（厘）; 10 li（厘）was equal to 1 fen（分）. However, all these definitions varied from one another, and none of them coincide with the prevailing measures at that time.

第十五章　农业典籍英译

文化外宣汉英翻译

（1）In the long process of history of humankind, China as one of the four ancient civilizations of the world once made splendid achievements in natural science and engincering technology. The scientific discoveries and technological inventions made by the ancient Chinese covered nearly all disciplinary fields. In particular, the Chinese nations scientific system represented by astronomy, calendar, agriculture and medicines, as well as the technological achievements represented by the Four Great Inventions, once produced a profound impact on the historical process of human development. Some of them spread out to different parts of the world where they either were directly adopted by the local people or inspired them to conduct related researches and make their own inventions.

（2）As pointed out by Dr Joseph Needham (1900–1995), the late foreign academician of the Chinese Academy of Sciences and an internationally renowned British sinologist, in many important areas of scientific discoveries and technological inventions of the ancient and medieval times, the Chinese were well ahead of the legendary figures who had created the famous Greek Miracles and were on a par with the Arabs who practically owned all the cultural wealth of the ancient Occidental world. Between the 3rd century and the 13th century, China maintained a level scientific knowledge which was too advanced to bear any comparison in the west.

(3) Winter starts with the Beginning of winter. People in this term should enhance the management of the three cereals (wheat, barley and highland barley) and rape. In order to ensure the seedlings to be strong enough to live through the winter. After the beginning of Winter, the temperature drops below ero degree and snow of limited volume begins to fall in the Lesser Snow. The field management of the overwintering crops should be emphasized to make sure the growth of autumn crops. The snowfall of the Greater Snow is heavier than that of the Lesser Snow and Chinese people believe in the proverb as, "A timely heavy now promises a good harvest." The more the snow is covering on the earth the better the environment is to destroy the harmful insects. On the Winter Solstice, the sunlight shines vertically on the Tropic of Capricorn, with the shortest daytime and longest night in the Northern Hemisphere, namely the coldest period of a year.

(4) The Pure Brightness derives from the southeast monsoon (pure and bright wind), when plants buds and weather becomes warmer and brighter. With regards to the farm works in this period, it is said "melons and peas should be cultivated around the Pure Brightness". Not limited to one of the 24 Solar Terms, the Pure Brightness is also a traditional festival in China, on which we will sweep tombs, offer sacrifices to ancestors and go out for a spring hiking. The Grain Rain is the last term of oring and its name is based on the old saying of ancient Chinese people "rain breeds cereals". The rain during the Grain Rain is beneficial for the five cereals' growth.

第十六章　地理游记英译

文化外宣汉英翻译

(1) The diction of the Four Great Inventions was first put forward by British scientist and historian Joseph Needham, referring to Chinas papermaking, printing, compass and gunpowder. British philosopher Francis Bacon once said, " The three inventions of printing, gunpowder and compass have changed the outlook and situation of things all over the world." The emergence of the Four Great Inventions has promoted not only China' s developments in history, culture, economy and other aspects, but also even the progress of the whole world.

(2) China is the world's oldest nation to breed silkworms for silk weaving. The ancient Chinese reeled off raw silk from silkworm cocoons for silk weaving. After being rinsed some residuary wadding was left on mat. By drying in the sun and then stripping down from the mat, such paper was called Rectangle Wadding (Fangxu). Since such paper was too rough to be used for clear writing, it did not play an active role in cultural transmission. In the Eastem Han dynasty (25–220), papermaking was improved by Cai Lun. He selected and used barks, hemp wastes, rags, old fishnets and other easily obtained raw materials, which would be treated in steps of dipping, smashing, paper-shaping, and baking. After the pulp was air-dried, the paper more suitable for writing eventually was made. As one of China's greatest inventions, papermaking acted as a"messenger" for the transmission of human civilization and technology. Papermaking was first introduced into the adjacent North Korea and Vietnam, and then spread to Japan and Arabia, and was brought to Europe via the Arab region. By the 19th century, Chinas papermaking has spread to countries all over the world.

(3) Compass, as an important tool for people to discriminate directions, the world's first compass, which was called South-pointing Ladle (Sinan), appeared in China in the Warring States Period (475 BC–221 BC) Made of lodestone, the South-pointing Ladle looked like a ladle, which could maintain a balance on a smooth chassis (a square metal plate). It could also rotate freely, and when it stopped, the handle of the ladle would point to the south. In addition to South-pointing Ladle, a more convenient guiding tool South-pointing Fish appeared in the Northern Song dynasty (960–1127). The South-pointing Fish was made of thin iron sheet cut into a fish shape. With a length of about 6.667 cm and a width of about 1.667 cm, the fish had a slightly concave belly, which looked like a boat. After the magnetization treatment, it would point to the south and north when floating on water surface. As the friction of liquid was smaller than solid, the South-pointing Fish could make a more flexible turning, and was more sensitive and accurate than the South-pointing Ladle.

参考文献

中文文献

[1] 安乐哲，郝大维．切中伦常——中庸的新诠与新译［M］．北京：中国社会科学出版社，2011.

[2] 安乐哲．孙子兵法（汉英对照）［M］．北京：中华书局，2012.

[3] 保罗·怀特．大中华文库：菜根谭（汉英对照）［M］．北京：新世界出版社，2003.

[4] 曹雪芹，高鹗．红楼梦［M］．北京：人民文学出版社，1974.

[5] 道本周，徐义保．大中华文库：九章算术（汉英对照）［M］．沈阳：辽宁教育出版社，2013.

[6] 冯友兰．庄子（汉英双语）［M］．北京：外语教学与研究出版社，2012.

[7] 傅惠生．大中华文库：易经（汉英对照）［M］．长沙：湖南人民出版社，2008.

[8] 辜鸿铭．*The Universal Order or Conduct of Life*［M］．上海：别发洋行出版社，1906.

[9] 辜正坤．道德经（中英文对照）［M］．北京：中国对外翻译出版社，2007.

[10] 辜正坤．元曲一百五十首（汉英对照）［M］．北京：北京大学出版社，2004.

[11] 胡晓阳．增广贤文（汉英对照）［M］．北京：对外经济贸易大学出版社，2001.

[12] 黄涤明，丁往道．大中华文库：搜神记［M］．北京：外文出版社，2004.

[13] 黄友义，等．大中华文库：聊斋志异［M］．北京：外文出版社，2007.

[14] 李伟荣．大中华文库：徐霞客游记（汉英对照）［M］．长沙：湖南人民出版社，2016.

[15] 李照国．大中华文库：黄帝内经（汉英对照）［M］．北京：世界图书出版公司，2020.

[16] 理雅各．大学（汉英对照）［M］．北京：外语教学与研究出版社，2010.

[17] 理雅各．大中华文库：尚书（汉英对照）［M］．北京：外文出版社，2013.

[18] 林戊荪．大中华文库：孙子兵法（汉英对照）［M］．北京：外文出版社，2007.

[19] 林语堂．老子的智慧（林语堂英文作品集）［M］．北京：外语教学与研究出版社，2009.

[20] 林语堂．东坡诗文选（汉英对照）［M］．合肥：安徽科学技术出版社，2012.

[21] 罗慕士. 大中华文库：三国演义（汉英对照）[M]. 北京：外文出版社，2000.
[22] 罗希文. 大中华文库：本草纲目（汉英对照）[M]. 北京：外文出版社，2012.
[23] 马来西亚汉学院. 群书治要 360 [M]. 世界知识出版社，2019.
[24] 潘嘉玢. 大中华文库：吴子　司马法　尉缭子（汉英对照）[M]. 北京：军事科学出版社，2005.
[25] 彭发胜，孟凡君. 三字经　千字文（汉英对照）[M]. 北京：中国对外翻译出版公司，2006.
[26] 沙博理. 大中华文库：水浒传（汉英对照）[M]. 北京：外文出版社，2009.
[27] 沈菲. 弟子规（汉英对照）[M]. 桂林：广西师范大学出版社，2016.
[28] 沈菲. 朱子治家格言（汉英对照）[M]. 桂林：广西师范大学出版社，2016.
[29] 汪榕培. 大中华文库：牡丹亭（汉英对照）[M]. 长沙：湖南人民出版社，1999.
[30] 汪榕培. 英译乐府诗精华 [M]. 上海：上海外语教育出版社，2008.
[31] 汪榕培. 大中华文库：诗经（汉英对照）[M]. 长沙：湖南人民出版社，2008.
[32] 汪榕培. 大中华文库：庄子（汉英对照）[M]. 长沙：湖南人民出版社，1999.
[33] 汪榕培. 大中华文库：汉魏六朝诗三百首（汉英对照）[M]. 长沙：湖南人民出版社，2006.
[34] 汪榕培. 大中华文库：陶渊明集（汉英对照）[M]. 长沙：湖南人民出版社，2003.
[35] 王宏，赵峥. 大中华文库：梦溪笔谈（汉英对照）[M]. 成都：四川人民出版社，2008.
[36] 王伊同. 大中华文库：洛阳伽蓝记（汉英对照）[M]. 北京：中华书局，2007.
[37] 王义静. 大中华文库：天工开物（汉英对照）[M]. 广州：广东教育出版社，2011.
[38] 韦利. 大中华文库：老子（汉英对照）[M]. 长沙：湖南人民出版社，外文出版社，2008.
[39] 韦利. 大中华文库：论语（汉英对照）[M]. 长沙：湖南人民出版社，外文出版社，1999.
[40] 许渊冲. 楚辞（汉英对照）[M]. 北京：中国对外翻译出版公司，2008.
[41] 许渊冲. 画说诗经（汉英对照）[M]. 北京：中译出版社，2019.
[42] 许渊冲. 唐诗三百首（汉英对照）[M]. 北京：中国对外翻译出版公司，2006.
[43] 许渊冲. 西厢记（汉英对照）[M]. 北京：中国对外翻译出版公司，2009.
[44] 许渊冲. 元曲三百首（汉英对照）[M]. 北京：中国对外翻译出版公司，2008.

[45] 许渊冲. 长生殿（汉英对照）[M]. 北京：中国对外翻译出版公司，2009.

[46] 许渊冲. 经典英译古代诗歌1000首·宋词 [M]. 北京：海豚出版社，2015.

[47] 杨宪益，戴乃迭. 大中华文库：红楼梦 [M]. 北京：外文出版社，2010.

[48] 杨宪益. 大中华文库：史记 [M]. 北京：外文出版社，2008.

[49] 杨宪益，戴乃迭. 楚辞选（汉英对照）[M]. 北京：外文出版社，2016.

[50] 杨宪益，戴乃迭. 大中华文库：汉魏六朝小说选（汉英对照）[M]. 北京：外文出版社，2006.

[51] 杨宪益，戴乃迭. 大中华文库：长生殿（汉英对照）[M]. 北京：外文出版社，2004.

[52] 杨宪益，戴乃迭. 关汉卿杂剧选（汉英对照）[M]. 北京：外文出版社，1958.

[53] 杨宪益，戴乃迭. 乐府（汉英对照）[M]. 北京：外文出版社，2001.

[54] 杨宪益，戴乃迭. 宋词（汉英对照）[M]. 北京：外文出版社，2006.

[55] 詹纳尔. 大中华文库：西游记（汉英对照）[M]. 北京：外文出版社，2000.

[56] 赵甄陶. 大中华文库：孟子（汉英对照）[M]. 长沙：湖南人民出版社，外文出版社，1999.

[57] 中华文明史话编委会. 戏曲史话 [M]. 北京：中国大百科全书出版社，2010.

[58] 宗福常. 大中华文库：颜氏家训（汉英对照）[M]. 北京：外文出版社，2004.

英文文献

[1] Arthur Waley. A HUNDRED AND SEVENTY CHINESE POEMS[M]. New York: The Vail-Ballou Co.,1919.

[2] Bernhard Karlgren. The Book of Document[M]. Stockholm: Museum of Far Eastern Antiquities, 1950.

[3] Burton Watson. Chuang Tzu: basic writings[M]. New York and London: Columbia University Press, 1964.

[4] Daniel Gardner. The Four Books[M]. Indianapolis: Hackett Publishing, 2007.

[5] David Collie. The Four Books[M]. Malacca: The Mission Press, 1828.

[6] David Hawkes. A Litter Primer of Tu Fu[M]. Oxford: Oxford University Press, 1967.

[7] David Hawkes. The Story of The Stone[M]. NY: Penguin Press, 1974.

[8] Ezra Pound. Cathay[M]. London: MCMXV, 1915.

[9] Herbert A.Giles. Chuang Tzu: Mystic, Moralist, and Social Reformer[M]. London: Bernard Quarich, 1889.

[10] Herbert Giles. Chinese Poetry in English Verse[M]. London and Shanghai: Kelly & Walsh, 1898.

[11] Herbert Giles. STRANGE TALES FROM A CHINESE STUDIO[M]. London: T. Werner Laurie, 1916.

[12] James Legge. The Chinese Classics - Vol. 3 The She King[M]. London: Trubner & Co.1876.

[13] James Legge. Record of Buddhistic Kingdoms[M]. New York: Paragon Book Reprint Corp., 1965.

[14] James Legge. The Chinese Classics-Vol. 2 The Works of Mencius[M]. Taipei: SMC Publishing Inc.1991.

[15] James Legge. The Sacred Books of the East, Vol. 16 The I-Ching[M]. Oxford : Clarendon,1899.

[16] James Legge. The Sacred Books of The East: The Texts of Taoism[M]. Oxford: Clarendon Press, 1891.

[17] James Legge. The Chinese Classics - Vol. 1 Doctrine of the Mean[M]. London: Trubner & Co.,1861.

[18] John Minford. Strange Tales From a Chinese Studio[M]. New York:Penguin Group, 2006.

[19] John Turner. A Golden Treasury of Chinese Poetry[M]. Hong Kong : Chinese University of Hong Kong. 1976.

[20] Kangshen, S., Crossley, J. N., & Lun, A. W-C. The Nine Chapters on the Mathematical Art Companion and Commentary[M]. Oxford: Oxford University Press.1999.

[21] Kenneth Rexroth, Ling Chung. Li Ching-Chao: Complete Poems[M]. New York: New Directions Publishing Corporation. 1979.

[22] Lam Lay Yong, Jiu Zhang Suanshu. An Overview, Archieve for History of Exact Science[M]. New York: Springer Verlag, 1994.

[23] Paul Rouzer.The Poetry and Prose of Wang Wei [M]. Boston: Walter de Gruyter Inc., 2020.

[24] Paul U. Unschuld. Huang Di nei jing su wen[M]. CA: University of California Press,

2003.

[25] Pearl S. Buck. All Men Are Brothers[M]. NewYork: The George Macy Companies, Inc., 1948.

[26] Richard Wilhelm and Cary F. Baynes. The I Ching or Book of Changes[M]. Princeton N J: Princeton University Press, 1967.

[27] Roger T. Ames, Henry Rosemont. The analects of Confucius: A Philosophical Translation[M]. New York:The Random House Publishing Group, 1998.

[28] Samuel Beal. Buddhist Records of The Western World[M]. Trubner & Co., Ludgate Hill, 1884.

[29] Sidney L.Sondergard. Strange Tales from Liaozhai[M]. Fremont: Jain Publishing Company, 2008.

[30] Stefan H. Verstappen. The Thirty-Six Strategies of Ancient China[M]. San Francisco: China Books & Periodicals, 1999.

[31] Stephen Owen. The Poetry of Du Fu[M]. Boston: Walter de Gruyter Inc., 2016.

[32] Stephen Owen. The Great Age of Chinese Poetry: The High Tang[M]. New Haven and London: Yale University Press.1981.

[33] William H. NeinHauser. The Grand Scriber's Records[M]. Bloomington: Indiana University Press, 1994.

[34] Witter Bynner. The Jade Mountain: A Chinese anthology; being three hundred poems of the T›ang Dynasty[M]. New York: Alfred A. Knopf, 1957.

[35] Xi Jinping. Xi Jinping: The Governance of China（Ⅰ）[M]. Beijing:Foreign Languages Press.2014.

[36] Xi Jinping. Xi Jinping: The Governance of China（Ⅱ）[M]. Beijing:Foreign Languages Press.2017.

[37] Xi Jinping. Xi Jinping: The Governance of China（Ⅲ）[M]. Beijing:Foreign Languages Press.2020.